"A most important book that will help the reader go beyond any self-imposed limitations." —Gerald Jampolsky, M.D., founder of The Center for Attitudinal Healing and author of *Love Is Letting Go of Fear*

"Visionary thinkers Land and Jarman provide a compelling framework and road map to create a future of unparalleled opportunity." —*World Business Academy Perspectives*

"An ebullient and abundant book filled with the crucial strategies that could make the future work." —Jean Houston, Ph.D., President, The Possible Society, and author of *The Possible Human*

"Nowhere has the cataclysmic change rocking the world been so well documented and have the prescriptions for living through it been so clear and valuable. Land and Jarman take us to the heart of change in a story of our world that is as gripping as a mystery and much more crucial to our survival." —Michael Ray, coauthor of *Creativity in Business* and Professor, Stanford University

"There are few books I'd endorse because there's great duplication of information, especially with books that are said to be 'breakthrough' pieces of literature. *Breakpoint and Beyond* is a breakthrough book because its message and information are unlike anything I've come across. It's important and relevant to everyone." —Ken Dychtwald, author of *Age Wave* and CEO of Age Wave, Inc.

"Fascinating reading! It very effectively applies the secrets of nature. It is a 'must read' for anyone responsible for transforming an organization." —Keith Goodrich, Chairman and Chief Executive, Moore Corporation, Ltd.

"George Land and Beth Jarman are clearly two of the most innovative thinkers of our time. They have had a tremendous impact on the success of our business. They broaden your perspective and make you think." —John Allison, Chairman and CEO, Branch Banking and Trust Company

"*Breakpoint and Beyond* should challenge anyone, regardless of the size of the company they're with, to think beyond some point at which they currently rest, or to seriously reexamine some of their fundamental thoughts regarding why we are here and where we are going." —Jerry Marlar, President, Intermedics Orthopics, Inc.

"Transformative change is taking place. *Breakpoint* is a guidebook for the journey. It helps to understand that 'we are normal' and that our experiences are shared and consistent with natural laws." —Herman Maynard, Industry Manager, E.I. DuPont de Nemours & Company

"*Breakpoint and Beyond* is a most articulate document that helps us welcome and embrace the future, not fear it. This is the book that will launch us into the next century with hope, meaning and purpose." —Doris Shallcross, Professor, University of Massachusetts, and President, Creative Education Foundation

"The world is transforming, whether we like it or not. This very readable book can contribute to more widespread understanding as to why this is happening, and must happen. It will help the reader to navigate the tumultuous rapids ahead, and its insight will help make the journey more exhilarating and less fearsome." —Willis Harman, author of *Creative Work* and *Global Mind Change* and President, Institute of Noetic Sciences

"Land and Jarman's outstanding book explores how we can express our potential at the highest level. To better understand the process of change, buy a copy today." —*New Paradigm Digest*

BREAKPOINT AND BEYOND

BREAKPOINT AND BEYOND

Mastering the Future—Today

George Land ■ **Beth Jarman**

HarperBusiness
A Division of HarperCollins*Publishers*

A hardcover edition of this book was published in 1992 by HarperBusiness, a division of HarperCollins Publishers.

HarperCollins books may be purchased for educational, business, or sales promotional use. For information please write: Special Markets Department, Harper-Collins Publishers, Inc., 10 East 53rd Street, New York, NY 10022.

First paperback edition published 1993.

The Library of Congress has catalogued the hardcover edition as follows:
Ainsworth-Land, George T., 1933–
   Breakpoint and beyond: mastering the future—today / George Land, Beth Jarman.
     p.   cm.
   Includes bibliographical references and index.
   ISBN 0-88730-547-4
   1. Psychology, Industrial.   2. Organizational change.   I. Jarman, Beth.   II. Title.
HF5548.8.A62   1992
158.7–dc20   91–33455

ISBN 0-88730-604-7 (pbk.)

93 94 95 96 97 PS/CW 10 9 8 7 6 5 4 3 2

Today, across the planet, millions of people are creating a future different from the past. Your individual efforts are moving us to a time when the world will truly work for everyone. We dedicate this book to you.

CONTENTS

CONTENTS

ACKNOWLEDGMENTS

During the writing of this book, we have received assistance from countless individuals and organizations from around the world. Bob Elmore at Arthur Andersen deserves special mention, as does Beth Ames Swartz, who continually encouraged us.

To our partners at Leadership 2000, Brenda Ringwald, Robert Daniels, Matt Day, Michelle Jarman, and Tom McNamee, we extend our heartfelt thanks for their patience, support, and good humor. Michelle Jarman provided invaluable assistance and untold improvements in the manuscript as our in-house editor. Special research assistance was provided by Brenda Ringwald and Diane Wiesen-Todd.

We deeply appreciate the significant contribution of Arnold and Selma Patent. Their insights and ideas continue to broaden our perspective and contribute to our living at a higher level of creativity, love, and joy.

A book such as this is built on the shoulders of countless great thinkers. Their creative research and ideas led us down the path of discovery. We particularly acknowledge Margaret Mead, Dr. Karl Menninger, and Dorie Shallcross, whose collaboration and stimulation over the years was unparalleled. Other pioneers who provided us with invaluable keys to understanding the Breakpoint phenomenon include David Bohm, Paul Davies, Jean Houston, Gerald Jampolsky, Ilya Prigogine, John Rice, Richard Scrivner, Humberto Maturana, Francisco Varela, and John A. Wheeler.

Breakpoint and Beyond would never have been possible without the vision, enthusiasm, and assistance of our publisher at HarperBusiness, Mark Greenberg, and our terrific editor Jim Childs.

INTRODUCTION

By Beth Jarman

The beginnings of *Breakpoint and Beyond* go back to January of 1974. I left one of the important meetings of my life trying to comprehend why my principal and superintendent, both good friends and ardent supporters of my career advancement, agreed that I would never have the opportunity to become a principal or a superintendent in their lifetimes or mine. They said, "Beth, this has nothing to do with your abilities or your commitment to education. Our telling you this is because we know this school district isn't ready for the kind of change that would result in appointing a woman to a top administrative post."

It didn't seem possible that my career in education could be sidetracked because a group of people couldn't see the value of changing the criteria for selecting administrators. Why did change threaten people so? Why couldn't the school board see the richness that comes from including those who have been previously excluded? Change, why was it so difficult?

I left education within two months and within a year was elected to the Utah legislature. I thought governmental institutions would be far ahead of education in their ability to embrace change. What I discovered was quite the opposite.

Out of my personal experiences, I became fascinated with change in all its dimensions. My own life was unfolding as a major experiment. I was the first person of my gender in many nontraditional positions. Not only was I a learning lab of sorts, but I started reading everything I could about change.

What I found were a myriad of articles and books describing the countless changes surrounding us. Anecdotal accounts of how individuals and organizations coped with change uncovered some helpful advice, but nothing particularly compelling or original caught my attention.

What I wanted was an understanding of change itself. Why did change happen? Why did people put up such resistance to change? What were the forces driving change? Why the unprecedented and massive changes sweeping through our lives today?

Because of my abiding interest in change, a friend asked me if I had read *Grow or Die* by George Land. She thought his concepts about change were expansive and original. I hadn't heard of George Land or his book. However, my curiosity was stirred.

Not a week later, when I was conversing with another friend about my sense of frustration working as a cabinet secretary in Arizona state government, she said, "It might help you to grasp the significance of your experience if you were to read *Grow or Die* by George Land. He discovered a Theory of Transformation that puts into perspective why and how individuals and organizations grow, change, and sometimes renew themselves. He also explains why organizations often find themselves incapable of changing."

At this point, I was more than interested. My friend suggested she bring her copy of Land's book right over and even offered to give her interpretation before I started reading it.

That she did, and begin the book I did, but not before another friend dropped two tapes on my door step with a note: "I think you will be very interested in the ideas presented on these tapes." I quickly looked at the tapes. They were a speech on the "Spirit of Business" by George Land.

Why were this man's ideas surrounding me at every turn? I had heard of serendipity. I also recognized I was probably in the middle of it.

INTRODUCTION

I was just leaving on a government trip, so I threw the tapes into my briefcase. A short time later, out on the open road, I put the first tape into the tape deck. I became intrigued with the simplicity of his explanation of how every system in nature, including organizations, goes through a process of change that can lead to renewal and transformation.

I don't know about you, but the last place I thought I would be looking for advice about how change occurs or about my own growth or how to renew my organization would be within the secrets of nature. Yes, I once read C.P. Snow's *Two Worlds,* and I realized that as a lay person I didn't understand science or nature. It was like a difficult foreign language. I knew it was important. Certainly great wisdom resided there, but I didn't have the inclination or time to learn it.

Here was a person presenting me with a way to understand nature as well as the opportunity to build a roadmap to the future from a most unlikely source. By equipping myself with an intimate comprehension of nature's creative processes, I realized I could enhance my own personal growth and that of any organization.

Land's Theory of Transformation explained why most leaders get stuck in a phase of growth that no longer serves them. They don't know how to integrate the new and different, that which was previously excluded.

His discoveries about how nature works put into perspective the last fifteen years of my life in major leadership positions as a state legislator, executive assistant to a governor, cabinet secretary to governors in two different states, and president of two corporations. After serving as a cabinet secretary for the second time, I was beginning to despair.

How could a woman in a man's world be heard? It seemed so obvious to me that my way of leading was different, and to my way of thinking, refreshing. I knew from experience that I wasn't fully accepted because I didn't follow the established rules. Here was a framework for me to understand why it had been so difficult. Here too was a way for others to understand that the changes occurring all around us are, in fact, the very ingredients for individual, organizational, and cultural renewal.

Suddenly I was armed with hope. Hope for the organization in which I had a major leadership position, a way to understand why all of those who resisted change, in my circle of the world, were unable to embrace change at the level I had anticipated, and most importantly, hope for the future.

When I finished listening to his "Spirit of Business" speech, I decided I was going to meet George Land. Six months later, we met. During that three-hour lunch, I was intrigued with his ideas about nature's creative process of change and how understanding nature provides a wealth of information about the way change really works.

George willingly shared how it all started and where his journey into understanding nature had taken him: "It came originally as a total shock. I was sitting quietly in my study after concentrating on a tough cell growth problem for work I was doing with a team of scientists in helping them to deliberately apply the creative process. Suddenly, I saw the image of cells floating around in my mind. What seized my attention was that these tiny cells were going through crucial changes that were exactly the same process as the steps I had discovered that people use in creative thinking. How could that be? How could simple cells perform the ultra-complex processes that all my research had identified as the special and totally unique properties of human beings? Could cells be creative?

"By the time I had conferred with a number of leading biologists, comparing creative thinking and the process of cellular growth and change, we had agreed that cells were, in fact, doing exactly what we call creativity in humans. In biology it just had a different name. My fascination with nature's underlying creative processes of growth and change began. I researched biology, genetics, chemistry, anthropology, psychology, cosmology, and atomic physics. In *every* case, I found the same essential natural process of creativity operating.

"What was even more significant is that this knowledge changed my life radically. It provided me with a context to understand how everything fits together and works. Suddenly what had seemed so disorderly and chaotic in my world made sense. It revealed how I could successfully deal with great changes in my own life and assist the organizations I worked with in applying the simple laws of nature.

"My odyssey has now lasted nearly twenty-five years. It was interrupted by my first book on natural creativity and change,

INTRODUCTION

Grow or Die, the Unifying Principle of Transformation. My most recent thinking has taken me to the frontiers of quantum physics. I've been trying to wrest the underlying secrets of the scientific reality discovered within the new physics into a form that can be understood and applied by the lay person. It's been six years now, and I've felt such frustration at times trying to unravel the paradoxes of the new sciences, but startling breakthroughs have finally emerged."

When that lunch ended both of us knew we would definitely work together. My firsthand experience and knowledge about organizations and personal change greatly enhanced and broadened George's theoretical discoveries. Together we knew our combined experiences would assist even more individuals and organizations in grappling successfully with the unpredecented changes surrounding us.

Our combined experience of over fifty years taps into a wealth of knowledge as change agents and leaders of change in our own personal lives and within education, government, business, consulting, communication, and the media. We have worked with senior executives of large organizations, advising on issues surrounding today's turbulent social and market changes or conducting very personal and intimate seminars dealing with profound personal transformation.

First and foremost, we do our best to practice these concepts in our personal lives and with our families. In addition, the concepts have been utilized by thousands of individuals in a multitude of organizations. These are not theoretical ideas. Individuals and groups around the world have applied these discoveries and ideas successfully in their own personal lives and in organizations large and small. We know they work.

Our great hope is that these unique new ideas have as lasting an impact on you and your family and loved ones as they are having on the individuals and organizations with whom we have had the opportunity to work.

It's taken this last five years for us to write *Breakpoint and Beyond*. Our commitment has been constant, to provide a compelling framework to understand how the forces of change really work and interpret this knowledge in such a way that a powerful new roadmap to the future can be created.

If you are at all like us, you want to know where the journey along the pages of this book will lead. In that spirit, we provide a brief synopsis of how we organized the book and a summary of each chapter.

AN OVERVIEW OF BREAKPOINT AND BEYOND

Part One

Breakpoint and Beyond is divided into two major parts. Part One, Chapters 1 through 5, focuses on uncovering the method nature uses to achieve creative growth and change. We explain what a Breakpoint is, how and why most individuals, organizations and entire nations have reached Breakpoint; and what the new rules for success are in moving beyond this great historical turning point.

CHAPTER 1 BREAKPOINT CHANGE This chapter challenges our assumptions about change and invites the reader to understand that nature's method of change is far different from what we've been led to believe.

CHAPTER 2 THE MASTER PATTERN OF CHANGE A natural creative process of evolutionary transformation creates Breakpoints where the rules change dramatically. Breakpoint change provides the basis for understanding how organizations, individuals, and society can take advantage of massive change to create a different and far better future.

CHAPTER 3 DYNAMIC ORGANIZATIONAL CHANGE AND RENEWAL Nature's method for dynamic creative growth and change becomes the key element in unlocking the mystery behind why most mature organizations are unable to successfully reinvent themselves.

CHAPTER 4 THE WORLD AT BREAKPOINT Applying the Master Pattern of Change to civilization provides the framework to discover that society today is at Breakpoint. We audaciously cover the history of civilization from 14,000 B.C. to the present to see how human society has moved through an evolutionary pattern to bring us to this juncture in history. The pattern of civilization has been exhausted, and in order to move to a higher level a new pattern must be created.

CHAPTER 5 MASTERING THE FUTURE   The principles uncovered by the revolutionary discoveries of quantum physics unleashed a new reality on the world. By uncovering what have appeared to be obscure and arcane principles and applying them to human beings, we too can revolutionize our world to meet the challenge of Breakpoint change now confronting civilization. The reader will understand, in order for the massive shifts we are suggesting to take place, that individuals will need to *alter their worldview*. This can occur when individuals take the natural principles discovered by scientists, which have revolutionized our world technologically, and apply them in their own lives. It is clear, at this juncture in the book, that we must change our minds about how the world fits together and works in order to apply nature's laws and evolve human development.

Part Two

In Chapters 6 through 11, nature's secrets are translated into practical skills and tools needed by individuals to handle the massive changes of our times. By taking each of the vital cornerstones of how nature works and breaking them down for individuals, readers can apply these concepts in their own lives.

CHAPTER 6 PARTING WITH THE PAST   Here we look at how to move beyond Breakpoint by applying the new rules of success. We provide specific examples of different ways individuals are resisting and creating a new worldview (the Creative Worldview). Our position is that it will take nothing short of a shift in worldviews to move beyond Breakpoint.

CHAPTER 7 CHANGING OUR MINDS   We begin weaving the essential threads in the tapestry of how individuals can integrate the Creative Worldview into their own lives.

CHAPTER 8 THE CREATIVE DRIVE   Every person is a creative being capable of bringing into existence what has never been before.

By embracing their own creativity and knowing where they are in their own process of growth and change, individuals can become the conscious evolutionary agent of their own development. The reader is provided with the essential tools of how to be more creative.

CHAPTER 9 THE POWER OF FUTURE PULL   By applying in our own lives how we are being pulled to the future rather than being pushed by the past, individuals can powerfully move into alignment with the power of Future Pull. This unique concept offers compelling evidence why the power of vision is fundamental to great organizations and the lives of great people.

CHAPTER 10 THE FORCE OF CONNECTING   The deep and abiding interconnectedness of all life applies equally to human beings. The specifics as to what stands in the way of our connecting at the highest possible level are presented as well as how we can enhance our ability to connect.

CHAPTER 11 A SOLID BRIDGE TO THE FUTURE   The final chapter provides the context for how to live creatively. This powerful chapter invites the reader to create the context for the creative spirit to pervade his or her own life. It also uncovers some of the deeply hidden invisible barriers standing between us and our willingness to embrace the Creative Worldview.

This book isn't intended as a quick read during which you skim through the pages gleaning a few new ideas or magic formulas to try out in tomorrow's meeting. It takes some resolve to integrate the concepts in *Breakpoint and Beyond* in a world firmly embedded in yesterday's truths. To understand how to apply successfully the principles of nature uncovered in these pages requires reading the entire book and then actively joining that growing world of intrepid explorers who are creating a new kind of future.

We suggest you approach this book as you would an exploration: Let go of preconceptions as you journey through an unexpected and original interpretation of a world undergoing unprecedented and massive change.

Paradise Valley, Arizona, 1992

PART ONE
BREAKING WITH THE PAST

1: BREAKPOINT CHANGE

> Unprecedented social, political and technological changes have occurred during this century. More profound changes lie ahead. To make the decisions that will be required, we must understand the nature of change itself—its causes and effects—its dangers and possibilities.
>
> The Smithsonian Institute,
> *The Phenomenon of Change*

A barrage of books, articles, television specials, and newspaper headlines all announce that things aren't the way they used to be—or even the way they were supposed to be. Everything is changing: family relationships, jobs, child rearing practices, technologies, political systems, economics, competition. The future has come upon us so fast and furiously that we're often left confused and unsettled. How can we equip ourselves or our organizations to deal with a world that is transforming before our very eyes?

To answer that question we have to reconsider our basic notions about change itself. Neither our traditional beliefs nor the opinion of experts offer much illumination. The experts claim that change today is certainly faster and much more complex. This information is of little help if you are dealing with global competition, street crime, collapsing families, or failing schools. A more customary explanation is that change is cyclical. The flower children were merely a repeat of the beat generation, and the greed prevalent in the 1980s was not much different from that of the robber barons. Some observers would have us believe that "the more things change, the more they stay the same."

A far more widespread explanation of change is that the past predicts the present and can be forecast into the future. Change has always followed trends. This perspective is evident in diverse areas, from the fashion industry to movements in the social political scene. This view claims that the way things change is continuous, incremental, and fairly predictable. For thousands of years this idea of the past guiding the future has served us well. This established interpretation of change presents us with our single biggest obstacle in dealing with today's world.

Today's change is not just:

> more rapid,
> more complex,
> more turbulent,
> more unpredictable.

Today's change is unlike any encountered before.

The surprising fact is that *change itself has changed!*

The process of change has moved away from its well-marked channels and into uncharted waters. When you buy an airline ticket, use a fax machine, purchase a VCR, heat leftovers in your microwave, try to reform the schools, or shift to a quality or customer-driven orientation in business, you are buying a ticket to a new—and different—kind of future; a future that follows rules contrary to those we have used so successfully throughout human history.

The old rules mandated changes of degree, not of *kind*. Advances were extended and extrapolated from the past. Conventional improvements in communications meant stringing more wires and sending quieter signals. The idea of combining radio transmission with space vehicles gave us the communication satellite. Today thousands of signals travel with *no* wires and *no* noise at the speed of light. Likewise, initially accepted methods for improvements in electronics produced equipment that got bigger, hotter, and more expensive. With transistors, enormous advances now come from making things much smaller, cooler, and far less expensive. Something totally new was created as the rules of change shifted 180 degrees.

These great leaps defy traditional wisdom supporting linear and progressive change. "The more things change, the more they stay the same," is a hopelessly outdated idea. Now, totally unexpected phenomena occur regularly. Alchemists used to dream of magic that would turn lead into gold. Today, nobody would bother. It has become routine to take sand, the most plentiful material on the planet, and turn it into transistors worth hundreds of times their weight in gold. This kind of totally unconventional change process has pushed us to the edge, teetering precariously between two eras.

We've reached a Breakpoint!

Breakpoint change abruptly and powerfully breaks the critical links that connect anyone or anything with the past. What we are experiencing today is absolutely unprecedented in all of humanity's recorded history. We have run into change so different from anything preceding it that it totally demolishes normal standards. It has swept us into a massive transformation that will completely reorder all we know about living in this world. It demands totally new rules for success.

The entire notion of change turns out to be amazingly different from what we have long thought it to be. Change actually follows a pattern that results in momentous and seemingly unpredictable shifts. Long periods of great disorder can shift abruptly to regularity, stability, and predictability. Equally long periods of incremental, continuous, and logical advancement shift to an entirely different kind of change—one in which unrelated things combine in creative ways that produce unexpected and powerful results. At Breakpoint, the rule change is so sharp that continuing to use the old rules not only doesn't work, it erects great, sometimes insurmountable, barriers to success.

In our work with hundreds of diverse organizations around the world, ranging from state governments and national associations to such companies as AT&T, Dow Chemical, and 3M to major American church bodies and monolithic foreign companies such as Mitsui and Takenaka, we have seen these natural Breakpoints appear again and again, always suddenly and sometimes devas-tatingly. Over the past decade, individuals in these organizations have been forced to abandon an entire body of accumulated his-torical wisdom and make epic shifts to entirely new, creative, and revolutionary practices—practices in alignment with new disclo-sures about natural change.

The effects of these shifts impact personal as well as organi-zational life. As one manager at Dow Corning put it, "We not only learned to work creatively together to make a new future for our company, but at home when I used these ideas I finally reached a good relationship with my teen-age children." Natural Breakpoint change touches every part of our lives—profoundly.

Extraordinary discoveries about how change works have driven the onslaught of technology that is revolutionizing our world. These fresh insights have been assimilated into transis-tors and satellites, into medical marvels and bioengineering. It's relatively easy to observe a new kind of change and manipulate new rules in the practice of science and engineering. We have only just begun to understand and deliberately apply these amazing findings in the more complex arena of human affairs.

What we learn when we dig deeply into how Breakpoint change occurs is that these giant leaps and crucial shifts in the rules that govern success are quite natural—even though they cleave massive gaps between what has always been and what can now happen. When human breakthroughs come about, when an antagonistic relationship turns into a creative partnership, when a dying organization suddenly discovers new life and vitality, when a brand new and surprising answer is found to an apparently unsolvable problem, it's because people are challenging conven-tional wisdom. They are naturally, intuitively, and unconsciously using a new kind of thinking.

The good news is that the principles of Breakpoint change can be understood and deliberately applied in all our human interactions in the same way they have been in technology. The new rules of change can be used to renew our lives, energize our organizations, and create an exciting and extra-ordinarily better future for everyone. Breakpoint changes in the human sphere are moving us into a whole new era of human possibilities.

THE HUMAN BREAKPOINT

The present situation is unique, without any parallel in the past.

MARGARET MEAD

Few, if any, of us living on the planet today are insulated from the profound effects of the maelstrom of Breakpoint change going on about us. Neither position nor power, wealth nor geography will protect us from the inadequacies of our traditional ways of solving problems that deal with change or the false assumptions that undergird those methods. The flaws are not just inadequate, they can be fatal.

At this point in our collective human history, we are up against an extraordinary circumstance—tomorrow is guaranteed to be nothing like today. Even so, surrounded by a rampage of phenomenal change—failures in education and business, global competition, disappearing jobs and industries, growing deficits, political upheavals, proliferating drugs and crime, cities running short on money and long on garbage—we continue applying age-old methods and solutions. This strategy simply will not help us solve the unique challenges we now face. Classical wisdom is of little use. The concepts, tools, and solutions that have proven so successful in the past have now become the tap root of our growing problems.

For those willing to move ahead with conscious awareness of the natural laws of change, the future offers unparalleled opportunity to reshape our lives, our organizations, and our world into what we want. For those who insist on clinging to traditional ways of looking at the world, change will continue to come so fast and in such unexpected forms that the future will no longer be a desirable place.

Some sense about the direction of the future comes when we realize the amazing changes that are now taken for granted. After eighty centuries of gradual change, in one short generation ancient and accepted male, female, and family roles have been totally redefined. A study by the traditionally conservative Credit

Union National Association concludes, "There is no longer a typical family." At the midpoint of this century, most households were still made up of a married couple supported by one worker. Today, only 14 percent of American households have one breadwinner! In all the thousands of years of recorded human history, the most basic and dominant family roles never shifted until now.

The radical restructuring of family relationships is only the beginning; the entire human equation is going through a Breakpoint. Time-honored and accepted inequalities and narrowly defined roles are being entirely reformulated.

Suddenly, in our time the human rights movement surges forward. Minorities, women, the handicapped, children, consumers, prisoners, and senior citizens actively claim their "rights." Individuals, not parents, pick their mates and choose their careers. Just think, in a world where, for 97 percent of all recorded history, almost 98 percent of all humanity had no rights, today even animals have rights.

In this topsy-turvy era, previously unheard of protections for nature itself are voiced. In the not too distant past, in what some refer to as "the good old days," if you owned a machine, a piece of property, an animal, or a slave you could do with them pretty much whatever you wanted. Those days are gone—forever.

A NEW WORLDVIEW

Even though we are standing on the threshold of a great historical turning point, the seemingly incomprehensible changes now besetting us can be understood, and new rules to deal with that change can be applied. Breakpoint change actually follows nature's most basic and ancient practices. Since other natural systems have successfully conquered such change, we will uncover what worked before and pick up the clues for what will work for us in these trailblazing times. We will make meaning out of the seemingly chaotic changes going on all around us.

Breakpoints shift any phenomenon of nature—from atoms to societies—into a completely different process. The silent drama of Breakpoint change is, in fact, found everywhere in nature, from the shift a tree goes through when it slows its growth and produces fruit to the more spectacular metamorphosis of the lowly caterpillar into a beautiful butterfly. The tree has become quite different, covered with plentiful fruit, and the butterfly will never return to be an earthbound caterpillar. As we move up the ladder of complexity to the changes experienced by individuals and organizations, nature ups the ante considerably. *The human Breakpoint requires us to change our basic thinking patterns and alter our worldview.*

What we are calling a "worldview" is that set of shared assumptions that make up our fundamental idea of how the world works—how things fit together. It is largely unquestioned, it is "the way things are." We accept the traditional wisdom of a worldview the way we do eating or breathing; we are not conscious of the thoughts forming our worldview. It is simply the way things have always been and always will be.

For most individuals and organizations our most fundamental rules are quite "natural." "Of course," we say, "you have to look at past results to plan for tomorrow" and, "Things must be controlled from the top." Naturally, "We need standard policies, practices, and procedures or things will go nowhere." Who would question the obvious good sense of sticking with "something that works," or that, "Nothing succeeds like success"?

If these uniquely human notions were truly natural, the tree would never change its process and bear fruit; the caterpillar would never become a butterfly, and human beings would never have appeared on the planet. In nature, the common sense way to do things is very different from orthodox human wisdom. The science of natural change and growth shows that at critical points in the development of anything the rules shift.

The tree, for example, as it matures, slows down its quantitative growth and changes to *qualitative* growth. It switches its internal relationships and starts suddenly to bear fruit. It enters into a new relationship with its neighbors, becoming an integrated part of a complex and interdependent ecosystem. It shares its space and provides shade, habitat, and nourishment for other plants and animals. It goes from independent, getting bigger, to interdependent, sharing, connecting, and developing deeper relationships. Unfortunately, most individuals and organizations don't respond this naturally or successfully to change. How can we learn the new rules for change?

SOLID GROUND FOR A BREAKPOINT LEAP

Strangely, amidst all our problems and failures, we are enveloped by extraordinary marvels created by science and technology. They have soared ahead of human progress for a very powerful reason. A few decades ago some revolutionary discoveries about nature forced scientists to fundamentally change their minds about how the invisible world of atoms really works and how change itself works in this domain. Despite the fact that the new knowledge violated a dominant body of traditional assumptions, the findings were clear and undeniable. Engineers moved right ahead and applied these newly found rules, inventing a world radically different from the one they had abruptly left behind.

Even though they may not be consciously aware of it, scientists and engineers applying the principles of the new physics are using Breakpoint change principles in a myriad of ways—miracle cures, computers, VCRs, microwave ovens, satellite communications, robotics, and lasers. Take the compact disk player in your home. That ultimate high fidelity system is made possible by a laser. The laser reads the microscopic code on the disk because light has been excited inside a crystal all the way to a Breakpoint. Once laser light hits a Breakpoint, the rules shift radically. Light changes from its usual chaotic pattern to a highly ordered or coherent state, making possible the translation of the microscopic code on a disk into the highest quality sound. Ordinary light that has not passed through a Breakpoint cannot do this.

Probably nothing has created more change within the organizational world than the Breakpoint change of computer technology. It has removed much of the mechanical drudgery from repetitious jobs and made basic operations such as inventory control and accounts receivable and payable easier, more accurate, and faster. However, since 1960, when computers were broadly distributed, increases in productivity have actually diminished. Why? Managers in industry, government, and education have employed computers primarily to assist them in storing and retrieving data to solve problems and help plan and forecast the future. Most managers tend to build the current five-year plan based on results from the previous five years. When a problem is encountered, they look to see how it was solved before. This management practice is totally consistent with normal and accepted methods—and totally violates the natural principles of change! Natural change operates on the principle of being Pulled to a Future unlike the past, not perpetuating past patterns into the future.

Locked into an outmoded worldview, computers have acted as an ever more efficient means of bonding us to the past and limiting our conception of what is possible. As Samuel Coleridge put it, most people use past experience, "like the stern light of a ship, which illuminates only the track it has passed." By storing and extrapolating historical data, the spreadsheet mentality guarantees that the future will be limited by the past. Foresight is overwhelmed by forecasting. If the use of computers had been introduced with an understanding of the natural processes of change, it would, instead, extend and enhance our human capacity to create a different and far better future. Computers would continually reference the vision of an organization and enhance creativity by asking stimulating questions. People would easily connect by way of computers with the people, information, and ideas to build a future different from the past.

With few exceptions, the human community has not followed the path of change laid out by new discoveries in nature. The deeper and more powerful rules of nature that have driven scientific contributions have been ignored. Thus, the meaning behind the seemingly chaotic changes surrounding us remains obscure. People still spend extraordinary time and resources to "manage" situations in orthodox and time-honored ways only to be plagued with failure. If science had allowed itself to stay stuck with its traditional viewpoint of the world, we would still be using the Pony Express instead of Federal Express.

Modification of our thinking patterns will not work. This new era requires a radical rethinking of the most basic and foundational ways we view the world.

BREAKPOINT WISDOM

Nature's evolutionary processes provide the key to a new worldview. Nature specializes in change; she's been in the business the longest. Understanding natural change processes will unravel many seemingly intractable problems we now face. It will show

how totally new phenomena spring into being, how long periods with little change lull us into complacency. Most important, we will look underneath change itself, interpreting how change really works, and what forces drive change.

The phenomenal effectiveness of adopting the natural rules of Breakpoint change can be seen in some organizations that have adopted natural change processes.

A natural principle of Breakpoint change is creating what's never been seen before—and couldn't be predicted by the past.

In the troubled financial services industry, confronted with the most chaotic, turbulent, and threatening changes, the Branch Bank and Trust Company in Wilson, North Carolina after ten years of decline defied the odds—and extraordinary competition. As its president put it, "We depended on the creativity of our people," to come up with new and different products and services, and novel kinds of branch offices and internal practices. To fully support their people's creativity, they even created a unique position in their system, "Vice President of the Possible," a position with no staff. Yet everybody in the bank worked in that department. The result: growth from a $100 million community bank to a $5 billion national success.

Another rule change at Breakpoint is the shift from independence to interdependence.

To compete in an industry that had moved offshore, North American Tool and Die in California created an environment of total trust and built new mutual partnerships, both inside among previously separate departments and functions and outside with suppliers and customers. They made the basic shift from "me" to "we" in everything they did. They created standards, systems, and products jointly with their vendors and customers. The most important person in the organization became the frontline worker, and the president became "Assistant to Everybody." By any standards—growth, profit, customer satisfaction—NATD has moved from the brink of failure to become one of the most successful businesses in the United States.

The power of Future Pull replaces the anchor of the past.

Every single cell in a tree, in a caterpillar, or in a human being grows and develops not based on its history but by being pulled forward by its internal picture of the possible future. That future is inscribed in the DNA, the genes that reside in the nucleus of every cell. That way, every part of the system can pull together toward the common future. In human terms, this translates into living with a powerful vision of the future. Apple Computer committed to a unique vision: "To change the world by empowering individuals through personal computing technology." They then used enormous energy in sharing the vision of the future throughout their organization, with their customers, and within their communities. Their vision became not only the driving force of the organization, but the primary criterion by which to make decisions. Choices are made not just "by the book" but by the vision. The pull of the future always takes precedence over the past.

Natural Breakpoint change gives us overriding principles and rules that can guide individuals and organizations in creating a dynamic tomorrow:

- Creating what has never existed before, not depending just on improvements to what already exists;

- Making deep and powerful interdependent connections with one another, not excluding people based on differences or separating functions;

- Being pulled to a new kind of future, not being pushed by the past.

These principles are simple to enumerate. Yet they mock historical knowledge. They run counter to our most basic, long-lived, and cherished beliefs and assumptions about how the world works. We will look in detail at each of these principles and how to apply them in subsequent chapters.

Our intention is to unveil the invisible reality of nature. You will learn how to apply these unique discoveries and interpretations about Breakpoint change in practical and useful ways in your own life, within the organizations where you work and the communities where you live.

Just as the scientists who created the technological advancements of our contemporary world had to change their minds about nature's laws, so too can we shift to a unique, but more natural, way of thinking. It was Einstein who recognized, "The world will not evolve past its current state of crisis by using the same thinking that created the situation."

2: THE MASTER PATTERN OF CHANGE

Humanity's survival depends on all of our willingness to comprehend feelingly the way nature works.

Buckminster Fuller

Braving the furies of today's change in positive and effective ways requires getting under the battering waves and penetrating to the deep currents driving change. To do that, let's consider change from a different perspective, seeing it as multidimensional rather than as a single phenomenon. Instead of the old question, "Why is change occurring?" we must ask, "What's going on within change?"

The Greek philosopher Heraclitus observed that "the only constant is change." What he did not know, and what we didn't discover until recently, is that the ceaseless process of change takes on unique characteristics at different points in time. The rules governing change shift dramatically and almost without notice. These Breakpoint shifts, however, follow the same master pattern whether they occur in one's personal life, in an entire organization, or within a single atom.

Nature's method of change, once understood, can be applied like other natural discoveries. The power that guides objects in outer space, for example, was a mystery until Newton saw that apples followed the same laws as celestial bodies. Identical principles could then be applied to all movement, from a baseball pitch to space rockets. Similarly, nature's master pattern of change can be applied to unravel anything from a mid-life crisis to organizational renewal; it is as useful in the classroom as the boardroom.

THE CYCLE OF CHANGE

Discovering the essentials of nature's method of change calls upon your creativity. Try to capture the imagination used by the astonishing Breakpoint thinker Albert Einstein. He penetrated the deepest marvels of nature by envisioning himself riding through the universe on a light beam traveling at the speed of light. In this case, imagine yourself as a passenger riding on the edge of a tiny particle of sand.

At this minute, your piece of sand, also known as silicon or quartz, is being subjected to immense heat inside a volcano. The temperature rises so much that your grain of sand becomes liquified. You're surrounded by confusion, turmoil, and chaos as other atoms hurl past in every direction. All is tumult and disorder.

Slowly, the heat dissipates, and as it does your tiny atom of sand begins to settle into a comfortable relationship with other silicon atoms. Slowly gathering together, the atoms form layers, fitting snugly into a tiny quartz seed crystal. As more and more atoms join the group, the world around you changes radically. The wild ride has settled down. Your trip has moved from disorder to order. You just passed through a natural Breakpoint!

The ride, however, has just begun. The hardening quartz, of which you are now an integral part, starts growing rapidly as additional atoms fuse together, forming large quartz molecules, growing ever bigger. Taking shape around you, the almost transparent crystal provides some rules of arrangement, order, and regularity. The ride is smooth and even, continuous and comfortable. The bonds between the silicon atoms have formed molecules that are so strong it seems nothing from outside can intrude on your secure world. Just as you are relaxing, expecting the gentle ride to continue indefinitely, the quartz crystal runs into an immense surprise. What is happening couldn't be predicted based on the past.

Suddenly, foreign atoms make their way into the crystal. Atoms of copper and magnesium intrude between you and other silicon atoms, spinning things around, grabbing loose atoms and electrons, changing the composition and arrangements of the crystal. Within the crystal new bonds are formed as old configurations vanish; the rules and orderliness you depended on have gone completely. Nearly overcome by confusion, you can't fathom what's happening. You just passed through another Breakpoint!

As you look around, you find that many of your new bonds with strange atoms are even stronger than before. Light is now refracted in many directions, suffused with beautiful colors. Actually, you notice that what was once a comfortable but rather dull neighborhood is becoming varied and interesting.

You have just taken a trip from plain old sand to become a quartz crystal and finally emerged as a precious amethyst. You have experienced two powerful Breakpoints where the rules around you shifted totally.

This same trip through Breakpoints is what happens when modern scientists and technicians copy nature's approach and grow silicon crystals, cut them into tiny wafers, etch them, and then add new and different atoms to bring a totally unique possibility into being. By going through two powerful Breakpoints, the cheapest and most common substance on the planet suddenly becomes the most expensive and important— a semiconductor, the basis of today's revolutionary transistorized technology. Instead of a powerful computer needing a giant, specially cooled building with complex and expensive vacuum tubes, it can use millions of transistors on several square inches of transformed sand run by flashlight batteries. The new system is many, many times cheaper, faster, smaller, and cooler.

Taking that ride on board a piece of sand to become an amethyst required a volcano and many years of cooling. Modern technology not only reduces this same process to days, but creates the special properties of a human-designed semiconductor. Over the last sixty years, individuals working in many fields have uncovered the secrets of how to shatter the Breakpoint barrier, causing a totally unpredictable technological revolution.

Probing into the experience of the silicon atom, we find that a cycle of change was encountered that includes three unique phases. (A *phase* describes an interval within the cycle of change between Breakpoints.) After a Breakpoint, the rules governing what works and what doesn't work shift dramatically. Successful methods in one phase actually become counterproductive in another.

These phases can be thought of by drawing an S curve that shows change across time. The horizontal movement shows the passage of time, the vertical motion indicates growth.

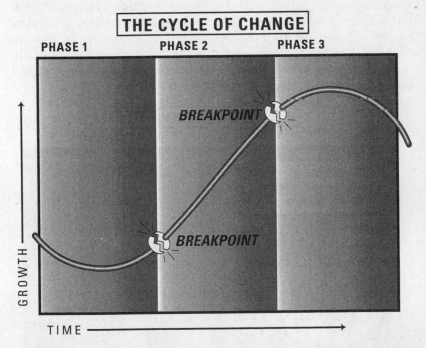

In order to understand what's going on within change an understanding of each phase becomes essential. The three phases are each distinct with unique qualities and characteristics that assure success.

PHASE ONE—FORMING

The First Phase of change consists of a disorderly probing and exploring of the environment. The aim is to discover what exists within the growing organism and in its environment and how these pieces can be brought together into a pattern—a pattern that can extend into and organize the larger environment. Exploration, experimentation, putting things together, and taking things apart are the change processes that go on in every first phase whether it be a quartz crystal developing or an entrepreneur looking for a pattern of success.

In the early part of the first phase, your imaginary piece of sand was quietly minding its own business inside a latent volcano. But suddenly inside the earth's surface, massive heat generated by the volcano led to great disorder. The atoms began moving faster and faster. It might appear to be total confusion, but only through turning silicon atoms into a turbulent, disorderly liquid can nature connect them into a pattern.

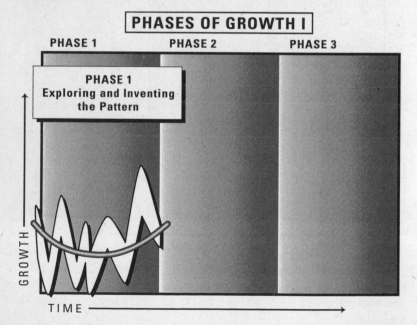

PHASES OF GROWTH I

PHASE 1 PHASE 2 PHASE 3

**PHASE 1
Exploring and Inventing
the Pattern**

GROWTH

TIME

Your piece of sand emerged as part of a special design once the slow cooling process ensued. Some of the silicon atoms linked up with one another to form the pattern of a seed crystal. No longer in disarray, the silicon atoms found a way to connect with one another in a regular, predictable arrangement. They reached the first Breakpoint. An inventor reaches this same point once a prototype is marketable, has been field tested, and is ready for production.

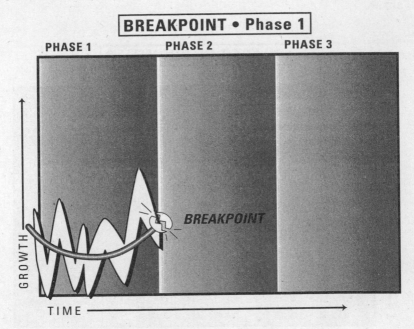

PHASE TWO—NORMING

Once a pattern takes form, the first massive shift in the change process occurs. Random experimenting ceases; the approach switches to an orderly building on the pattern. In the first phase, energy is spent on trial and error. In the second phase, replicating success concentrates energy efficiently; it builds on the extension of likeness. Extending, improving, and modifying the central pattern, while discarding what does not fit, make up the method of change and growth in the second phase.

The silicon atoms in the seed crystal resonated with one another and kept attracting other atoms like themselves until they formed large molecules. Organizations behave in a similar way once they find a workable pattern. By standardizing procedures, policies, product lines, and methods of production and distribution, an organization efficiently grows larger in its second phase.

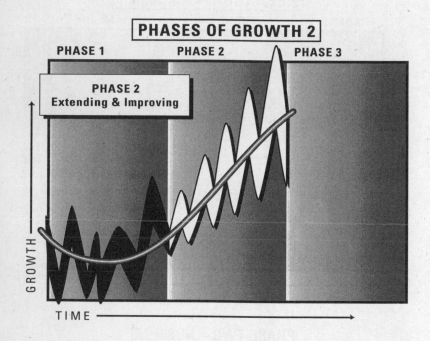

Every growing organism in the second phase will ultimately exhaust its ability to grow by building on the standard pattern. It uses up the environment and extends itself beyond its ability to maintain the limits and boundaries of its stable pattern. Whether it be a quartz crystal, a person, or an organization, any growing thing will hit another natural Breakpoint.

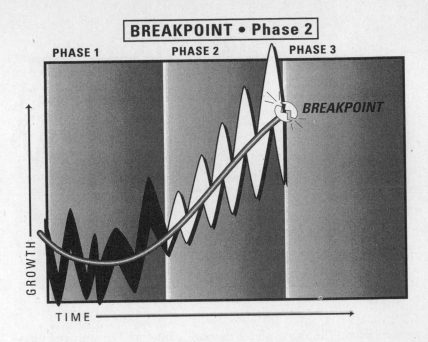

PHASE THREE—FULFILLING

Nature's method of growth moves ahead, attempting to fulfill the potential of the growing organism. To continue growth, the original pattern must be broken, rearranged, and then restructured. The new configuration must include elements that were rejected in the second phase. Only by combining the new and different and what was previously excluded can the growing entity fulfill its potential. Disordering, reordering, and innovating all make up the method of change in the third phase.

The quartz crystal, in order to become an amethyst, opened up its molecular bonds and allowed in the new and different. Foreign atoms joined and bonded with the silicon atoms.

Just like the third phase in a quartz crystal, crossing the powerful second Breakpoint barrier requires human organizations to bring in what was previously excluded. In the second phase of mature organizations a comfortable and routine environment is

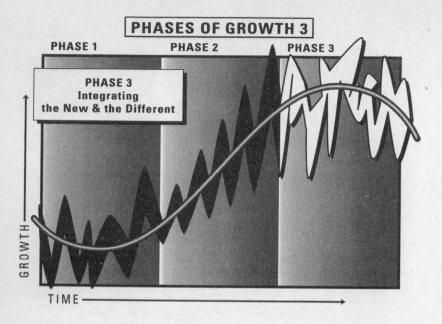

established. The third phase demands new and disparate behaviors such as innovating, partnering with customers and suppliers, adding new value to products and services, opening up the system to involve women and minorities, and taking on community and environmental responsibility.

Each phase of the change cycle adheres to its own specific procedures governing success. The rules change completely each time the system moves beyond a Breakpoint, otherwise growth would drift, slow down, halt, or even backup to a prior phase. The confusion in understanding the pattern of change comes from the fact that each phase is so different from the others.

Just like the changes going on around us today, the accumulated experience and wisdom of the past within any system presents no precedent or reason to lead us to believe that a totally new kind of change and growth could occur.

If we look deeper, behind the everyday occurrences in our lives, we can see that in many common experiences the rules change just as they did in something as common as simple sand becoming a quartz crystal. A couple meets, begins dating, and becomes better and better acquainted. In the process they fall in love. They have much in common and delight in discovering more about one another. Six months later they have established a wonderful and mutually reinforcing pattern in their relationship. Some years later the pattern starts to wear itself out; monotony and boredom set in. Suddenly, new, unexpected, and seemingly unnecessary tensions arise. The relationship is calling for new rules. Do they shift to phase three and bring new life back into their relationship, or do they resist the change and go slowly downhill, risking the possibility of the relationship completely breaking apart? Even the "second honeymoon" doesn't work for long. Phase three demands not more of the same but a new kind of relationship.

Likewise, the inventive entrepreneur takes what appears to be wild risks building a business where everyone said no business could exist. Yet after successful production and marketing begins and the company has a set pattern, she is told by the professional management team she hired, "Slow down, quit inventing." The rules changed on her, too.

Years later, after the founding entrepreneur grows bored with the sterile environment of her phase two business and leaves to continue inventing, the organization finds that it needs her fresh and different kind of thinking. But no one knows how to fit her unique style into the rules and tight structure. Like the marriage that hit the wall at Breakpoint, organizations most often settle down into a siege mentality and hold on, staving off complete failure as long as possible. These responses violate nature's formula for continuing growth and success.

For most people, to leave the comfort and security of the past behind and enter unknown and untried territory is difficult, at best. Second phase success lulls us into complacency and sometimes even arrogance. The rules and successes of parting with the past and entering a new domain are unfamiliar. It seems as if mastering the future would require the same rules that were used to achieve success in the past, but that isn't the way nature works. Nature parts with the past. For many, going ahead in the absence of some security appears forbidding and frightening. However, knowing nature's pattern of change offers safe passage to a different and far better future.

EXPERIENCE THE CYCLE OF CHANGE

In many ways, this voyage of discovering the natural pattern of change will take on the aspect of what Plato called "anamnesis," the opposite of amnesia. He believed that all learning was remembering. You will find that remembering and applying the knowledge that nature has already given you will prove essential to make change a productive partner. Then, even with Breakpoint change running so fast that anything is possible, you will be able to call on that storehouse of internal wisdom in any situation.

The natural cycle of change is something practically everyone already knows—intuitively—and has experienced in a myriad of different ways. It is particularly apparent in things we do that are imbued with natural fun and enthusiasm. Learning a sport, for example, gives us a somewhat larger view and personal sense of the inherent naturalness of this three-phase process.

Let's say you're taking up something like golf. In the beginning, the first phase, you explore, experiencing a trial and error process, picking up the pattern one piece at a time: the procedures, the stance, how to hold the clubs, which ones to use, how to swing. It's confusing at first, but little by little you assemble a complete pattern. Now you can put it all together and begin to really play the game.

In the second phase, you gradually improve your game; you get a better swing, select just the right club, and begin to test the green for speed. Your game gets better and better with practice. One day, just as you're getting ready to make another good drive, a fellow player remarks, "Why don't you hold your hands this way," and demonstrates her unique way of crossing her fingers over each other. We all know where you might want to tell her to go. Instinctively, you know not to tamper with success. So you go on playing, gradually improving your game. You may play successfully for years and years, but inevitably one day you hit a plateau; not only does your game stop improving, but the harder you try the worse it gets.

At this point you scratch your head and seek out the player whom you once told to keep her suggestions to herself. "How did you say to hold your fingers?" you ask. Now that you have a secure style—and you're not getting anywhere—you'll experiment with ideas that are different. In most cases, however, trying new things really doesn't take you to a much better level of play. The catch is, you've hit an invisible Breakpoint barrier. Most players never get past it.

But you've heard about some unique practices in the sports world; things such as "inner golf" and "Zen tennis" that can make major improvements in a person's game. You are determined to change your game so you go to one of the new breed of sports coaches. You get what seems to be very odd advice: "Don't try," he says. "Don't think, let go and become one with your club and the ball, visualize the result, not how you're doing it." It all sounds pretty strange, to say the least. These curious notions don't fit with much of anything you've spent so much time learning.

For the people who have mastered a sport and are willing to completely break with the habits brought on by past successes and bravely enter this new kind of world amazing results lie in wait. Those people move to third phase rules—rules that are very different but that are in tune with a more accurate, much deeper, and more powerful reality; they adopt nature's pattern of change.

OUR LINK WITH NATURE

There is no greater miracle than the continual, successful reduction of the rich complexity of nature to simple principles comprehensible to humankind.

REPORT TO CONGRESS, NATIONAL ACADEMY OF SCIENCE

Deeper and more profound insights about the natural cycle of change become available by understanding how simple cells evolved billions of years ago. The three phases that made up a cycle of change in silicon or improving a golf game or revitalizing a marriage or a business were identical to the billion years it took nature to create early life on this planet. That the patterns are essentially the same demonstrates our wonderful and profound links with nature. It also exposes how we can evoke vital lessons from the far eons of time to deal with the massive Breakpoint changes surrounding our organizations and personal lives in today's turbulent world.

4.5 Billion B.C.

Let us step far back into the world of early life to penetrate the secrets of change from yet another essential vantage point. Not long after the birth of our planet, over four and a half billion years ago, nature began a creative and inventive process as it searched for a pattern for life itself.

FIRST PHASE   During the earliest days of our planet, complex groups of molecules floundered around in the primordial chaos. They probed ceaselessly for the bits and pieces of our world that could be assembled into a repeatable pattern of self-sustaining growth. They tried out a myriad of experimental forms; most didn't survive. Ultimately, these ancient first phase entrepreneurs were able to piece together internal machinery to take in and digest food, membranes to defend themselves from the environment and, most important, they conjured up a nucleus of DNA, the blueprint of life. After over a billion years of experimentation, cell evolution reached the first Breakpoint; the rules shifted 180 degrees.

SECOND PHASE   With a nucleus of information that governed pattern repetition, these tiny cells, much like today's bacteria, could efficiently manufacture likenesses of themselves. They entered the second phase. Their success at multiplying themselves and reshaping our planet was unprecedented. These ingenious replicating cells dominated life on the planet for the next billion years. They extended, improved, and modified the original pattern through mutation and other means of exchanging genes, evolving into organisms with tremendous vitality and resilience.

If nature were truly after mere survival, she would have stopped with phase two nucleated cells. Descendants of these tiny creatures are the all-time world champion survivors. They can be found living successfully in polar ice caps, in hot springs, in air samples taken at 60,000 feet, and even in the deep canyons of the ocean where sunlight never reaches. Survival and quantitative growth is, however, but one critical step in the growth process. Just like the quartz crystal, repetition served to propel the cellular system to the second phase Breakpoint.

THE SECOND BREAKPOINT   The growth potential of any system is fulfilled by connecting with the different and dissimilar rather than building on similarities. This huge shift in the pattern of growth reveals one of nature's more useful secrets. A mature organization or an individual who feels stagnant after a long period of success, or feels the excitement of a career vanishing can get some real help by looking at what nature does.

The alarming news is that most people and most organizations don't understand what's happening when strange third phase phenomena suddenly appear in the environment. They usually respond like the imaginary executive board of "Nucleated Cells, Inc."

The time is Thursday morning at 8:30 A.M., 900,000,000 B.C. The executive committee is meeting and the president has just presented the five million year plan. Based on past performance, it was easy to project at least a 10 percent increase in growth. General agreement ensued. However, one of the managers at the back of the room interjected, "Before we finalize our numbers, I think we ought to take a look at something very strange which seems to be occurring out in the bushes in my district. I think we may need to make some big changes . . . "

The president quickly cut her off, reassuring her and the other managers that odd things had always happened out in the bushes. It was just a minor annoyance. As always, it would go away. The manager just had to tighten up and get back in control of her district. After two billion years of success, Nucleated Cells, Inc., would continue business as usual.

What our interjecting manager had observed in the bushes was the business of A and B getting together in a new kind of partnership; producing unique new cells. What she hadn't seen clearly was that these new cells were eating the A's and B's for breakfast, lunch, and dinner. Technically, gene recombination and hybridization had begun. This is also known as sex. It caught on. As things evolved, we can imagine that Nucleated Cells, Inc., ultimately filed for the cellular equivalent of Chapter 11.

At this cellular Breakpoint, a totally new process came into being. Nothing like it had ever existed before in the entire history of life on the planet!

THIRD PHASE—FULFILLING   Third phase integrating began as nature fulfilled the potential of cellular evolution. Cells combined and integrated differences that had kept them apart for countless millennia. Nature once again adopted the divergent process of creativity by combining the characteristics of parent A with parent B to create a unique hybrid in the new cell C. This occurred by opening up the internal bonds that had kept cells locked in a tight pattern.

Nature's way of bringing entirely new possibilities into existence necessitates crossing a Breakpoint barrier. Millions of years ago, the cellular Breakpoint occurred when cells began sharing differences rather than simply building on similarities.

Crossing the second phase Breakpoint has now become common because scientists have uncovered many of nature's secrets. For instance, corn yields gradually increased over thousands of years to reach finally about 23 bushels per acre in the 1930s. With hybrids, corn production catapulted to over 100 bushels per acre. Crossing a Breakpoint to produce alloys in metals invokes the same kind of amazing result. Combining titanium with iron didn't just add strength, it multiplied its tensile strength from 40,000 pounds per square inch to 200,000 pounds per square inch—and with a weight reduction of 60 percent. Without the crossing of this Breakpoint barrier, jet airplanes couldn't get off the ground and the transportation revolution wouldn't have happened.

A Breakpoint powerfully breaks the critical links with the past and brings into being what never existed before. Cycles of change build on one another bringing about continuous evolution.

Reinvention—Transformation

A vital clue for how evolution continually occurs comes in understanding that nature doesn't stop at the third phase. Fulfilling the system occurs simultaneously as another, essentially invisible cycle of growth begins. Nature enters a new first phase, inventing the next cycle at a much higher level of complexity.

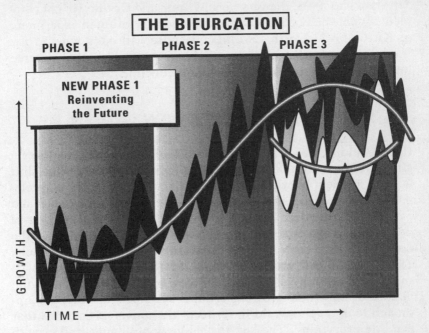

Compared to the incredible and overwhelming success of hybrid vitality, this parallel probing for something new appears almost indiscernible. It's often so different and alien to what's going on in the dominant third phase system that it seemingly doesn't deserve attention. In cell evolution, cells started joining in extensive interlinked, interdependent colonies, starting another first phase. It set the stage for the next great cycle of life, tiny multi-cellular plants emerged. This is a *transformation*.

The kind of transformation that leads to the reinvention of any ongoing enterprise is usually totally neglected. This is why the airplane industry was not invented by railroads. Experiments with odd vehicles in the air not only appeared foreign, but occurred when the railroad industry was at the zenith of success. We can all imagine the boardroom conversations. One well-published critic estimated that "the flying machine which will really fly might be evolved by the combined and continuous efforts of mathematicians and mechanics in from one to ten million years." The date was 1903, the very year Wilbur and Orville Wright completed what many claimed was a crazy, hare-brained experiment at Kitty Hawk, North Carolina. Because railroads ignored the "noise" of flight and the opportunity to transform, they entered into a period of gradual, yet inevitable decline.

A WHOLISTIC VIEW

Understanding how nature's method of change works requires a different kind of thinking. Peter Drucker concluded that the shift is from "a view in which the accent has been on parts and elements, to a configuration view, with the emphasis on wholes and patterns." Rather than beginning with the pieces of the puzzle and proceeding to construct the puzzle, we begin with a picture of the puzzle and place each piece by constantly referencing the whole. The change in cell evolution could not be grasped by taking a snapshot of an individual phase. It required looking at a moving picture of the whole growing cellular system. This wholistic approach looks at the world in terms of the universal patterns that pervade everything. The key to this view of change and growth is the knowledge that every single thing found in the universe is involved in the same evolutionary change process when observed over time.

Evolution has been thought of as survival of the fittest. To conquer the challenges of change we must ask, "Fit for what?" The reality of evolutionary success demonstrates that "fitness" is not simply about "adapting to an environment," but rather the continuing improvement in the capacity to grow and to build ever more connections in more varied environments (we define growth and evolution as continuously making more extensive and increasingly complex connections inside the growing organism and with the varied outside environments).

As we have seen with cell evolution, the whole became greater than the sum of its separate parts when nature built such broad, deep, and interpenetrating connections that hybrids were created. This would have been impossible to predict based on looking at any individual phase of growth or on the cellular system's past. This unending chain of connecting can be traced all the way from silicon atoms joining with molecules to form an amethyst, to cells evolving to create hybrids, to businesses connecting with new markets.

The ongoing cycle of evolutionary change finds the third phase overlapping with the new first phase. In this wholistic view of nature, an unending cycle of evolution occurs as one cycle with three phases of growth and change gives way to new, larger, and much more elaborate cycles—with capabilities and expressions of life far more complex than their predecessors. At one point, billions of years ago, it might have seemed that the phenomenal creation of hybrids was nature's finest hour. However, the creative evolutionary journey continued as complex organisms evolved into plants.

NATURAL PRINCIPLES

When we move inside the process expressed by ancient cells, we see that not only are the methods identical with how silicon atoms become an amethyst or how a relationship becomes revitalized, but the conclusions that can be drawn are far beyond what we would consider a traditional view of how our world works. They violate the orthodox and standard concepts that the world is logical and straightforward, made up of things that are separate from one another and that progress into the future as a continuation of the past.

Nature does not operate in a logical, regular, and predictable progression, but is engaged in a dynamic creative process, bringing into being what never before existed. Nature follows a very special pattern. She weaves in and out of ordering and reordering, encountering Breakpoints along the way. The phenomena that are often labeled "disorder" and "randomness" actually operate to provide necessary opportunities to develop deeper, broader, and more complex connections among people, ideas, and things both internally and with the outside environment as it moves through the three phases of creative growth and change. This allows nature—including us—to create giant, unpredictable leaps of evolution and creativity. New species appear! Unique cells, plants, animals, and varied forms of organized life emerge. Constant creative change hallmarks our planet—and our lives.

BEYOND CONVENTIONAL WISDOM

How does nature's dynamic creative change process correspond with what a person normally learns about change? In school, mathematical descriptions of change, whether it be a ball rolling down a hill, the trajectory of a bullet, or the acceleration of an automobile, build and reinforce the belief that change follows a straight-line and predictable path. Rarely, if ever, are we invited to question the assumption that change is uniform, orderly, and regular. The sad fact is that we are taught very little about change, at least not natural creative change. Conventional wisdom has it that "The only constant is change," but also that, "The more things change the more they stay the same."

The revolution in understanding nature disrupts such opinions. Over this last decade, pioneering research into such areas as biological evolution, chaos and catastrophe theory, self-organizing systems, and fluid dynamics has revealed that natural and abrupt, nonlogical changes from ordering to reordering and from disorder to order are found everywhere in nature. Over time, these processes of change lead inevitably to more ordered, more complex, more interrelated states. Nature is engaged in a dynamic creative change process that over and over again brings into being what never existed before. Thus, nature creates!

Individuals engaged in the creative process encounter exactly the same kind of vacillation between disorder and order that occurs in cells and other natural systems. Starting with a goal or problem, individuals first dynamically explore mind and environment, generating large numbers of alternatives and unusual combinations of ideas. Using an exploratory, open, nonrational, imaginative process, they allow connections to be made with the most unlikely associations.

After putting together enough bits and pieces, creative thinking moves to select the most promising combinations, discarding those ideas that are unworkable. A basic pattern takes form. Finally, after people have tested the initial pattern, they assemble or "synthesize" a complete solution. In this way, they integrate and embrace different possibilities into a unique, original expression. Thus, people create!

NATURE'S CREATIVE DYNAMIC

To see how people apply the creative process, look into the life of a person imbued with the creative spirit. People thought Edison was completely crazy as he experimented with everything he could get hold of to make a filament for a light bulb. He tried over 10,000 different materials. He even tried putting current through spiders' webs and Limburger cheese to see if it would work. Finally, by applying what he had learned from filaments made with burned thread, he synthesized and integrated some of his earlier experiments and ended up with a workable solution. The world was illuminated!

Even though some have long maintained that a few chosen humans are special because they are creative, the undeniable fact is that even atoms behave in ways that could only be defined as "creative." So do molecules, cells, plants, and animals. They invent novel forms, shift to new behaviors, combine in unpredictable—and unprecedented—ways. Far out in the outer reaches of the universe, stars form and galaxies coalesce in a creative process. The noted scientist and philosopher Karl Popper concluded, "The greatest riddle of cosmology may well be...that the universe is in a sense, creative."

Unleashing the creative spirit within each of us will happen only when we recognize the natural creativity that lies within everything and everybody—and willingly remove the tight barriers that have us convinced that only a few special people are creative. Only then will we be able to begin the exciting process of moving beyond Breakpoint.

Nature's creative method that conquers Breakpoints is not only something anyone can do, but it's also something that everybody intuitively already knows. Creativity is not only a natural process; it's *the* natural process. Once we are willing to tap our creative potential, we will move to doing what nature does, creating the impossible; not just doing things differently, but doing different things. The basic approach moves from solving problems and getting things back to normal to formulating original opportunities. Attitudes shift from applying the "right," tried-and-true, traditional answers, to energizing the production of unique possibilities.

Only by fostering major breaks with the past will organizations and individuals meet the challenge of Breakpoint change.

Some companies such as 3M, Dow Corning, Merck, and P & G, to name just a few, are attempting to do just that. In addition, non-profit organizations such as the Girl Scouts and United Way have made innovative breakthroughs in membership services and expanding their cadre of volunteers. All of these groups have made creative innovation the watchword of progress. A great deal of attention is given to learning the skills of creative thinking and to building teams in which groups use unique methods to discover unexpected opportunities that break with the past. In education, the Creative Education Foundation devotes its programs to teaching creative processes to individuals and organizations throughout the world. Experts in creativity are being utilized in organizations as never before.

When people tap their natural creative potential on a regular basis, their lives become energetic and vital. What other people call problems are for them opportunities to invent original solutions. Rather than daunting them, change invigorates. The true creative geniuses are all around us—they might be solving a plumbing problem in the basement, rearing children, or fishing. Vibrantly alive and involved with the world around them, they are living fully. The great inventor Buckminster Fuller summed up our human situation, "Everyone is born a genius. Society de-geniuses them."

The secret to recapturing the genius inside us—and success-fully crossing those invisible Breakpoints that face us today—is in getting a clear picture of the essential steps involved and of what works best. The secret is in knowing that everywhere in nature change follows the same three-step creative process, along with accompanying Breakpoints.

NEW RULES FOR SUCCESS

Once you understand nature's master pattern of change and growth, it can be applied to almost any situation that you encounter. You can see where your family, your relationships, your volunteer organization, and even society are in fulfilling their possibilities. You may find that your family is in phase two, your career at Breakpoint moving to phase three, and that your volunteer organization is just inventing a pattern. We will uncover the unique rules for each phase, and you will learn how you can integrate these rules fully into your life and work.

You will be able to understand when family relationships change, and you will know how to adapt to those changes. James Rumora of Arthur Andersen's Business Systems Consulting group realized he and his wife had been in a successful second phase pattern of relating to their two daughters. But when his oldest daughter was about to turn eighteen, the family relationship began to get chaotic. The traditional methods he and his wife had used with their daughter no longer worked. "For the family relationship to grow, we had to break apart the old ways of relating and integrate new and different behaviors. We had to view our relationship with our oldest daughter in a new light and from a different perspective." A shift to the third phase of change was essential for the Rumora family to thrive.

If you feel undervalued by your organization or unable to make the contribution you want to make, you will be able to diagnose the problem and figure out how to create within it. You will know when you are approaching a Breakpoint or when the rules themselves have already changed. The tools and skills to build a new approach to any situation will be available to you.

The seemingly chaotic change assaulting our individual lives, organizations, and society is understandable. Only by crossing over the Breakpoint barrier and releasing our traditional patterns, opening up and bringing in the new and different, will there be a transformation of our personal lives, the workplace, and our larger society.

The organizational ineffectiveness of schools, government, businesses large and small, the judicial system, medicine, the legal profession, to name but a few, demand not more intensified solutions from the past, but a willingness to ask totally new questions about what is possible. The environment they have encountered will continue buffeting them, demanding radical change. Organizations simply cannot use the same worn-out patterns to get to the future. The time has arrived for all of our major institutions to diverge creatively, to explore their total environment to find out how they can renew the enterprise. The question that must be asked is how can they create what has never before existed?

THE MASTER PATTERN OF CHANGE

Organizations deserve our interest and focus because they are the building blocks of society. Individuals build organizations; organizations build the world. The most important and critical organization is the family. From the smallest family to the largest multinational organization, it is imperative that moving beyond Breakpoint becomes a natural process rather than something to be resisted. The great challenge is to understand the process of organizational transformation and then to construct a new roadmap for organizational success in this new era.

3: DYNAMIC ORGANIZATIONAL CHANGE AND RENEWAL

> The whole world is being swept forward in a tremendous economic revolution which promises to dwarf the impact of the industrial revolution. Top management must be committed to science-led change.
>
> Sir Kenneth Durham,
> Chairman, Unilever Corporation

The annual Association of Manufacturers' meeting is always lively. Managers, academics, and consultants vociferously discuss what mix of improved product quality, management delegation, employee training, personal empowerment, customer service, plant productivity, niche marketing, and advanced technology will help their members meet increasing global competition and the challenges they are confronting with customers. Almost identical dialogues echo in universities and volunteer groups across the country. When organizations are viewed through the lens of the natural process of growth and change, we realize that these discussions miss the point of how to succeed in today's world. A much more basic and far-reaching shift is required.

Breakpoint changes are sweeping us *not* toward doing things better, but forward to a monumental revolution that will redefine the way work is organized and performed—and the very nature of

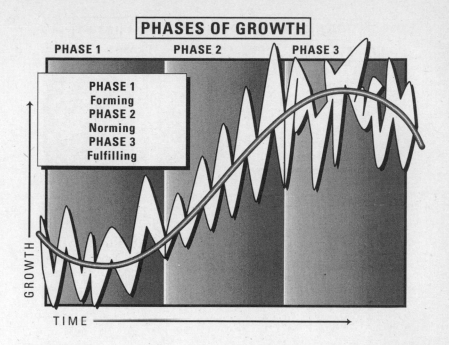

PHASES OF GROWTH

PHASE 1   PHASE 2   PHASE 3

PHASE 1
Forming
PHASE 2
Norming
PHASE 3
Fulfilling

GROWTH

TIME

organizations themselves. An astonishingly new system of human endeavor will send shock waves throughout organizations that will eclipse the impact of the industrial revolution.

The familiar *S* curve will be used quite differently from the usual exposition of birth, growth, maturity, and decline of an enterprise. Our exploration of this growth and change process will show how natural growth leads to extraordinary Breakpoint shifts in the way organizations must operate for initial success to occur, how this is followed by different forms of quantitative growth, and how the usual decline and demise of a successful organization can be replaced by renewal and reinvention of the enterprise. (Horizontal movement shows the passage of time, the vertical motion indicates growth of the organization.)

Let us follow the growth and change of an organization to reveal exactly how the hidden drama of Breakpoint change unfolds.

PHASE ONE—ORGANIZATIONAL FORMING

When any organization starts out, it instantly becomes subject to the dynamic rules of nature's method of growth. Organizational start-ups, whether they be in education, business, volunteer groups, or government, are trying to discover an efficient and effective pattern in order to grow and survive.

The first phase of an organization is the entrepreneurial stage. Entrepreneurs believe, for any of a diverse number of reasons, that they have an idea for a product or service that will solve someone's problem. They are convinced, with a deep fervor and obsession, that their idea will be needed and wanted in the marketplace; it could make a real contribution.

The entrepreneur:

■ Imaginatively probes and explores the environment in extremely creative and dynamic ways to learn everything possible

- Experiments by attempting all manner of things to find what succeeds and what fails

- Rebounds between the terror of survival and having fun, bouncing ideas around and trying things out and

- Brings together an essential blueprint of success with the desirable resources that marries the product or service with the market.

This period is very ingenious and unpredictable, a time of trial and error, of success and failure, of untold frustration and great triumphs. Yet, it certainly isn't a period to merely survive, but to find, in the most creative and inventive way, how to operate and structure the enterprise in order to connect with the larger environment. The successful entrepreneur is, in the words of Peters and Waterman, "a maniac with a mission."

Edwin Land of Polaroid fame personifies the entrepreneur. He had such tenacity that he wouldn't be stopped from realizing success with instant photography. Many people, observing his inventive style, concluded that he could never succeed. He worked in a laboratory atmosphere of chaos and confusion. He and his associates weren't "manageable." The young George Lucas, the guiding force behind the *Star Wars* epics, experimented with producing backyard carnivals and went on to try new kinds of films like *THX 1138* and *American Graffiti*. He admits that in the first *Star Wars* film when he wanted to star two robots, "They said I was nuts." When Tom Watson of IBM wanted to replace punch cards with invisible electronic signals, the experts regarded him the same way. Lillian Vernon, Chairman and CEO of her own company, started out with $2,000 and an ad in *Seventeen* magazine forty years ago. Today she runs an incredibly successful mail order catalog business. Vernon believes that, "entrepreneurs never feel they are going to fail. They have a sureness in their path. It is an innate feeling."

The type of creativity in phase one is *invention*. At its most elementary level, behind the process of imagination and exploration is the basic drive to find a repeatable pattern of success.

Because of the tremendous difficulties in creating a new pattern, if the entrepreneur does not have a clear goal, exceptional determination, and commitment, along with ideas, resources, and an ability to cultivate good market contacts, success is unlikely. The entrepreneur must explore the environment relentlessly, almost obsessively, to discover that special pattern and then go out and win acceptance for it. This period requires great flexibility and adaptability to meet the unpredictable circumstances that inevitably appear.

Most first phase organizations, whether for profit or not for profit, fail to find a pattern of success. In nature, new cell mutations typically fail well over 99 percent of the time. One acorn out of thousands will grow into a healthy tree. In business organizations, 84 percent of those that make it past the critical first year fail within five years. They don't find or invent the successful product or service, or they don't discover a real need. Some entrepreneurs just give up too soon. Business is totally "natural" in that most small businesses fail to find that critical pattern of success.

The start-up period has little or nothing to do with the classic idea of management. It has everything to do with inventiveness, decisiveness, commitment, and flexibility. We characterize the most successful entrepreneur in phase one as a sort of benevolent Genghis Khan. Quick decisions, bold initiatives, and resourceful ways of solving problems are the only standards. To the entrepreneur, none of this is risky; it is necessary! The underlying success factor in phase one is the willingness to fall down, pick oneself up, and start all over again. The rules—do it, try it, fix it— totally agree with what happens in the beginning for everything in nature.

PHASE TWO—ORGANIZATIONAL NORMING

The trap that can ensnare organizations as they attempt to grow is that each phase in this cyclical pattern is extraordinarily different from the others. Movement from one phase to another brings about an all-out shift in the rules that govern how the system connects internally and with its external environment.

Once an organization finds a workable pattern, the first Breakpoint occurs—with a 180 degree shift in the rules. In order to grow in the most efficient and effective way, the dynamic disorder so characteristic of the entrepreneur is replaced by focusing on a pat-

DYNAMIC ORGANIZATIONAL CHANGE AND RENEWAL

tern. Henry Ford standardized the manufacturing of automobiles, moving the auto industry into its second phase. Scores of first phase automobile manufacturers soon disappeared. The American public school movement found a successful pattern when state monies and compulsory education became the law. Public education became institutionalized and with it the vast array of educational choices vanished.

TRANSITION PROBLEMS

At this Breakpoint, if the entrepreneur keeps inventing and introducing new products into the environment, it can be disastrous. A number of recent corporate examples of entrepreneurs not making the shift from phase one to phase two have become legends. Steve Jobs and Steve Woycniak, the creative founders of Apple Computer, were successful entrepreneurs. Woycniak left Apple after the adventuresome entrepreneurial phase. Adjusting to a phase two management system with rules and regulations was not conducive to his creativity or propensity for invention. Steve Jobs stayed on and ultimately ran into trouble because he continued inventing when Apple needed replication. John Sculley, the chairman of Apple Computer, suggested that if he were writing a want-ad for an entrepreneur like Steve Jobs, it would read, "Wanted: Impresario to orchestrate a workshop of wizards."

At Control Data, Bill Norris continued to invent new and untested services when the company needed to stabilize and maintain its successful product-driven pattern. The resulting losses were phenomenal. At Polaroid, the huge investment made in instant motion picture development by Edwin Land at the time when the company needed to move into mass production and marketing of a cheap still camera almost took the company under. Knowing when and how to make the big shift to the second phase is critical to the success of any organization.

SECOND PHASE RULES FOR SUCCESS

The rules governing success in the second phase change totally. The primary objective at this point is to set up methods to repeat, extend, and improve those things that work and to discard those things that don't fit the pattern. Managers at this point talk about the "best surprise is no surprise," "solid bottom line," and "running a tight ship" with "clear lines of authority." The opportunities for growth are now very different from the entrepreneurial situation. The wasted energy of trial and error in phase one must be replaced by policies, practices, and procedures that guarantee the repetition of the successful second phase pattern. The rule becomes "When you find something that works, stick with it."

Leaders everywhere in the postindustrial world know the second phase well, for within it are based the ideas of traditional organizational management: plan, organize, staff, and measure. The shift from the freewheeling, ingenious inventiveness of the entrepreneur to the narrow limits of management is a massive leap. Second phase management success factors conform to orderly, established routines with predictability and control. If these management practices don't take over from the entrepreneurial style, the enterprise will fail.

DYNAMIC ORGANIZATIONAL CHANGE AND RENEWAL

A thriving phase two business regulates its internal processes, supplies, manufacturing, product lines, and selling methods and continually seeks to extend and improve its particular group of activities. During this stage, organizations strive to achieve uniform methods, efficiency, and effectiveness; a system that will support pattern repetition and extension. Clear direction from the top—policies, procedures, and measurements—is established to limit activities to those already proven successful in the past. It is a period of *growth through limitation*. Because the energy in the system can be focused on replicating the success pattern, growth in the second phase is usually very rapid.

One of the most fascinating things that happens once phase two begins is that walls are erected to exclude anything that does not fit the basic pattern. The ruling method of growth in phase two builds on *similarity and likeness*. Anything that might disturb the basic pattern is eliminated or discarded.

Fast food chains specialize in limited types of food and service with standard quality and low price. Domino's Pizza and McDonald's, for example, focused on particular products, services, and market segments. UPS and Federal Express didn't try to compete with the postal service in all areas. They selected very restricted market niches, excluding anything that didn't fit their particular pattern. The system works because of well-established limits.

Creativity does not disappear in phase two; it is focused on incremental improvements in the system. Speeding and scaling up production, reducing waste, maximizing investment in inventory, eliminating bottlenecks, and lowering defects make up a few of the areas on which second phase organizations focus. Trends such as *Management by Objectives, Just in Time,* and *Total Quality* dominate organizations. Breaking original patterns or innovating by introducing the *new and different* are not appropriate or welcome. The natural fact in the second phase is that thinking too differently is actually dangerous to continuing success and sometimes even threatens the survival of the enterprise. It is unsuitable. Good managers know this and far-ranging creativity is discouraged, if not completely killed. One primary purpose of management in the second phase is *to limit and control the creative potential of the people in the organization.*

SECOND PHASE RULES AND TRAPS

Consider the ideal working rules of successful second phase systems:

- Management procedures, processes, and controls are geared to maintain order and predictability.

- Reward systems motivate the preservation and expansion of past investments and routines. Compensation is standardized and competitive.

- Quantitative measurements are used to judge the health of the system.

- People connections are narrow and specialized. People know little about what is happening outside their own area, and problems are seen as not relevant if they are outside one's own department.

- Internal organizational priorities, resource allocation, and political problems have precedence.

- The organization maintains an atmosphere of agreement. A "don't rock the boat" mentality prevails, thus reinforcing past practices. Solutions to many problems and experiments or innovations are viewed as disturbances.

- New, incompatible, and unexpected customer and competitive changes are not noticed or investigated; reality is what is communicated within the system's regular reporting processes, and malfunctions and misdirections may not be detected for long periods, particularly if they are not in the area of such normal quantitative indicators as costs, sales, or production figures.

As a consequence, although these rules work well in a predictable, stable second phase environment, when organizations encounter a third phase environment, they naturally resist change that involves doing things differently. They will resist change *regardless of obvious need or changed conditions*. The result is that unpredictable modes of failure regularly occur, often where least expected. The organization will not be able to make the vital changes needed for survival and growth.

Let's examine some second phase traps in more detail. Often they are so insidious that they are almost invisible.

Trap Number One—Measurements Become the Mission

Second phase organizations concentrate on planning, organizing, and evaluating. Linear, logical, rational, empirical thinking becomes the ruling paradigm. A variety of standardized measures are installed to ensure that the system is working. Measurements become so important that many successful organizations in the middle of the second phase make a subtle but critical shift in how they look at the business, and the measurements actually become the mission. The original entrepreneurial vision of meeting an important need is lost. A spreadsheet mentality takes over and numbers begin to drive the organization. People in the company lose their focus on why they are there, and quality—solving a customer's problem in a superior way—suffers. The motivation to be a part of providing a product or service needed by customers is replaced by short-term bottom line results.

Even in the halls of academe the measurements have also become the mission. The "publish or perish" syndrome forces faculty members seeking tenure to put most of their emphasis on research and writing rather than teaching, even though the claim is continually made by university officials that teaching is a professor's most important contribution. In elementary and high schools, measurements are so important that students are given training on how to take tests rather than on learning how to think and how to understand material in various subject areas.

Trap Number Two—Past Assumptions Go Unquestioned

As voter turnout has decreased over time in the United States, the major political parties have decried this circumstance as an indication that responsible citizenship is being eroded. If the Republican and Democratic parties wanted to look underneath the numbers, they might discover that the voters are delivering a clear message that the traditional limits of the two-party system are no longer acceptable. The communist bloc has collapsed within a dynamic third phase global environment. Attempting to build the future using centralized control or tyrannical rule proved fatal.

The entrenched public educational establishment continually opposes genuine educational reform. Competency-based education, the voucher plan, parents choosing where to enroll their children—all are vehemently opposed. The powerful educational lobbies claim that what education needs is more money. Even though more money has been allocated to education by state legislative bodies for the last thirty years, test scores plummet and drop-out rates escalate. The public has begun to believe that perhaps educators are unable to look beyond past assumptions to truly transform education.

Trap Number Three—Embedded Investment

Traditional assets often anchor organizations to obsolescence. Letting go of what have served as foundations for success is so difficult that many organizations suffer paralysis. The U.S. steel industry was so mired in its procedures, basic technologies, and past markets—and the pressure to make continuous high levels of profit—that it did not see the consequences of new technologies, foreign competition, or even the rapidly growing demand for new and highly specialized products. When the light dawned, it didn't have the time or resources to make the change.

The more subtle embedded investment of knowledge and expertise forms an even more compelling trap than having to write off hard assets. A host of information-intensive industries remain dependent on so-called experts and managers who cling tenaciously to outdated and obsolete knowledge. Replacement solutions then emerge from organizations whose people are free from the weight of the past.

Excluding women from entering the priesthood in major religions has been an unquestioned practice for some fifteen hundred years. Recently it has come under attack, and the upheaval in some denominations around women becoming part of the clergy has led to controversy, protests, and divisions within these religious groups. Embedded practices are hard to overcome.

With escalating budgets for higher education, governors, legislative bodies, and the public want a more accountable system. The public asks, why duplicate degree programs throughout a state university system? University administrators, faculty, and governing boards have a knee jerk reaction. Cutting programs and eliminating duplication are often met with a lobbying effort that holds fast to the embedded investments of the past.

Trap Number Four—Blaming Others

A history of success leads many people to look outside for the sources to their problems. Many industries once dominated by the United States, such as textiles, electronics, and tool and die making, fall back on the usual excuses of "regulatory limits," "cheap labor or raw materials," "foreign government incentives," and "unfair practices." These don't add up when we see such companies as Honda, Sony, and Panasonic building highly successful plants in the United States with methods available to everyone.

Traditionally there has been ample blame to go around whether it's labor versus management or management versus labor. Both sides find ways to blame the other for whatever ill is sweeping through an industry, organization, or company. Until recently, anything that was based on cooperation was looked upon as collusion.

Trap Number Five—Maximizing Profit

It was in 1970 that General Motors announced that its mission was making money, not cars. It didn't take the American consumer long to figure that out. Unfortunately, the mission statements of many mature companies have moved from being service- or product-driven to maximizing profit. A classic example was Southland Corporation, the legendary 7-11 chain. Its mission was "building the long-term market value of shareholder equity." This is hardly the original vision that the founding entrepreneur set out to achieve. This shift most often leads to the misuse of resources and long-term disaster. The deeper tragedy, however, is that the people in the organization no longer feel they are meeting a valuable need and become cogs in an impersonal machine designed merely to generate sales and profits.

Trap Number Six—Information Filtering

Another deceptive trap awaits the successful second phase organization. Repetition of success by building on likeness is so crucial that it becomes an inherent and unseen problem. Like-minded people with similar backgrounds and education are hired and promoted. As their experience and body of knowledge grow, they tend to feel threatened by internal or external challenges. *Selective attention takes over.* Perceptual screens are constructed to filter out information and ideas that could interfere with rote pattern repetition. Tragedies similar to what is happening in American education, health care, and heavy industries abound. The people in the system are unable to see the changes that are happening in their environment. Often the data that people ignore have to do with factors that could literally drive them out of business.

Some years ago one of our clients, an American car manufacturer, was given a report that a nation in the Far East could produce a car within the next ten years at a cost of $995, compared to nearly $10,000 for the American equivalent. One of the members of the executive management team said, "Oh, we did a study much like that." He looked around the room, "What was our number?" No one responded. No one on the executive committee remembered what the report said.

The study was finally unearthed, and it turned out their own researchers estimated that by applying new manufacturing processes and plastic/ceramic technologies a car might actually be built that would cost as little as $935. In carefully reviewing how a report with that kind of impact was virtually forgotten, it became obvious that the executive committee was able to dismiss it because it was not within their frame of reference; it was just too different. They had built in mental barriers to shield them from information that did not fit the pattern they had come to know and expect. It fell outside of their perceptual screen.

Trap Number Seven—Tight Control

Losing control presents great risks to orthodox management. Uncertainty, ambiguity, unpredictability, and surprises are discouraged. Tremendous pressure from top management for bottom-line results often generates fear about losing one's job and leads to managers imposing even tighter controls.

The search for certainty and predictability, so characteristic of second phase organizations, leads to building bureaucracies that insulate the top echelon from what is really happening. These bureaucracies become too big, too complex, too bureaucratic, and too insulated from the problems to see what is going on without opening up the system to include the previously excluded. All of the governments in Eastern Europe collapsed under the oppression of a tight second phase pattern before their leadership saw what was happening. By then it was too late to loosen the bonds and bring in the previously excluded.

A major institutional example in the United States is medicine. Samuel Thier, former president of the Institute of Medicine in Washington, D. C., said medicine's successes have caused it to "fall prey to the equivalent of a bureaucracy. It has come to compromise both its intent and purpose, to protect the corporation instead of the principles." The tight control of the medical bureaucracy, from the American Medical Association to the fifty state associations, has led to medical care becoming impersonal and expensive. In essence, just like other organizations, much of medical practice has lost its original purpose in bureaucratic red tape. The very people it was set up to serve lose out because the desire for control from the top fails to serve the desires and wants of the client.

Trap Number Eight—Internal Competition

Tremendous energy is expended at the end of phase two in doing more and getting less. One major reason for this loss in productivity comes from the enormous vitality lost in internal competition for resources. Separate departments try to "go it alone" to prove their value to the organization. Members of the research department of a major American company swore one of the authors to secrecy, revealing a discovery of how to make great savings by eliminating waste. The research department was unable to implement its discovery and wouldn't turn it over to the production department because the research department wanted credit and bonuses for the big savings. Two years later, the idea had not yet reached the production floor. Whether it is an individual, an organization, an atom, or a developing cell, every system must ultimately make the massive shift to phase three interdependency and sharing of resources in order to grow. The very things that contributed to the success in the second phase stand in the way of making the move to third phase advancements.

Within the executive branch of government, whether it be at the federal or state level, there often emerges competition between the chief executive's staff and individual cabinet members and their staffs. The fighting for turf between the Secretary of

State and the head of the President's National Security Council has emerged over the years as nearly inevitable. Different cabinet secretaries vie for the chief executive's favor and funding. Valuable time is focused on in-fighting for position and power.

In American politics, allegiance to political ideology and party differences often takes precedence in the Congress over the nation's business. Squabbling over petty concerns obscures the real issues and results in time and money being squandered.

Trap Number Nine—Vendor Competition

Traditionally, the practice of organizations buying from suppliers on a tough price-competition basis made good sense. Today, with rapidly changing markets, creative partnerships with vendors can add new value for customers. Part of Wal-Mart's success is due to its unique collaborative relationship with key vendors. Wal-Mart and its vendors collaborate in product development, packaging, and merchandising. This allows Wal-Mart to move from merely providing the lowest price to providing superior value. Third phase preferred vendor relationships, in which buyer and supplier work together to create new value for customers, add new elements to the mix. Mutual sharing of critical—and usually secret—information to jointly bring about higher value replaces cut-throat competition.

NOTHING FAILS LIKE SUCCESS

In every system, there are finite limits to growth. This happens in two ways. First, *the very success of an organization changes the environment.* By meeting the initial need, the organization impels the emergence of new and different needs. Second, a point is reached when the whole organizational system becomes so large and complex it exhausts its ability to grow just by following its standard and rigid ways. Standard practices become increasingly out of touch as change accelerates. What was simple in the first phase ultimately becomes extremely complicated—and expensive—late in the second phase. Any mature phase two organization so increases and stretches its linkages, both internally in production and in the external distribution and marketing environment, that it uses up the normal pattern and must shift its basic methods in order to continue growing.

American TV networks "used up their environment." They so sophisticated their viewers and standardized and formularized their offerings that they automatically made room for the "surprising" success of cable TV. No one in the industry predicted how this phenomenon, with its tremendous revenues and profits, would grow. The same has happened in a movie industry once controlled by a few big studios. Now, small, independent producers are the big multimillion dollar successes.

McDonald's was mentioned as a phase two example—but it didn't stop there. McDonald's enjoyed tremendous success, expanding and modifying a successful phase two pattern that was extended worldwide. Eventually, McDonald's faced the natural laws of change; competitors such as Wendy's, Burger King, and others saturated the market. McDonald's had the flexibility and foresight to move to third phase marketing. It opened up the standard system and integrated the new and different. Now, throughout its markets, McDonald's is offering many other items besides hamburgers. It is building unique McDonald restaurants that are not the rubber stamp, golden arches of the past. The standard and predictable has become rich with variety.

SHIFTING TO PHASE THREE

The Breakpoint shift from second phase management to third phase Breakpoint leadership is even more difficult than the previous leap from the entrepreneurial to management phase. Tremendous resistance can arise to make forces within the organization gear up to fight—and defeat—the change. Organizations must develop early warning signals as to when standard management will begin to produce diminishing returns. Then, it must reenter the divergent part of the creative process—in a totally new way!

The organization must open up to permit what was never allowed in to become a part of the system, not only by doing things differently, but *by doing different things.* This de-structuring the

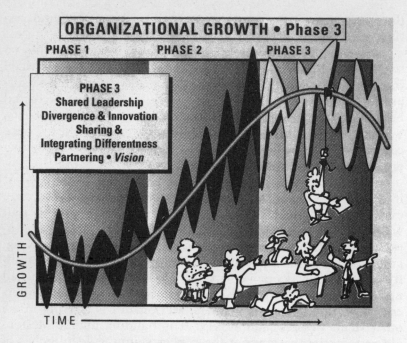

old and re-structuring to integrate the new is the natural creative process at work.

The de-structuring process at Breakpoint in the business environment seems, at first glance, very disorderly. We find common symptoms that indicate that a business organization has reached the second to third phase Breakpoint:

- Rapidly increasing internal and market place complexity in such areas as product proliferation and market divisions

- Internal competition for resources

- Increasing costs of manufacturing and sales

- Diminishing returns

- Declining share of market

- Decreasing productivity gains

- Growing external pressures from regulators and influence groups

- Increasing impact of new technologies
- New and unexpected competitors

Today's organizations in the United States and other postindustrial nations face a new kind of change. Never before has America's posture in world trade, health care, education, and production been challenged with such vigor on so many levels. The strategies that were so successful in the past are no longer working. And because today's forecasts are based on past performance, many businesses are finding that continuing growth and expansion no longer ensure profitability. The uncertainty of current trends and projections, as well as the frequency of economic and political surprises, clearly indicates that change is an irrevocable necessity, that organizations have depleted the carrying capacity of second phase patterns.

As Robert Horton, chairman of British Petroleum Co., declared, "In the 1990s, corporations that achieve the greatest success will be those that manage surprise." The environment has shifted enormously: from local to global, from stable markets and supplies to fluid markets with shifting and uncertain supplies. New corporate and community pressures have also emerged: responsibility for environmental impact; need for community and social involvement; accountability for political influence, ethical standards and open information—public disclosure, open accounting, and pressures for truth in advertising and truth in lending.

The winds of change blow from unpredictable quarters. We must now deal with a new two-tiered global marketplace: the transnational competitive organization and individual consumers who buy what they want regardless of where it comes from. Today, in order for a business to work, there must be both national and international purposes as well as extreme sensitivity to the rapid variations in individual customer needs.

Versatility and target marketing now has vast potential. The break up of standardized markets and production is occurring throughout a wide range of products, rapidly replacing mass-produced commodities with diversified, high value-added, almost custom-made products. The magazine industry is an excellent example of this trend away from mass production. Rather than a few magazines with huge circulations, the industry is now based on literally thousands of magazines with relatively small circulations, each targeted for special groups.

Mass-produced commodity businesses are a second phase phenomenon and rest on outmoded notions of large-scale production, standard management, and mass marketing. The third phase shift to many small, special markets integrates ideas and material that were neglected in the second phase pattern. These changes include specialized consumer needs, market niches, vendor and consumer partnerships, quality over quantity, and products that are almost custom made.

A THIRD PHASE WORLD

When the Breakpoint from phase one to phase two occurred, many possibilities were eliminated in order to achieve a pattern that allowed growth to take place. Those possibilities that were excluded or discarded in the first phase did not disappear, however, they lingered outside the growing system. In phase three, they are noticed and brought back in. It is remarkable how easy it is to ignore those things that were there all the time. Suddenly, many of these discarded elements can generate fresh successes if the system starts seeing them and using them in new and different ways.

A classic example is the new movement to "High-tech—high-touch." Pre-industrial methods in organizations were necessarily high-touch, but as the industrial age developed, they were replaced by more efficient mechanized processes. Now, the unique value of human relationships has re-emerged. Banking, for example, once a completely people-centered business, became highly automated. Today, depersonalized banking has rediscovered "relationship banking" into which human caring and contact are integrated.

In the second phase environment, minorities and women have been part of the organizational work force for a long time, but they have been asked to behave according to the rigid expectations, rules, and policies of a phase two system. The work force grows more diverse daily, with women and ethnic minorities becoming a dominant force. No longer is it a question of affirmative action,

DYNAMIC ORGANIZATIONAL CHANGE AND RENEWAL

but clearly essential to have Hispanics, Blacks, Asians, and other important groups contributing their insights and viewpoints to building the future. It is just being discovered that women and minorities can bring unique perspectives and totally new ideas into the workplace. Capitalizing on the contributions such differences can bring to organizations is a major key to success in opening up the system in phase three.

REINVENTION OF THE ORGANIZATION

In phase three, two activities occur simultaneously. While the mainline or core business grows around creative innovations, a simultaneous renewal phase is completely reinventing the enterprise. This is technically called a bifurcation. The result will be the beginning of a new first phase. The renewal line is based on new inventions. The mainline or core business is based on innovations.

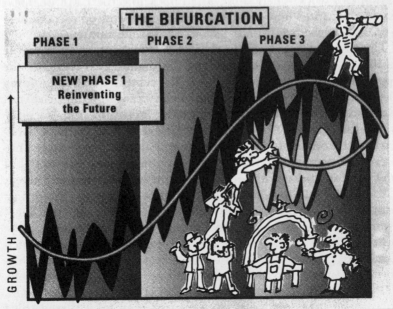

Even though the two processes are occurring in tandem, they require completely different kinds of creativity, leadership, and ways of doing business. They must be kept away from one another or the resulting confusion will be extreme. Entrepreneurs and core managers operate differently. The two enterprises can and will powerfully interfere with one another. The invention process is very "noisy." It looks alien. In the beginning, since there is no detectable pattern, it cannot even be recognized as relevant. In fact, if an effort does look relevant to the core business, it probably is not part of the invention process.

In practice, a useful approach is to keep the two efforts geographically and physically separated from each other with a well-organized information-sharing process. In many cases, each undertaking can incorporate discoveries made by the other. What can't be shared is the type of creativity that will assure success. Innovation doesn't mix with invention. The initial success of IBM's entry level division in Boca Raton, Florida and its creation of the business personal computer industry far away from corporate influences in Armonk, New York, shows how well such separation can work. Their integration back into the main business also demonstrates how creativity based on invention can quickly be squashed in a traditional second phase environment.

The group reinventing the enterprise, operating away from the mainline or core business, is given the mandate to recreate the organization—in a totally new way. The central question guiding this group is, "How can we put ourselves (the core enterprise) out of business?" This is done by exploration, invention, repatterning, and trial and error. The ultimate objective is that the core business and the reinvented enterprise merge in late phase three into a recreated company with the same organizational purpose, but doing it in an entirely different way from what anyone expected.

Today, the public schools, large mature businesses, the transportation industry, the energy industry, medicine, and the legal system, to name just a few, need groups totally dedicated to the question, "How can we reinvent ourselves?" Without a dedicated effort, even giant industries could slide into the backwaters of history to be replaced by those who didn't recognize the impossible.

While the reinvention activities go on outside the mainstream, the core business itself also changes substantially in the third phase. The core business continues with what has become essentially a commodity. Distribution is large and margins are low, lower than in the usual second phase. Other parts of the core business are, at the same time, integrating new and different elements into the core and also providing very new products and services aligned with the core. The global accounting and auditing firm of Arthur Andersen has broken the old patterns by offering management consultation, systems designs and applications, litigation services, and many other new and different offerings to their clients. Services such as these are aimed at special markets and add considerable value. They enjoy very high margins and extremely high return on investment.

Organizations in the third phase have to be extremely careful in making new investments. The usual criteria of low, 10 percent to 20 percent return on investment signifies they are still in the second phase; they have not innovated to meet customer needs, and they are not adding new value. Nonprofit organizations often fall into this trap more easily than for profit organizations because their accounting practices and orientation aren't focused on return on investment. This invisible snare can be devastating because the organization can deplete limited resources by continuing past patterns and not have an adequate level of investment capital to support new types of customer research, technology, training, and innovation.

Unfortunately, the question of adequate return on investment for innovation is rarely discussed in most organizations. Most have not seen the need to enter on the path of either core business innovation or the reinvention of the enterprise. Long periods of success dig deep trenches and make it hard to peer out over the edge—where it could be dangerous. Recent history in the use of new technologies shows that the old second phase blinders have consistently led to disaster. The rail transport system, for example, saw experiments with airplanes as irrelevant to their business—except for very limited use with passengers and special cargo. Thus, they continued to invest in a business that would go into major decline rather than enter into the creation of the future.

General Motors did exactly the right thing by bringing in Ross Perot, the inventive genius who created EDS, the successful computer processing company. Ross Perot personifies the first phase inventor. He could have been given the assignment to recreate the company away from the core business. But what happened? Those who held power rejected Ross Perot's very different approach in dealing with people, and his ideas about what technologies to integrate and how to shift General Motors to being a third phase innovative and inventive corporation.

Perot didn't fit a second phase view; he simply did not share the same perspective as the executives and board of directors of General Motors. They couldn't open up the system and accept this unique entrepreneur because they were locked into the success of phase two. They couldn't even see the relationship between automobile use and the emerging trend of telecommuting in which computers and telephones eliminate the need for a good deal of automotive use. In fact, the management and board of General Motors found Perot so different and disruptive that they paid $700 million dollars to get rid of him ... and get "back to normal."

AVOIDING THE PROBLEM

Having watched scores of companies and countless other organizations in government and education that are at the transition from phase two to phase three, we recognize that most enterprises (like other extinct species in nature) will make the same mistakes and the same choices as General Motors did at this critical juncture.

Most organizations think improving on their past successes will solve their problems. They begin by recentralizing control, cutting out the fat, reducing costs, eliminating unnecessary people and programs, and trimming management down to a lean, mean team. Numbers are watched with magnifying glasses. Accountability dominates. Departments compete ruthlessly for scarce resources, salespeople wheel and deal in the marketplace to make their quotas, and supervisors push workers to the wall to get production. The entire organization moves into a siege mentality to defend itself from any threats, real or imagined. This is what we have come to call the *Back to Basics Bump*. It is seen as the ultimate solution for getting out of the temporary downturn.

Unfortunately, normal accounting and auditing practices support the illusion that going Back to Basics is a solid strategy. If management's major attention is focused just on the bottom line,

THE "BACK TO BASICS" BUMP

PHASE 1   PHASE 2   PHASE 3

BREAKPOINT

BREAKPOINT

GROWTH

TIME

The BUMP

Healthy Growth

going Back to Basics in late phase two appears to pay off. Sales and profits rise over the short term. The audits look good. At the same time, everything not directly related to making the numbers is set aside. *Any innovation or change that might not produce immediate and certain results is squashed.* Even competition edging into market segments with new products and services is ignored. No one wants to rock an already unsteady boat by asking for significant changes in products or procedures. Everyone knows what happens to messengers carrying bad news. What never appears on audit sheets are the absolutely critical elements like:

■ Fostering creativity

■ Amount and rate of product and process innovation

■ Knowledge about customers' and prospects' needs

■ Employee morale and turnover

- Developing leadership skills
- Information about competitors
- Commitment to a common vision

Because of the shortage of information in these essential areas, following the Back to Basics cure ultimately kills the patient.

One of the world's preeminent college textbook publishers brought this lesson home to us in a very powerful way. Several years ago, sales and profits began to slip. Managers knew that economic pressures were hard on students' budgets and that books were getting more and more expensive as paper and distribution costs rose and authors prepared bigger and more elaborate textbooks. At a planning meeting, a lonely voice brought up the possibility that students might buy more used books. He was boldly reassured that professors were in the habit of changing new editions and that the used book business just couldn't make it. Used book buying had always had an inconsequential share of the market, but it would never be a big competitive factor. The company moved to cutting costs and pushing sales wherever possible in an effort to get a solid balance sheet.

In the meantime, an entrepreneur who knew nothing about the self-imposed limitations of publishing developed and put into place a national computerized used book buying and selling system. Within a short time it captured nearly 30 percent of the market. The pitiful fact is that management knew such a possibility could happen but nobody really wanted to talk about it. Traditional wisdom was that authors and publishers generated no profit from used book sales. As is always the case with today's problems, the situation was impossible to correct with past solutions. The company is now barely surviving.

The textbook publishing story can be repeated endlessly from industry to industry: major chemical companies ignoring small specialty manufacturers and pushing sales of commodity products; steel companies refusing to move to different ways of producing and distributing; automotive monoliths defending themselves from changing their production-line, economy of scale, styling-driven mentality; entertainment giants tightly controlling their products. The corporate graveyard is full of once major enterprises unable to shift gears.

This Back to Basics mentality is fully operational today in countless organizations from government to education to religious groups. The report of a distinguished panel of American educators entitled, "A Nation at Risk," suggested a Back to Basics solution for America's educational crisis. The outcome today is classic. The initial response was to require tougher graduation requirements for high school students, elminate so-called frills from the curriculum, and impose more stringent testing. Over the short-term improvements were seen, but very quickly the dropout rate increased, test scores plummeted, and the prospect of a long-term decline in public education still looms.

Many mature enterprises are now going through this tragic reaction to today's form of turbulent third phase change. When an organization finally realizes that its environment has changed beyond its capacity to satisfy its new needs even with a Back to Basics strategy, it then attempts to do things in a radically different way.

CHANGING THE PROBLEM

Some businesses try to solve their economic problems by aggressive acquisition and diversification. The results of this strategy have produced a litany of failures. Instead of avoiding the problem, as Back to Basics does, this is an effort to *change the problem* by entering another business. The vast majority of these undertakings by big companies to diversify their business lines since 1950 have ended in failure.

According to Michael Porter, a management expert at Harvard Business School, companies that fail in diversification typically choose the wrong businesses, spend too much for them, or ignore whether the linkages truly add anything to either side. In a study of thirty-three of the largest U.S. companies, Porter looked at 3,788 entries into new businesses through acquisitions, joint ventures, or start-ups from 1950 to 1986. The results showed that diversification succeeds only when the old and new units transfer skills back and forth or share activities. The disaster of the huge Polly Peck conglomerate in England illustrates what can happen. It had companies dealing with products as dissimilar as electronics and food. Creditors are likely to recover only half of the $4 billion in assets from this portfolio management strategy of a conglomerate of unrelated businesses. Alcoa expanded nonaluminum production to 50 percent of its business. Not surprisingly, the CEO of Alcoa, Charles Perry, and his strategy are gone. *Acquisitions can work in the third phase but only if they complement the core purpose of the business and provide fuel for innovative combinations.*

Without question, all organizations that resist the Breakpoint leap from phase two to three will eventually go out of business. In nature, this results in the extinction of a species. In political terms, it results in the collapse of parties or governments. The big question is how to make that great leap from the past to the future.

MAKING THE BREAKPOINT SHIFT
TO THE THIRD PHASE

When we consider the changes that must occur in the usual organization to succeed in a highly competitive, fast, and unpredictably changing third phase world, solutions include such shifts as:

- From mechanical technology to electronic technologies
- From uneducated, unskilled, replaceable workers doing simple physical tasks to educated, skilled, career workers performing complex mental tasks
- From mass production to specialized and global markets
- From a "factory-out" product focus to a customer-focused system
- From functionally organized systems to integrated, multi-functional, multicultural teams organized around markets
- From clear and sharp divisions between controlling managers and directed workers to managers as supportive resource finders and workers as self-managers
- From making incremental improvements to adding significant value through innovations

- From price competition with vendors to long-term, value-added relationships

The Breakpoint shift to the third phase is difficult because it requires:

- Valuing and trusting employees and others who have an interest in the organization

- Shifting from repeating and improving to creative innovation

- Committing to and being guided by an inspiring and compelling vision

- Recognizing the interdependence of the organization, its employees, the community, constituents, and customers in a global setting

In that process the organization unearths and asks completely new questions, it lets go of the limits of management control and understands that those within the organization are no longer the preeminent experts, that customers, employees, owners, community members, and vendors must truly become valued partners in creating the organization's future.

Unfortunately, many leading management theorists, consulting firms, and colleges of business continue to focus on how to become successful second phase managers. The traditional business cycle shows an enterprise going from birth through robust growth to maturation and decline without either a phase of innovation or a cycle of rebirth. They show no third phase. It is accepted that innovation and replacement traditionally come from outside the industry, not inside it. Motels were not created by the hotel industry, softcover publishing wasn't the brainchild of the hardcover publishers, desktop publishing did not grow out of the printing establishment, air travel was not invented by the railroad industry. Recreating the enterprise is as difficult, in fact probably more difficult, than the shift from phase one to phase two.

MOVING BEYOND BREAKPOINT (ALMOST)

The past is a foreign country, they do
things differently there.

L. P. Hartley

The new reality at this turning point in history is a great opportunity to go beyond Breakpoint. Once we recognize that solutions from our past second phase simply won't work any more, we can move to the unequaled challenges before us and apply totally new rules for success.

Today, as organizations abruptly encounter a third phase environment they have begun to undergo the processes of third phase integration. They realize it makes good sense to organize to meet a new set of needs. Those needs could be stated as:

- Unleashing the creative capacity of employees
- Responding rapidly to customer changes
- Innovating to meet competition
- Adding new and different value to products and services
- Partnering relationships with customers
- Manufacturing and selling to new, different, and smaller market segments around the world
- Planning geared to anticipate emerging problems and opportunities
- Understanding and working with outside pressure groups
- Producing quality within a work environment where managers and workers trust and value one another
- Integrating new technologies
- Integrating diverse cultures in the organization

In order to meet these new needs, organizations have employed a variety of contemporary techniques. The methods range from participative management, global marketing, and quality circles to employee involvement and innovation teams. Organizations enter upon programs to change the culture and replace the management hierarchy with a horizontal structure. They practice strategic planning, segmented marketing, and "management by walking around." All of these solutions have value. *Most have failed to bring about the desired results.* In fact, in the hundreds of organizations we have worked with and studied, we observed that implementing these changes has usually created more problems than it has solved. Introducing the new and different has so interfered with the way the organization has always worked that natural resistance to change rears its head and either openly or unconsciously sabotages the solutions.

In one client organization which manufactured business products, it became clear that the sales force would have to make several critical changes. In order to compete, salespeople would have to know their customers much better and be able to offer new value-added services to complement their standard products. This meant reorganizing around customers instead of geography and also changing the selling relationship from order-taking to consulting. A year after the discovery of this need, the authors visited the company and found that nothing had been done. When asked why nothing had been done, the company president responded, "The sales force and the sales managers don't want to do it." He added, "They own the accounts!" So, rather than work on the central issue, management decided to see if they could sell their new services over the telephone. Sales have been consistently declining ever since. Layoffs have maintained profits—so the problem has been solved!

REAL BREAKPOINT CHANGE

The great challenge facing organizations today goes far beyond what can be accomplished by introducing a new program or using cookbook techniques. Organizations defeat their best intentions by continuing to operate with essential beliefs that automatically perpetuate the second phase.

The most obvious sign of these basic obstacles is that of the continuity of a management system. In normal second phase organizations, management exists in a tightly controlled hierarchy in which managers are unquestioned emblems of authority. The manager's function—to control, organize, and predict—is critical and necessary in any second phase organization. Otherwise the processes of replication, improvement, exclusion of differences, incremental increases, and standardization could not work. *Yet the fact is that management's primary role is to limit the potential of the organization!*

One of the few things you can predict about the third phase is that many of the things an organization said it would never do while it was in the second phase, are exactly what it will be doing in the third. Barriers crumble, values shift, and rules change, very dramatically—more dramatically than we can easily imagine.

One of the authors gave a speech at an IBM management conference in 1972 when IBM was nearing the peak of its second phase success pattern. He said, "Someday IBM might even sell small computers in retail stores." After the meeting a friend in the upper management of the company warned the author not to bring up such ideas again because it would reveal how little he knew about their business. It took a decade for IBM to manufacture PCs and begin selling them in retail stores.

We are entering a period that demands that we operate in such a way as to empower the incalculable assets of human intelligence and creativity. The major distinction, for example, between old and new methods lies not in the methods themselves, but in the ability to integrate human beings into meaningful work. The new world requires humans to function as essential information and idea resources, creating solutions we have never seen before. In this kind of situation, human labor is no longer a disposable commodity, but a unique creative resource, in which an *individual's development is as valuable as the organization's growth.*

The most basic and entrenched thinking patterns, the worldview dominating traditional organizations, fits humans into parts of production machines. This worldview clings to the past as a guide to the future. It values logic and reason above imagination and creativity. Consider these examples:

■ A major communication company created a new customer-centered marketing effort, it remained a separate department—and manufacturing and service could not meet its demands.

■ A manager at an automotive company set up new teams to solve problems, he fulfilled his responsibility and gave them clear directions—but they could not think beyond those limits.

■ A *Fortune* 100 chemical company needed innovation, it selected special R&D people to think up the ideas—but they were so far from the customer that their ideas were rejected in the market.

■ A new government initiative was tried and turned over to the bureaucracy—but it was put through normal channels, and it died.

■ A consumer products company set a new vision, it was to reach $10 million in earnings—but workers just weren't motivated by the vision of generating increased manager and stockholder profits.

Everyone of these thrusts into the future failed because the essential nature of today's change has been misunderstood.

The main current of creative change in the third phase is the fulfillment of the organization's potential. In human and organizational terms, it is characterized not just by accepting and bringing in the previously excluded, the new, and the different, but by the people in the system functioning in trusting and interdependent relationships, by committing to a vision and long-term purpose, by acknowledging the unlimited creative potential of its people and by connecting with those outside the organization in creative and mutually benefiting partnerships. This kind of behavior violates the basic principles of logic, control, predictable order, and results that worked so well in management for so very long.

Just as when cells shifted from copying themselves to exchanging DNA in hybrids, the shift from phase two to phase three in organizations is revolutionary; growth no longer occurs through the limited extension of likeness or similarities but in sharing, exchanging differences, creating what has never before existed, and fulfilling the unrealized and unknown potential of the system.

Many nonprofit organizations and foundations are making the third phase shift far more successfully than entrenched government bureaucracies, the education establishment, or mature businesses. The Girl Scouts, founded in 1912, has continued its dedication "to inspiring girls with the highest ideals of character, conduct, patriotism, and service." Committed to innovative ways to reach young girls, the Girl Scouts today extends its programs to homeless girls in inner cities and has expanded its volunteer program at a time when volunteers in nonprofit organizations have fallen precipitously. The rapid changes in family structure have had a dramatic impact on the lives of young girls, causing the organization to extend its programs to girls who are five years old rather than the customary age of seven. The Girl Scouts continually shifts its programs to meet special conditions, whether it be nutrition counseling, working with children of divorce, or offering a stable hand in time of crisis.

The United Way was forged through the creative cooperation of the profit and not for profit sector. By using the broad base of employee giving in organizations and their commitment to volunteering, United Way has experienced tremendous success and has reduced the number of community-wide drives for charitable giving.

The Ys, whether they be YMCAs or YWCAs, have experienced stunning changes since 1844. Even though dedicated to fostering a Christian orientation, the Ys around the world today serve millions of people of all faiths, callings, and beliefs. The Ys bring together people of both sexes and all ages, incomes, abilities, races, and religions. They embrace a sense of worldwide understanding through programs that build healthy bodies, minds, and spirits.

Strikingly few examples of successful phase three businesses exist and, for the most part, they are relatively small and nonmainstream organizations such as Herman Miller in Michigan, Johnsonville Foods in Wisconsin, North American Tool and Die in California, Branch Bank in North Carolina, The Body Shop in England or company divisions such as the Business Systems Consulting group at Arthur Andersen, the Palo Alto Group at Xerox, and the Saturn Plant of General Motors in Tennessee. This is understandable because the massive cultural forces surrounding organizations have reinforced second phase rules and beliefs. As we will see in the next chapter, it is very difficult, if not impossible, to move far beyond where the society is moving. This is why we have not, until now, begun a large-scale organizational shift into the third phase. Today's emerging culture makes shifting to the third phase both necessary and possible.

The central and overriding barrier to making the Breakpoint shifts resides in our basic thinking patterns, the beliefs that guide all our activities. The critical dimension of organizational change is in the realm of redefining the belief system that undergirds the entire idea of management. This is very easy to say and very hard to do, because it literally requires understanding a new reality. It requires fundamentally *changing our foundational assumptions* about how the world really works.

The next chapter opens the door to this new world. In it we discover the roots of the deeply embedded beliefs we all share. The understanding of where our beliefs came from will help us adopt natural thinking processes that will allow us to transform our organizations and our world.

4: THE WORLD AT BREAKPOINT

So quickly that few have recognized what is happening, a society that lasted for ten thousand years has begun to dissolve. In its place a new society has been growing up, one in which the mores, habits, and goals of a hundred centuries are being profoundly altered. Some might take longer than others to recognize this colossal reorientation; many will undoubtedly spend the rest of their lives resisting the new direction of humanity. But it is real.

William Glasser

Nearly a year after delivering a series of seminars on organizational growth to managers at 3M, a division head telephoned one of the authors, "I've done everything you said and it hasn't worked!" He went on to explain that he and his management team had created a vision; they had instituted programs and training in creativity techniques and put together cross-functional teams. The prescription had been taken, but the patient was not doing well. What was wrong? The answer to that question took five more years of research, experimentation, and hard-won experience to discover.

At the time of those seminars, we didn't have a deep understanding of what was really required. The challenge extends far beyond setting up change programs in organizations. *What is called for is a massive change of mind.*

This requires examining that set of beliefs and assumptions that make up the common and unquestioned explanation of how our world fits together and works. It is based on what seem to be down-to-earth and obvious facts, the kind that everyone knows, that go without saying. These beliefs guide our everyday actions, holding together our sense of how our world works. We call this set of primary and implicit assumptions a *worldview*.

The underlying assumptions that make up the worldview of most people are actually contrary to the deeper reality that will move us beyond this Breakpoint in human evolution. In order to meet the challenges of our world, a fundamental shift in thinking is required. Unfortunately, a worldview is very difficult to change.

Although shifting from one worldview to another is a monumental undertaking, the comforting news is that this kind of major change has happened before in the annals of human history. The last Breakpoint occurred between 8,000 B.C. and 6,000 B.C., when humanity shifted from living as nomadic hunters and gatherers to living in permanent settlements. With that shift a different worldview emerged to guide humanity's progress along with its accompanying values, mythology, and mindset.

The story of how the shift from one worldview to another occurred, how long our present beliefs have been with us, and how tight these beliefs hold us to the past is of critical importance. Just like breathing, these undergirding assumptions of how things work usually go unexamined. Our journey into the future will be much easier if we step back and see how we arrived at this present Breakpoint in history.

Our reason for asking you to embark on an exploration that recounts a fair amount of history is not for the sake of historical fact, but to craft meaning from the past. How does the past keep us captive? What challenges are we undertaking to free ourselves from these bonds? Where will the resistances occur? How can we overcome them? Nature's process of creative growth and change will be our overlay as we sketch the journey of humanity. Through this unique lens, we will see how we reached this monumental social Breakpoint between our past and the extraordinary future that lies ahead.

THE WORLDVIEW BEFORE CIVILIZATION

Humanity's sojourn on this planet has extended over a period of perhaps two million years. Yet, only during the last 8,000 to 10,000 years have humans experienced the life we associate with civilization. By civilization, we are referring to people living in cities with complex social, political, and economic interactions.

An attempt to recapture the ancient past must, of necessity, rely on conjecture and inference since no written record exists. The archaeological evidence indicates that prior to about 10,000 B.C., nomadic clans lived in small communities, wandering in search of food and shelter; their daily existence was dominated by nature. Dealing with shortages of game or plant life and other natural calamities was a constant reminder that controlling nature was impossible. These hunter-gatherer clans lived with great respect for the mysteries of nature.

The unearthed evidence of the past combined with research into the few remaining primitive tribes left on the planet, indicates that early people believed that events were guided by invisible, uncontrollable, supernatural spirits. Nothing could be done to change that fact. If a tree fell on someone in the clan, it happened because the spirit residing in the tree deemed it to be. Everything in nature was imbued with life and spirit.

A nomadic tribe, with whom one of the authors lived for a year, explained patiently that if a person ate a particular plant and died, that plant's spirits were angry. Happy spirits inhabited other plants and those were all right to eat. The members of that tribe followed the complex dictates of myriad supernatural beings.

Ancient peoples observed nature closely, constantly learning about its cycles and movements. The seasons came and went with little separation of the past from the present and future. Some Native American traditions express this viewpoint of seeing everything in life on a continuum as a "long body" of time. All life experience fits together and what happens in early life is the beginning of the "long body"; it all connects and interweaves as part of the whole.

Experience and intuition guided the actions of the people. To protect the clan's survival, rigid icons, totems, and taboos became deeply intertwined with daily living. Songs, dances, and incantations reinforced the powers of the spirit world and maintained the clan's connection with an imponderable and deeply mystical world.

Among early people, roles were defined by ability. The fastest runner automatically became the leader of the hunt; the person who knew the most about local herbs became a healer. An elder who could remember a water hole became the guide, at least for that day. The midwife was given power and authority because she was most skilled at helping a woman through the travail of childbirth. These weren't inherited positions but were conferred on the most adept individual. The shaman was particularly respected and given authority because of the experience and power he or she held in the spirit world.

Before the advent of civilization, the social system was communal. Small clans worked together to guarantee their survival and there was *no elite class* that expected to be served. Nomadic clans lived in the present. In fact, to many of us today there is something attractive about their disregard for time. They punched no time clock, had no watches. Their concern about the past or the future played little part in their daily life. Work was not segregated from play. At any given moment, they could be catching the day's fish in the local stream, laughing and playing, or conveying their traditions through stories, dance, or song.

It is likely that these ancient people developed a psychology radically different from our own—what modern psychology would refer to as altered states of consciousness. Through dreams, trance states, listening, and communicating with the spirits by drumming and dancing they accessed ways of knowing and solving problems that many would like to recapture. Out of the everyday life of these people came their worldview. They built a complex belief system with great spiritual and psychological depth along with guidelines that shaped everyday action. Built on great reverence for the mysteries of nature, what we call the spirit-guided worldview prevailed.

The beliefs and assumptions of the spirit-guided worldview were that:

- Specific spirits controlled the world. Humans attempted to evoke these forces to serve their needs.

- There was little distinction between the past, present, and future.

- Animals, plants, the earth, the sky, the water, *and even humans* were an integral part of nature.

- The social system was communal, and roles were defined on the basis of ability. Power and authority belonged to those with the appropriate skills and knowledge.

This way of life dominated human beings on the planet for thousands upon thousands of years. It isn't known exactly how or when, but testimony from existing ruins indicates that some nomadic clans started altering their thinking and the way they lived as far back as 15,000 B.C. Ripples of change appeared, foretelling the inexorable journey toward people living in cities with complex social, political, and cultural arrangements.

CIVILIZATION'S FIRST PHASE

When the last great ice age had subsided, bands of hunters and gatherers found themselves greeted with regular sunshine and fertile soil where neither had existed before. At the same time, nature provided abundant new grasses growing along river banks. Some unheralded genius, or perhaps a number of geniuses, figured out that there was a relationship between the seeds that fell on fertile soil and the grains that were sprouting. Suddenly, a completely new idea took hold—deliberately planting seeds might cause edible crops to grow, and it worked!

Ingenious inventors ultimately wove together a repeatable and sustainable method of planting and harvesting. In parallel, other life-enhancing inventions multiplied: shelters became permanent; flint and stone made fire; metals were melted and made into ornaments and tools; clay was shaped into pots and bricks; roads and carts transported the now abundant produce and products further and faster. A flood of new technologies totally transformed life.

Our view of this distant past often fails to recognize the amazing and inventive creativity of these people who put together the many pieces of the pattern for all civilization to come. The domestication of plants and animals alone required inventions that rival

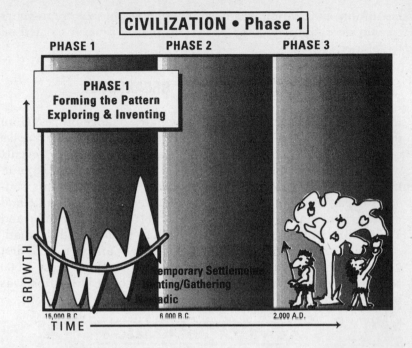

CIVILIZATION • Phase 1

PHASE 1   PHASE 2   PHASE 3

PHASE 1
Forming the Pattern
Exploring & Inventing

GROWTH

Temporary Settlements
Hunting/Gathering
Nomadic

15,000 B.C.   6,000 B.C.   2,000 A.D.

TIME

the most ingenious scientific discoveries of the twentieth century.
Master toolmakers created an array of inventions numbering in
the hundreds: the plow, harness, spade, nail, bellows, loom. In
such an environment, the richness of what was happening multiplies, according to J. Bronowski, as each "new device quickens
and enlarges the power of the rest."

Breaking with countless eons of tradition, these prehistoric
entrepreneurs unknowingly invented the Neolithic Revolution of
Agriculture. It would become the greatest change human beings
had ever experienced—most of all, it brought with it a fundamental shift in worldviews.

Just like any first phase in nature's process of creative growth
and change, the first phase of civilization was characterized by
a high level of inventive, exploratory activity. The human beings
inventing civilization maintained a high level of disorder as they
divergently explored the environment searching for the bits and
pieces that could be assembled into a cohesive pattern. In this
phase of discovery, through perpetual trial and error and experi-

mentation, civilization was born. These first phase entrepreneurs created an extremely complex system that had never existed on the planet.

CIVILIZATION'S FIRST BREAKPOINT

Like all natural systems moving through the change process from the first to the second phase, sudden and discontinuous breaks with the past occur. An extraordinary pace of revolutionary events surged forward at civilization's first to second phase Breakpoint. Like a firestorm moving across a prairie, tiny settlements suddenly began congealing into large, organized cities. Uncertain and precarious nomadic ways transformed abruptly into regular and predictable routines. People's lives shifted rapidly and dramatically. In historical terms, it took but a blink of an eye for the first great city to appear on the planet. By 6,000 B.C., at least 3,000 people were living within the walls of Jericho. Civilization was born. Humanity had entered its second phase.

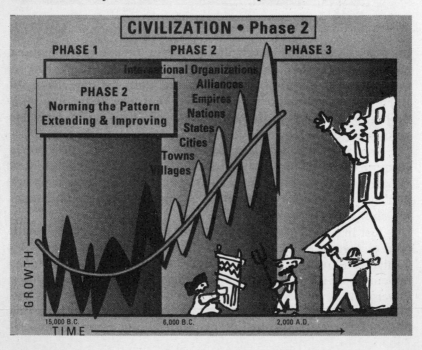

With the birth of civilization, people in large numbers lived in close proximity to one another, and two entirely new and very basic questions needed to be answered: "Who will decide what must be done?" and "How will things be organized so it can happen?"

On entering the second phase, every society we know of accepts a need for some form of centralized authority. Someone must be in charge, someone who also carries forward the power of the first phase spirit world. This is not to say there was a linear progression throughout the world. The Breakpoint changes between phase one and phase two of civilization varied by thousands of years depending on when agriculture was invented. Coupled with this was the overlapping of the spirit-dominated worldview with the new worldview emerging. It took thousands of years for the spirit-guided worldview to lose ground.

J. Bronowski spent years studying the shifts that took place during this period. His research confirms that a remarkably tight social structure was constructed with one person in charge, the civil and spiritual head of state. The peasants, soldiers, craftswomen, and craftsmen all worked for this one person. Over a period of time, this same person became the "religious incarnation of godhead." Lewis Mumford relates how this fusion of sacred and temporal power had great consequences for humanity. It created a new institutional form of power, "dominated by an elite who were supported in grandiose style by tribute and taxes forcibly drawn from the whole community."

Incalculable changes took place when a central authority intervened. People could be organized in ways that led to feeding and housing thousands of people and to the building of monumental structures. Centralized control and authority loomed as powerful testimony that human beings had the capability to make exceptional things happen. Individuals took on assigned tasks, almost like human parts to a machine. With crop surpluses, entirely new forms of work emerged so that each person was assigned a special duty and role in order to meet the immense work necessary in imposing public works projects. For the first time, such things as management control, functional specialization, and schedules developed into an essential aspect of the culture. The carefree spirit of the nomadic clansperson was no longer tolerable. Time was of the essence, and to get people to conform, rigid rules and regulations were implemented. If people didn't adapt, coercion and social pressure could always be used to get them in line. The result was a set of operating principles that has now guided civilization for the last 8,000 years. The basic patterns of government, education, religion, and commerce were set so deeply that they have lasted until today.

One of the major changes in human life took place as warfare evolved. Because bands of nomads were still wandering around, implements of warfare were needed to defend the cities against the attack of the remaining "uncivilized" marauders. Riane Eisler claims that this was the "great change—a change so great, indeed, that nothing else in all we know of human cultural evolution is comparable in magnitude." The consequences of the change have been widespread and profound. After war came upon the scene, a dominator class emerged that has been a major influence on civilization ever since. The primary reason for war was the existence of material prosperity and the new notion of ownership and inheritance. Then, the necessity for record-keeping emerged once a surplus of goods and the notion of ownership came into being. Accurate record-keeping was possible once writing was invented, bringing with it the massive shift from an exclusively oral tradition to a combination of writing, storytelling, and singing.

The beliefs and assumptions of this new worldview were a radical change from those of the nomad. They were based on the assumption that human beings could cause things to happen and effect controllable and predictable outcomes. *This belief in the logic of cause and effect created a totally new worldview.*

The beliefs and assumptions underlying the logical worldview were that:

- Humans control their own destiny through the logical manipulation and control of nature.

- The establishment of a centralized temporal and spiritual authority, including a hierarchical power structure; a rigid social system based on unequal relationships; rules, regulations, and standards; coercive physical power; defense and warfare.

- Divisions between things: functional specialization, time dependence and scheduling; ownership and inheritance, record-keeping and exchange; mechanized production, and the separation of humans from nature.

- Dualistic thinking: right and wrong, good and evil, black and white, male and female.

- Scarcity and limits of the resources available to share and the power to determine how to share them.

By 5,000 B.C., in Ur, Sumeria, and Babylonia, humankind was moving quickly beyond its first Breakpoint. With rules shifting 180 degrees, the life of the nomad characterized by disorder, randomness, and chance shifted to one of greater stability with a degree of prediction and some control over one's life. People began to build their lives on the logical relationship between the cause of things and their ultimate effect. No longer were humans totally subject to the whims of the spirits; they had some control over their own existence.

The notion that the application of logical principles could lead to control over nature differed radically from the first phase spirit-guided worldview. The invisible fuel behind the towering revolution that built civilization was a belief in the power of the human mind to cause things to happen. This belief in a logical cause leading to a specific effect, which began as far back as 8,000 years ago, has progressively gained momentum. Today this same belief holds us captive.

DELAYED AWARENESS

Many centuries later, only after much of the world had drastically changed, more contemplative human beings would connect the invention of civilization with an enormous change in the fundamental beliefs about how the world actually worked. In the Western world, a relatively small group of Greek philosophers and mathematicians brought to conscious awareness the change of thinking that enabled hunters and gatherers to create the Agricultural Revolution.

In this pioneering exploration of humanity's inner mental processes, the western world would be changed forever. These Greek philosophers and mathematicians discovered that underneath all the activity required in building civilization resided special mental processes—logic and reason. Once known and understood, these mental tools could be rigorously applied even more effectively to control nature.

Logic had been discovered much earlier in China and India and practiced with great success in Egypt prior to the Greeks uncovering its power. But when the Greeks said, "Let's be logical," the results in the Western world were epic. The Golden Age of Greece, the Roman Empire, and all of Western Civilization built customs, traditions, and beliefs on the foundation of rationally causing and controlling one's own destiny. Homer captured the essence of the great shift from a mind that believed in spirits to one governed by human rationality when Circe said to Odysseus, "There is a mind in you no magic can touch."

While early African and Middle Eastern cultures invented civilization by using their rational rather than their intuitive mind, they did so in an unconscious way and thus, with uncertain results. People would plant crops and then, carrying forward the old spirit-guided worldview, say, "The spirits made it happen." They held tenaciously to ancient beliefs in order to explain the new phenomena creating the Agricultural Revolution. From 6,000 B.C. until the Greeks, the ancient spirit-guided worldview existed side by side with the emerging worldview of logic and reason. The two opposing ideas clashed and collided as the principles undergirding them stood in opposition to each other. So, while the Agricultural Revolution took root between 8,000 B.C. and 6,000 B.C., the impact of carrying forward the early belief system of a spirit-guided worldview slowed down the process of change. It took centuries before logic and rationality became the prevailing worldview.

Over the expanse of history even religion began to apply logic to the concept of divine order. The once novel notion of a cause and effect world was ultimately taken for granted. It settled into humanity's collective unconscious. It made sense out of everyday life. It not only became "the way things work" but also was tacitly accepted as "the way things *are*." By the industrial age in the Western world, logic had become automatic. Over time, a complex edifice of beliefs and assumptions grew from the root notion that any event could be traced to a cause. Explanations for anything could be found in history. The future could even be predicted based on the past. This was a great shift from the beliefs of ancient people who were guided by their inextricable and unpredictable connection with nature.

CIVILIZATION'S SECOND PHASE

In applying the dynamic creative process of growth and change to civilization, we discover that phase two of civilization grew by repeating, modifying, extending, and improving a tested and proven pattern. The rule became, "When you find something that works, stick with it." By maintaining established order, civilization moved forward on an incremental, traditional and experience-based path.

Once nature finds a connecting pattern, it seizes it and shifts the system from open exploration to growth that follows rules within limits. Civilization was no exception. The new pattern was based on unequal relationships, control through hierarchies, and a belief that the past both controls and predicts the future.

Throughout the long history of the second phase of civilization, individuals have been informed in countless ways that their lives and the lives of their children have been preordained. With the exception of natural calamities outside of human control and the regular, violent confrontations over who owned what real estate, life was regular, orderly, and comfortably predictable. Change happened as an extension of the known past.

As we consider civilization's history from Greece, to Rome, to the Byzantine Empire of Constantinople, across the Middle Ages to the Renaissance and up to the present, we see that powerful and constraining rules guided civilization's progress. In every second phase society, individuals conform to the mores, norms, traditions, and obligations of the culture. Doing "the correct thing" appropriate to a person's position in society is expected and if it is not adhered to, the individual is punished or ostracized. The work of Riane Eisler concluded that this long second phase of humanity's journey can best be described as a "dominator" culture where a few people hold power and dominate the masses.

The values and assumptions making up the second phase worldview thrived in a snug corner of unquestioned, inherent, and tacit truth. The undergirding beliefs kept things simple. Rulers were rulers and peasants were peasants. It had always been so. It would always be so.

Differences from the established, accepted norm inspired incomprehensible injustices that make today's advocates of human rights shudder in disbelief. In "democratic" Athens, 25,000 free individuals did not have to spend energy on everyday concerns because their work was done by some 200,000 slaves. The taking of other humans as slaves was accepted as an indisputable right for almost all of recorded history. Slaves, after all, were different from "civilized" people. Such a practice held sway because belief in building on similarities and excluding the different is such a compelling and pervasive force in second phase civilization. The need for others to adopt this worldview was so powerful that the crusades in the Middle Ages were waged to eliminate the heretic and the infidel. People wore natural mental blinders allowing oppression to be practiced throughout history.

Government and religion serve to ensure that the second phase patterns endure whereby the different are excluded and the accepted values stay firmly in place. Religion even controlled creative art, beginning with Egypt and continuing unabated until the eighteenth century. Only in such secret and private papers as the notebooks of Leonardo di Vinci do we see the precursors of future breaks with the habitual and familiar. He saw deeply into nature, grasping clues of a future that would leave the traditional and orthodox behind.

Systems of laws, rules, and regulations have been used over the last 8,000 years to foster and perpetuate order. This was a natural and vital process in the evolution of civilization. Repetition provided stability; skills could be developed, daily life was organized and predictable, and thinking and problem-solving were simple. If marauding and uncivilized "barbarians" were allowed to roam at will, moving in and out of early cities to plunder and destroy, civilization would never have survived. Outside threats, as well as internal iconoclasts and malcontents, were dealt with severely as civilization spread across the globe.

Population grew enormously, yet the quality of life for the vast majority of humans did not shift a great deal. Personal income, for example, changed little. The noted economist Simon Kuznetz in his Nobel Prize acceptance speech pointed out that, in 1960 dollars, global per capita income in the year 1 A.D. was about $100 per year. In constant dollars, in 1780, with a 3000 percent increase in population, per capita income was still $100! In civilization's long second phase, the rich stayed rich and the poor stayed poor.

Something else was happening, however, something that did not immediately affect the quality of people's lives, but that eventually led to qualitative changes as dramatic as the giant increases in population. As civilization's success spread across the planet, the natural pressures were bringing people—different kinds of people—ever closer together.

No longer were villagers isolated and untouched by the world. Merchants, traders, missionaries, and entertainers brought with them the diversity and wonders of an unknown world. Unique races of people were brought into contact with one another; novel customs and traditions intermingled. What a shock when Marco Polo announced the astonishing discoveries of a giant and well-developed culture in Asia! Widespread contact with other cultures gave people irrefutable evidence that things could be different than they had been in the past. The continuing wave of human connections sowed the seeds of change that would grow into civilization's second Breakpoint.

The penultimate grand adventure of phase two civilization was the British Empire. Igniting the Industrial Revolution, England wove a new web of brilliant linkages using factory workers, steam power, shipping, commerce, mechanized farming, banks, joint stock companies, and a great navy. The richest nation in the world extended its common laws and language to all of the empire, subjecting entire populations to the British way of doing things. Spreading out in colonies from an isolated island realm, in 200 years the British built the empire "upon which the sun never set."

THE SIGNS OF BREAKPOINT

Ironic as it may seem, the forces that would ultimately undermine the great second phase pattern of empire were being laid at the exact time that the empire was enjoying its greatest success. This is completely natural as are the unseen forces of creative change that lay buried beneath the surface.

Every culture grows within a finite environment. Every society will reach a point when extending and repeating the pattern introduces diminishing returns. Less and less is achieved using increasingly more resources. This overextension is a natural and inevitable outcome of all successful second phase systems. Just like other effective natural organisms, civilization devours its environment and puts pressure on its ecological niche, consuming the resources that allowed success in the first place. Any growing organism will become so complex, so extended and wasteful that it literally exhausts its ability to grow. It discovers its hidden potential only when it reaches its natural and self-imposed limits.

CIVILIZATION'S SECOND BREAKPOINT

The first massive challenge to the indisputable power of rulers occurred in civilization's most successful empire. In the 1600s, the sparks of change ignited legal equality and freedom. Influenced by John Locke's social contract, the notion of individual consent as a basis of political authority stimulated the thinking for Breakpoint change. In the mid-1600s when Oliver Cromwell and his followers successfully overthrew the King of England, the seamless continuity of the reign of kings was shattered for the first time in English history. All at once, an entirely new set of possibilities lay before human beings.

The new flame took just over 100 years to fully ignite. The explosion came in a most unlikely place, a British colony, in a place called the new world. Led by a band of freedom fighters, the words of the Declaration of Independence heralded the most momentous break with the past since the first to second phase Breakpoint that gave rise to the Agricultural Revolution.

We hold these truths to be self evident, that all men are created equal and that they are endowed by their Creator with certain unalienable Rights, that among these are Life, Liberty and the Pursuit of Happiness.

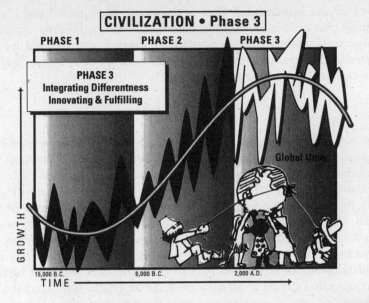

Anyone living on the planet in the eighteenth century could have legitimately asked, "Self evident to whom?" Never in all of human history had men been "equal." Only rulers had ever enjoyed "unalienable rights." Even in democratic Greece, less than 10 percent of the population had enjoyed the few rights granted to citizens—and their lives and liberty were forfeit at the whim of the ruling few. As for "pursuit of happiness," the nobility alone could follow that path. The American Pilgrim leader John Winthrop epitomized the eternal and official truth: "...you will quietly and cheerfully submit unto that authority which is set over you."

Nothing in all the annals of history prepared the world for the impact of those few words in the Declaration of Independence. They marked the beginning of the end of civilization's second phase, profoundly altering not just the United States, but the entire world. In rapid succession, common people rose up against their divinely endowed and appointed rulers and began creating a totally different world. Civilization was catapulted into its second Breakpoint. The future could be different than the past!

America offered the world something utterly new. Eric Hoffer pointed this out: "All civilizations we know of were shaped by exclusive minorities of kings, nobles, priests, and the equivalents of the intellectual. It was they who formulated the ideals, aspirations and values and it was they who set the tone. America is the only instance of a civilization shaped and colored by the tastes and values of the common folk. No elite of whatever nature can feel truly at home in America."

FREE AT LAST

The American Revolution laid the seeds for the ideas of freedom, democracy, and human rights. Allan Bloom pointed out that the American Revolution was the "greatest transformation of man's relations with his fellows and nature ever effected." What followed was the massive impact of the French Revolution on most of Europe. Over the next century great revolutions across the world freed humankind not just from the rule of royalty, but from the tyranny of the past. The most powerful single belief that had guided civilization—that a person's destiny was sealed at birth—was unveiled to reveal an illusion. Like an earthquake that shakes the ground and unleashes the pent up pressure of a volcano, social revolutions set free latent human power to create a new kind of future.

Individual freedom to break with tradition, to ask forbidden questions, to search out and apply new ideas advanced relentlessly across the globe. One by one, creative inventors and scientific explorers, pioneers in unleashing the human spirit, ignited new flames of change. These flames were kindled where technical expertise and the right social environment merged. These factors were found in Great Britain and France at the beginning of the Industrial Revolution and within time swept to the United States, Germany, and the rest of Europe. There were many instances of simultaneous inventions. Elisha Gray of Britain and Alexander Graham Bell of the United States filed for telephone patents the same day. Aluminum was discovered by Charles Martin Hall, an American, and Paul L. T. Herout, a Frenchman, independently and almost simultaneously. Both Sir Henry Bessemer of Great Britain and William Kelly in the United States made steel by blowing air through molten iron to burn out the carbon. All of these inventors set themselves free from the bondage of the past.

Beyond the second phase Breakpoint, the static system of civilization destructured, allowing in the new and different, the previously excluded. Latent creativity burst upon the scene. The harbingers of Breakpoint change came from around the world. James Watt of Scotland invented the steam engine; Karl Benz and Gottlieb Daimler of Germany collaborated on the internal combustion engine; Louis Pasteur and Madame Curie of France made startling breakthroughs in medicine; the father of the periodic table was a Russian, Dmitry Ivanovich Mendeleyev; the wireless was invented by Marconi in Italy; and Benjamin Franklin and Eli Whitney paved the way for even greater inventions in the United States. Not only were their inspirations astounding, like electricity, which illuminated the world, but some of the great Breakpoint thinkers such as Albert Einstein, Louis de Broglie, and Max Born were born into this new era and could now ask questions that would completely redefine the nature of fundamental reality.

PARTING WITH THE PAST

As we reflect on the history of the first great turn of the river of civilization, from first to second phase, we discover a key to dealing with the monumental challenges now facing those of us caught up in the maelstrom of civilization's second Breakpoint.

What ushered in civilization's first phase Breakpoint around 10,000 B.C. was that doers, not thinkers, started the big changes leading to the Agricultural Revolution. Moving from hunting and gathering to farming, people were caught up in a flood of powerful and tangible tools and technologies that altered their daily lives. Little if any time or energy could be given to probing for the meaning or forces behind all the changes.

The growing river of civilization was far into its second phase turn before people became consciously aware of the force of logic driving their lives. It wasn't until the Greeks that humanity became conscious of the magnitude of the thinking shift that created Western civilization.

The myriad forms of transformational change occurring on the planet today are *pulling us toward the same kind of delayed realization*. For over a century, the practical application of a radically different set of natural principles has unleashed a technological revolution flooding us with wondrous products. Like our first phase Breakpoint ancestors who were engulfed by the concrete changes involved in city life, we too have become overwhelmed by an onslaught of technological "stuff" that is rapidly and radically refashioning our daily existence.

Only a small percentage of the population invented the patterns and made the discoveries that have so extraordinarily broken with the past and changed our present day world. The vast majority of people, without much thought, have concluded that these breakthroughs are either extraordinary creations of rare and gifted geniuses, or simply an extension of a logical worldview. These conclusions have about the same validity as the use of magical incantations to grow crops. Today's prevailing thinking represents the carrying forward of an obsolete second phase worldview. Emulating those few Greek philosophers and mathematicians who discovered logic in the Western world, we need to step back and contemplate. The questions we must ask today are how we can understand and apply the deep underlying principles that are recreating our world and how these powerful natural principles can move us beyond Breakpoint.

5: MASTERING THE FUTURE

> Nature! We are surrounded and em-
> braced by her: powerless to separate
> ourselves from her.... She has neither
> language nor discourse; but she cre-
> ates tongues and hearts, by which she
> feels and speaks.... She is all things.
>
> Goethe

The natural forces driving change are propelling all of humanity to a future far different from the past. This began
when eighteenth century "doers" blatantly defied popular and
traditional wisdom. They boldly took hold of nature's secrets and
created totally new possibilities. Many historians and sociologists
agree that probably only 2 percent of the population discovered
the unexplored patterns that the rest are following today. *The
method they employed to begin creating this unique world remained
unseen.*

Although the Greeks had analyzed what was happening
around them and unearthed the concept of cause and effect in
addition to logical reasoning, it wasn't until the early part of the
twentieth century that scientists began uncovering nature's deepest and most hidden truths. These discoveries reveal that these
early third phase Breakpoint thinkers, who intuitively parted with
the power of ancient and accepted traditions, were actually oper-

ating in harmony with nature. They were not breaking the rules but just using a new—more accurate—set of rules.

The great challenge is to look beneath these new discoveries and interpret the new rules in a way in which a large portion of the population, not just 2 percent, can take advantage of their unused power. With civilization being pushed more and more rapidly by technology into the third phase, our first clue to understanding these new rules is to examine concepts that were important in civilization's first phase but left out of the second phase pattern. The question to ask is, "What was left behind that might help us move more effectively to the future?"

The most crucial aspect of ancient cultures was that *people saw themselves as an integral part of all of nature*. This idea was eliminated from the tight belief system of the second phase worldview. In fact, prevailing traditions in the long second phase of civilization taught that not only were human beings separate from nature but that nature was an adversary to be conquered. Human beings were to take dominion over nature and subdue it. For early people, who had always been subject to the whims of nature, this was a powerful idea indeed.

It's becoming clearer every day that this outmoded notion of "humans versus nature" no longer serves us. Growing awareness of our global ecological interdependence has demonstrated that it is one of our most dangerous and limiting beliefs. But ecological awareness is not enough to fully reconcile us with nature. Our imperative opportunity is to integrate the profound new discoveries about nature that have been made in this century. Just going back to the superstitious viewpoint prehistoric people had about nature would not be useful. The scientific revolution has now opened the once closed book containing nature's secrets. The goal is to open up our thinking to embrace and integrate these profound scientific insights not just to develop more new technologies—*but to use them in our daily lives to create revolutionary changes in our personal lives and within our organizations.*

SCIENCE DISCOVERS HOW NATURE WORKS

Scientists at the turn of the century began probing the deepest forces of nature, asking questions that had never been asked before about how our world functions. They completely departed from established scientific thinking. For thousands of years individuals interested in nature approached understanding its workings by *imagining and describing how nature ought to work.* Twentieth-century scientists took the opposite course. They decided to *observe nature closely and attempt to explain how she really works.* What they discovered about the material world was completely different from what their second phase logical worldview had always told them.

Logic had told them that the "stuff" from which everything was made was like tiny individual billiard balls. These little hard objects called atoms were assembled in various configurations to make up the world. They were thought to be separate from each other and distinct from such energies as heat, light, or electricity. They were conceived of as having an "objective" existence independent of whatever else was around them. The idea that the most fundamental matter making up the universe consisted of tiny and separate particles goes back as far as Aristotle. It was carried forward to Newton, who envisioned the universe as a huge cosmic machine assembled as individual parts.

The old way of looking at nature was to take things apart and examine each part separately. Modern scientists found that atoms couldn't be studied as "snapshots" of separate objects because they existed in a state of perpetual motion. They had to be studied as dynamic and enormously energetic moving objects. As it turned out, when scientists were able to get inside this astounding world, atoms were found not to be hard particles at all but were actually bundles of tremendous, vibrant energy. Not only that, but far from being separate and independent, they were intimately and powerfully connected with the other atoms around them.

Far more amazing than those revelations, however, was the fact that the logical cause and effect relationship assumed to be everywhere in nature was nowhere to be seen. The subatomic world behaved illogically and unpredictably.

These revolutionary Breakpoint discoveries dumbfounded those who made them. Neils Bohr, one of the pioneer explorers of this new world, concluded that anyone who was not dizzied by these discoveries simply didn't understand a word about what was being uncovered. Werner Heisenberg, another of the vanguard thinkers of the new physics, wrote, "I repeated to myself again and again the question: Can nature possibly be as absurd as it seemed to us in these atomic experiments?" Max Planck, in his Nobel Prize acceptance speech, described the situation; it was, he said, "entirely new, never before heard of, which seemed to call upon us to basically revise all our physical thinking."

While these breakthroughs may not have pleased the scientific community, when this new set of rules was applied, rules that completely violated orthodox logic, they worked—*better than any idea that had ever been proposed about the workings of our world.*

The enormous energy that was revealed to be enclosed deep within atoms presented powerfully convincing evidence, and today the gigantic technological revolution surrounding us presents daily reminders of just how well these strange new rules of nature do work. The deep probings of the atom created shattering Breakpoint change. Unfortunately, there has never been a concerted effort to translate the meaning of how individuals can apply these Breakpoint truths in their own lives or within their organizations.

Our current situation closely resembles what happened to the people who invented agriculture and ignited the fuse leading to the second phase Breakpoint of civilization. Their ancient first phase superstitions told them the spirit world dominated their existence, yet they found that incredible progress could be made through applying the logic of cause and effect. If they planted grain and gave it enough water, it would grow. For the first time, people had a constant supply of food and didn't have to wander or forage for an existence. They didn't know why it worked, it just did. So they continued doing it. Only many centuries later did people consciously realize the new second phase rules and the thought patterns they had automatically adopted.

The scientists and technicians that manipulate the molecular, atomic, and subatomic world are going forward with radically new concepts about nature to create a third phase of civilization. Today's transportation, communication, medicine, industrial production, and economy depend on using the new rules of science. Science will continue creating even more astounding technological breakthroughs in the years to come.

The onslaught of more technology will continue to create more problems than it solves because humanity continues reaping the benefits of third phase technology but lives within the rules of second phase thinking. The time has come for human beings to take the knowledge that has revolutionized our world technologically and apply these momentous discoveries in their own lives and within their organizations. Without this incredibly significant knowledge, the revolutionary breakthroughs so desperately needed on the human level will be impossible to create. Patchwork programs and solutions will continue to fail. The result will be the continuing inability to meet the extraordinary challenges of Breakpoint change.

Like the Greeks, who discovered the underpinnings for the logical worldview, we believe that it's time to find the meaning behind what is happening at the deepest level of nature. This requires constructing a new worldview to replace the second phase belief in the logic of cause and effect. We also believe nature can be understood in a way that will provide deep personal meaning, and her secrets can be utilized by everyone to build better lives and revitalize organizations.

We're embarking upon a journey into nature that is foreign to most people. The momentous discoveries of science have been of little interest except to those in the scientific community. We're going to look at these discoveries and present three foundational concepts that uncover how the newly discovered breakthroughs in nature can be applied in down-to-earth ways. It's the best information we have to date about how the world fits together and works. These bedrock principles form the foundation for what we're calling the *Creative Worldview*.

This Creative Worldview really arose from necessity. Our third phase world is beset with problems that cannot be solved with either the traditional worldview or by existing interpretations of the newly discovered laws of nature. A Creative Worldview offers us consistency and simplicity in solving these problems. It does this with just a few basic concepts, concepts that agree with the facts, not only from physics, but from the other natural systems of chemistry, biology, psychology, anthropology, and sociology.

Understanding the three cornerstones of reality provide the foundational support for applying the Creative Worldview. These are:

One: Dynamics of the natural process of change—how does change happen?

Two: Relationships among things—how are the individual parts
        of a growing system connected with one another?
Three: Forces driving change—what impels change to occur?

If we have an authentic idea about how change happens; about
how the process of building deeper, more interpenetrating connections work; and about how the actual forces propelling change occur, it will be possible to move beyond Breakpoint and transform
today's momentous problems into extraordinary opportunities for
enhancing our lives.

   First, let's examine each of these foundational ideas from the
orthodox and traditional view of science. This second phase thinking pattern with its logical worldview has guided civilization for
thousands of years.

One: How does change happen?

CHANGE IS A STEP-BY-STEP INCREMENTAL PROCESS. THE WORLD WORKS
IN A LOGICAL AND RATIONAL WAY.   The second phase logical worldview sees change as a progressive and cumulative process. From
the time of Aristotle, this classical scientific view has expected
the world and the people in it to operate in a regular, recurring,
logical, and linear way, with straightforward step-by-step progres-
sions. It was thought that everything conformed to orderly rules.

Two: How are things connected with each other?

MATERIAL OBJECTS EXIST AS INDEPENDENT ENTITIES.   From the
time of Aristotle, atoms were conceived to be the basic building blocks of the material world. As we have established, atoms
were regarded as hard objects having an objective and separate
existence from anything around them. These tiny balls of matter
were unlike such energies as light, electricity, or heat. The conclusion of traditional science has been that everything in the world
is separate and distinct. Everything exists by virtue of its own
autonomous and individual material nature.

Three: What really impels change to occur?

EVENTS ARE DRIVEN BY, AND ARE A RESULT OF, PAST CAUSES; THE
PRESENT IS DETERMINED BY THE PAST.   The prevailing view is that
every effect or event has a traceable material cause. A leads
to B, B leads to C, and so on. So whatever happens has been

caused by something in the past. This idea also originated with the Greeks, was modified and polished by such philosophers as Descartes and Hume, and completed by the great scientist, Newton. Classical science said that if you knew the original conditions when the universe was set in motion, it would be possible to predict all subsequent outcomes. There was an original cause that gave rise to a definite effect, and the future of any part of a system could be predicted with absolute certainty if its state at any time was known in all details.

Over the last half century, each of these dominant ideas about the workings of our world has been totally overturned. Let us turn to the discoveries that provide a more solid foundation for living effectively in our changing world.

THE THREE CORNERSTONES
OF THE CREATIVE WORLDVIEW

When we tap into the meaning behind the Breakpoint changes discovered by the thinkers working in the area of the "new physics," we expose the new rules that are so desperately needed in this third phase of civilization. Although these new concepts are broken down here into three different points, and serve as separate cornerstones, they are deeply connected and depend on one another.

A critical dimension of all of these discoveries is that they ask us to enter a previously *invisible* world. Within all of nature, the true power behind everything is unseen. Unobservable forces hold all matter together, the might of imperceptible gravity holds the stars, planets, and us in place. Our thoughts are unobservable. Radio waves in the air, magnetic fields in a television tube, x-rays and atoms changing state in transistors are all unseeable. Even the almost trillion dollars that are moved daily in the world's economic system move by invisible electrons. The notion that you can "believe it only if you see it" has long since been shattered. Today, 99 percent of the major changes impacting human life are happening at the invisible level!

Albert Einstein noted that, "a courageous imagination" was needed to realize that not the behavior of bodies, but the behavior of something between them, that is, the field, is essential. As we review the cornerstones of the Creative Worldview, we are also called upon to exercise a courageous imagination. Our challenge is akin to the ancient idea of picturing the invisible angels once thought to guide the stars—we have to see the unseeable. By engaging our imagination, an understanding of what is going on at the deepest level of nature can be constructed and placed within a framework where these discoveries can be useful in our ordinary lives.

The indispensable requirement to cross today's Breakpoint is to imagine what cannot be seen. Only in this way can we, like the scientists who created the technological revolution, unlock and apply nature's powerful forces in our own lives. Let's examine the key points.

One: How Does Change Happen?

LOGICAL WORLDVIEW: CHANGE IS A STEP-BY-STEP INCREMENTAL PROCESS. THE WORLD WORKS IN A LOGICAL, RATIONAL WAY.

VS.

CREATIVE WORLDVIEW: THE CREATIVE PROCESS FORMS THE DYNAMIC OF ALL NATURE. Nature's dynamic creative process fosters Breakpoint change by allowing differences to come together and form something totally new. The potential of how any growing organism, whether it be a quartz crystal, an individual, or an organization is fulfilled requires understanding the invisible world of atoms and how they work. Since the atomic and subatomic world are the building blocks of everything, understanding how atoms behave is crucial to comprehending the dynamics of how change happens. This understanding will reveal that the belief in the logical, step-by-step progression of nature can be replaced with a more accurate view—namely that everything in nature is dynamically creative.

Within the invisible realm of the atomic world, modern science has totally demolished the notion of an orderly and predictable cause and effect material world. All matter was found to exist in two simultaneous states—as *both* a material particle and as something new and previously unseen, something called a *wave*. The puzzle here is that a particle is a concrete physical object with mass that occupies a definite and limited space, somewhat like a tiny billiard ball. The wave reality that accompanies matter is made up of an invisible field, it spreads out in space and cannot be localized like an object. It has no mass, no material substance. *It became clear that everything in our universe has aspects that are somehow both solid and invisible—at the same time.* The world was not just the objective matter one could detect with the five senses. It was also found to be neither logical nor rational.

The term *wave* is used by science not to designate something like the wave that appears when we drop a pebble in water but a pattern in space and time that accompanies matter. This kind of wave is more like a crime wave or a wave of selling on Wall Street. A wave in physics is actually *a description of the probable futures of a material particle.* All the building blocks that make up our physical world carry in their present state a wave of future potential. *They are both being and becoming at the same time.*

PARTICLE WAVE REALITY

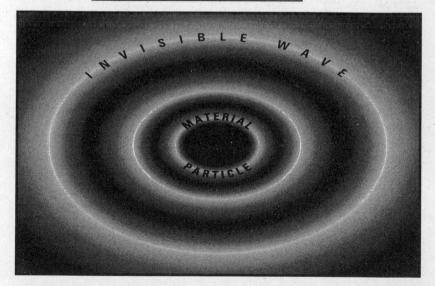

The wave state of an atom carries the potential for neutrons, protons, and electrons to achieve an enormous variety of possibilities. Without the wave state, new creative possibilities could not occur. Atoms would be inert or dead—incapable of growing and connecting. The wave is nature's method of connecting and bringing together atoms and molecules. The wave phenomenon holds our world together. Without the wave of their potential, atoms would just hit each other and bounce off. They wouldn't be able to merge. Because the waves of an atom can join with another atom, new possibilities can come into being. This is just like you reaching out and connecting with another person. A whole new realm of possibilities emerge.

The wave of our potential is primarily our beliefs, attitudes, and assumptions. Our invisible thoughts, actually our invisible waves, provide one of the most forceful ways for us to connect with or disconnect from each other.

Heisenberg, one of the great physicists once described this wave state: "It meant a tendency for something. It was a quantitative version of the old concept of potentia in Aristotelian philosophy. It introduced something standing in the middle between the idea of an event and an actual event, a strange kind of physical reality just in the middle between possibility and reality."

Neutrons, electrons, and protons carry a wave that is as real, concrete, and *important* as the object itself. It's real because the future carried in the wave *is* going to happen. If you don't know that a wave is part of matter, you'll miss the opportunity to use its possibilities. This was a major discovery in unlocking the secret of the atomic and subatomic world. Only with this knowledge and the use of the wave reality could the amazing breakthroughs of modern science and technology have happened.

You may ask, so what? How can I use this information in my own life, with my family, or to help my organization? As part of nature, you also exist in two simultaneous states—being and becoming. As a human being, your invisible—and real—wave state consists of all your thoughts. You carry your future around with you—right now—in your mind. Your thoughts make up your wave potential. Your invisible wave state carries within it the probable future states of your life. Your wave of potential, the wave of your children, your organization's wave are the most significant factors in creating the emerging future.

Extraordinarily successful people intuit this wave reality—and use it. Henry Ford observed, "Whether you believe you can, or whether you believe you can't, you're absolutely right." Countless individual stories of exceptional achievement and numerous research studies have confirmed the power of self-fulfilling prophecies. Belief—or nonbelief—in a future possibility dynamically influences results. Sören Kierkegaard, the Danish philosopher, continually challenged people to make what he called a "leap of faith," to tap their hidden resources of creativity and work toward making their dreams come true. A case in point is Debbie Fields, who held onto a dream of selling her homemade cookies nationwide. Without exception, experts told her it couldn't be done. She followed the dream and Mrs. Field's Cookies can now be purchased in countless locations across the country.

An idea becomes self-fulfilling only when someone chooses to make the leap. We can now see that a dream is actually the leap to embrace another form of reality—*if we really believe in it*. It creates a genuine and actual wave of potential that will guide us to the future. We can make a *leap of reality* based on the new facts uncovered by modern physics.

Each of us carries a picture of who we are at this moment, along with another picture of our possibilities. That picture of our probable future is not some kind of a vague dream. It has its own basic and powerful reality. The invisible image is as tangible as the world we can touch and see and feel. We're carrying two pictures with us at all times—what we are and what we could be. Both are equally critical to life. One is visible and concrete, the other is invisible and intangible. Your creativity is embodied in those pictures. The wave is the unexpressed potential of any system. In your wave of becoming lies your unexpressed potential.

The wave state potential of the world of matter has been manipulated through technology to unleash a world even alchemists never dreamed possible. As we have seen, the ability to convert common sand into silicon chips has proved even more valuable than gold. Considering what has been accomplished by scientists working at the atomic and subatomic levels of matter, imagine what human beings could do if they started deliberately manipulating the reality of their own wave function. When human beings begin taking advantage of the potential of their minds in totally new ways, the probable future states of humanity cannot even be fathomed. We get teasing samples from the lives of those creative people who have intuitively grasped their natural possibilities. After observing what happened in his own life and with many others with whom he has worked, Norman Cousins concluded,

"It's certainly a very exciting prospect even to contemplate the kind of world we can make once we allow the possibilities of development to assert themselves. We're still an unfinished species." In human consciousness, we see only the physical material or the substance of things—the reality of the wave of possibilities is invisible. It can be seen only in our imaginations.

Carl Jung observed, "Psyche cannot be totally different from matter, for how otherwise could it move matter? And matter cannot be alien to psyche, for how else could matter produce psyche ...If research could only advance far enough,...we should arrive at an ultimate agreement between physical and psychological concepts."

If we combine what we know about the workings of our inner nature and psychological processes with what we are learning about the nature of our physical world, we can resolve a number of paradoxes that have long baffled traditional science. If our minds contain, as the noted scientist Sir Arthur Eddington maintains, the "stuff" of the universe, there is every reason to believe that our mental processes reflect and extend the basic laws guiding our physical world. As ancient cabalistic magicians put it, "As above, so below." There is no essential difference between the phenomena of the world at large and the microcosm; just as there is none between the workings of the mind and matter.

CREATING THE OTHER HALF OF REALITY

Think back about the possibilities you hold for your future. When you imagine the possibilities for your future, you create not only your future but your *present*. You are creating, in your mind, the wave reality. Just by imagining possibilities you expand or contract your reality. Put another way, *the possibilities you imagine for anything actually make up half of its reality!*

Let's consider this again. The book you are holding has its "particle" reality. It has a being that is its own. It also is made up of its own set of probabilities, its *wave of becoming*. You also have your own being, what you are at this moment and, at the same time, you can imagine your own invisible wave of the future. The two waves, the book's and yours, interfere or interact with each other. They create a joint possibility. When you imagine something about the book, you are actually changing both your own and the book's present reality.

The material reality of waves—of possibilities—only reveals itself as time passes. As it must. How you choose to merge with, to blend your wave of possibilities with the book's possibilities creates the complete and ever-emerging reality. Any whole knowledge of reality would be incomplete without conveying the hidden nature of the wave potential.

When people say, "You create your own reality," we're sure that many of you would react as the authors have. "That's crazy, I didn't create this book. I didn't create this chair or table or building." And we were right—half right. The facts of the physical world and now the facts of common sense say something else, something totally different. We do create exactly how we will perceive and interact with the book or the chair or the building. We create something new, we create a reality of becoming—from our minds and our choices.

The reality of this very moment is in your mind. As you read this book you could be imagining a great array of possibilities, including such options as making it into a paper weight or passing it on to a friend. Those thoughts bring a new world into being—at this very moment. That world could be one in which your loose papers will be more secure because the weight of the book is holding them or it could be one in which the friend you give the book to will be inspired to create a very different future for herself or himself. The possibilities are endless. And they are part of the real world!

The continual creating of waves has yet another and astounding consequence—how these ensembles of waves act together. This brings us to our second cornerstone foundation of the Creative Worldview.

Two: How Are Things Connected with One Another?

LOGICAL WORLDVIEW: MATERIAL OBJECTS EXIST INDEPENDENTLY OF EACH OTHER AND THEIR ENVIRONMENTS.

vs.

CREATIVE WORLDVIEW: EVERYTHING EXISTS AS SETS OF CONNECTIONS WITH THE WORLD AROUND IT. New information discovered by scientists working in the realm of the new physics demonstrated that every part of every atom was actually a bundle of energy that was *not* independent of its environment but was intimately bound to the things around it. In fact, the nature of these minute universal building blocks verifiably changed even in the act of observing them, and depending on how one chose to observe them, they would change in different ways! Harold Fritzsch of the Max Planck Institute describes this process of relating as "a system in constant interaction with all other objects in the world. Nothing is or can be completely isolated."

The wave nature of our future possibilities interfere with each other. They intersect—and affect each other. They co-create. Another way of saying this is that they connect with each other. The physicist, Henry Stapp, testified as to the facts of physical reality for the Atomic Energy Commission as "a web of relationships between elements whose meanings arise wholly from their relationships to the whole." Everything—including us—exists as sets of relationships. *How anything relates to those things around it determines what it is!*

In recent years another startling fact has emerged. The physicist J. S. Bell and his colleagues have shown that all things are connected—at all times and instantaneously at any distance. This idea was proposed many years ago by the great thinker Ernst Mach. Simply using gravity as a basis, he pointed out that every tiny movement anywhere in the universe would automatically affect everything else. The noted physicist David Bohm concluded, "Thus, one is led to a new notion of unbroken wholeness which denies the classical idea of analyzability of the world into separate and independently existent parts."

In other words, the ancient notion that all things are separate is factually wrong. Everything and everybody is connected. Everything affects everything else. No matter how different, no matter how far away, we are all part of an interconnected whole. In the light of the most recent findings in physics, the fact is that no real division can be found between ourselves, other people, and the world around us—*unless we create it in our minds.*

The myth of the ancient and accepted second phase ideas of separation can now be exploded. As the world grows more and more interdependent, the more we reinforce the archaic illusion that things are separate, the less able we will be to solve our growing problems, let alone courageously imagine a world that works for everyone. When we ignore nature or wage war we inevitably end up having to repair the damage. The more we are disconnected from the rest of the world or from other people the worse we feel. Pitting humans against nature, black against white, or nation against nation results in cutting ourselves off from a future with unlimited positive potential.

Once we overcome the second phase delusions of separation we see why the idea of people working as a team is so important in organizations. It is critical in a third phase world that everyone in an organization be joined as part of a total unity. We see the practical necessity for organizations to find new and better ways to connect internally among different functions, with customers, and with the communities in which they operate. Even competition in business can be viewed beyond the separation of winning and losing and return to its original concept of a deep connection pulling everyone to reach further and do better.

The ongoing creativity and the connectedness of everything in nature moves onward, incessantly reaching out, extending beyond the boundaries of the past. This brings us to the third cornerstone of the Creative Worldview.

Three: What Impels Change to Happen?

LOGICAL WORLDVIEW: EVENTS ARE DRIVEN BY AND ARE A RESULT OF PAST CAUSES; THE PRESENT IS DETERMINED BY THE PAST.

vs.

CREATIVE WORLDVIEW: THE MOST POWERFUL FORCES DRIVING CHANGE COME FROM THE FUTURE. As if the wave/particle discovery was not enough to transform scientists' understanding of nature, there was another totally unexpected result of understanding the workings at the atomic and subatomic level. This provides an astonishing illustration of the true forces driving change.

For a moment, we must look at how physicists study electrons or other subatomic particles. By doing this, we will uncover the force propelling change. Let's engage in a simple experiment that most of us have seen in science classes. The idea here is to observe electrons hitting a target after they have passed through two minute openings in a screen. Instead of simply passing through and continuing on a straightforward journey to the target, they end up at the target forming parallel bands at the point of impact.

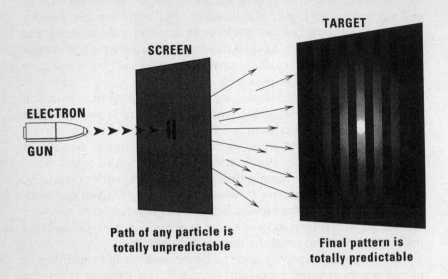

Path of any particle is totally unpredictable

Final pattern is totally predictable

This doesn't make any logical sense. Subatomic particles are like little bullets, so why does the pattern happen? Also, since countless experiments have shown that the path of any single electron passing through the openings is absolutely unpredictable, the final pattern should end up in a random distribution. Yet, mysteriously they somehow collectively "know" what to do and where to go and how they fit together. The same patterns are always created.

To add to the enigma, it doesn't matter whether the electrons are fired at the target rapidly in a group or *one at a time over a very long period of time*. In some extraordinary way they know where to go to form the same pattern. In no way can the cause or source of this pattern-making of particles be found in their past— or even in their observable material present. A physicist might study the track of one of these atomic particles and make a prediction based on its past direction and the result will always be wrong. On the other hand, *predicting the future pattern of many particles is always right*. Complete order comes from total disorder! How can randomness and disorder add up to predictable order?

This may appear to be a rather obtuse finding that might interest only scientists, but it carries profound and far-reaching meaning and power in all of our individual and collective lives. It has to do with how each of us creates our future, our wave of possibilities and the results we get. Most of our limits come from the assumption that has prevailed for almost all of recorded history, that is, that the present is a result of past causes. This automatically leads us into recreating the past instead of being able to fully create the future we want. We have been defeating nature. Let's take a look at how we can change our idea of the future.

THE DIRECTION OF CHANGE

The strange behavior of subatomic particles brought the law of large numbers and the laws of probabilities into being. Take the activity of a radioactive atom. It is known that such an atom will disintegrate over time, but when each nucleon will leave the atom is completely unpredictable. It has nothing to do with either the atom's past history or its present situation. Some invisible force is acting on it, something far beyond a past or present cause. Since it is unpredictable when any single nucleon of an atom will leave the atom, any *reasonable, logical* mind could conclude that the atom might occasionally emit most or even all of its nucleons at once. It never does! Astonishingly, however, half of the nucleons will decay in precisely a fixed time frame—every time. This is what gives radioactivity its well-known half-life.

This adding up a large number of unpredictable events and ending up with predictable results is what is often referred to as the law of large numbers. Although no logic can explain how it happens, it is very useful. The great mathematician John Von Newmann referred to this bizarre behavior as "black magic." The magic of probabilities, however, works! It allows insurance companies and gambling casinos to turn a regular profit. Statistics show that six and a half words will be added to the English language every day of this year, seventeen out of a hundred ties bought will be for Father's Day, one out of every eight restaurant bills will be incorrect. It is predicted that one in six teenage girls in the South Bronx will become pregnant. And that exactly one half of the nucleons in any carbon-11 atom will decay in twenty minutes. Uncertainty transforms into certainty!

The catch is, how do people know how many ties to buy and for what purpose? Who will tell which girls in the South Bronx to get pregnant? Do restaurant workers all over the United States get together and decide when to stop misfiguring bills? How did carbon atoms calculate exactly when to start and stop emitting nucleons? Arthur Koestler felt either this phenomena was due to blind coincidence or we are "driven to opt for some alternative hypothesis."

The resolution of the paradox appears when we shift our viewpoint and search for another explanation. A shift away from past cause to one of *Future Pull* provides just such a concept. It allows the enigmas of the new physics to join as factual background to the unceasing and relentless evolutionary process of life. It, moreover, gives us a new kind of common sense to apply to our turbulently changing third phase world.

The paradox appears only because of the ancient second phase assumption that causes come only from past events. If we step around to the other side of the events and imagine that *events can also be caused by the future*, the mystery dissolves. If natural events, atomic to human, have a direction, if they are being pulled to the future, then while single events may stray, the total system will always assume a predictable—and interconnected—pattern.

A simple thought experiment demonstrates the concept of Future Pull. Take the experiment we began with in which random electrons end up as predictable bands on a target. Imagine taking a box of metal tacks and throwing them out at random on the top of a table. What would be the result? A disorderly arrangement naturally happens. What if we put a large magnet under the table? Again we throw the tacks out randomly. This time, while each tack will land in its own unique place, the final result will be very different: *The bunch of tacks will be attracted to the magnet and will automatically arrange themselves in a predictable and orderly pattern*. The statistics of the magnet-pulled pattern of tacks just happens to match the statistical results assumed by electrons when they hit their target.

While the past surely effects whether the electrons exist in a particular spot in the first place, in the end they act like they were attracted to some kind of a magnet. They are pulled by the invisible forces of the future just as surely as the magnet pulled the tacks.

Just so, when two people join to create a child, although the past is represented in their genes, the future is based on the unique way those genes combine. That wave of potential pulls the trillions of cells forward to self-organize into a unique human being. A hybrid plant pulls a flower or fruit—never before known—into being. In exactly the same way, the resonance of the waves in a particle of quartz pulls it forward into a crystal.

We have reached a critical point in our journey together: recognition of the most vital quality of the change process. *Change is not only constant but change has a direction; it is pulled to the future.*

What is that future? Seeming miracles, such as the emergence of our continually evolving planet, the creation of life, or the appearance of human intelligence, are but commonplace and continual creative activities of nature's world. The concrete scientific evidence daily accumulating in the study of life, evolution, the development of civilization, and our own thinking processes shows a world progressing inevitably toward more complex relationships and deeper connections. This could only happen if change had a purpose.

In his book, *Chance and Necessity*, Nobel Laureate Biologist Jacques Monod stated, "One of the fundamental characteristics common to all living beings without exception is that of being objects endowed with a purpose." Or as José Ortega y Gasset puts it:

Life is a series of collisions

with the future; it is not

a sum of what we have been,

but what we yearn to be.

Change is driven by the pull of the future to connect everything at broader, deeper, more interpenetrating levels.

The pull of the future manifests itself in our lives, our dreams, our visions, our hopes, our waves of possible futures. Look around you, most everything you see and take for granted is an outcome of someone's idea of a possible future. Often those ideas were considered to be crazy or idealistic. "Wouldn't it be wonderful," someone once thought, "if a house could have holes in the walls you could see through and still be protected from the weather?" "How about having heat or cool air whenever you want it?" No power is greater than ideas and ideals, the waves that continually create the future.

We have not realized until now the *reality* we create with our visions. Yet, as we look at the people or organizations enjoying great success, we find in every case it was no accident. They allowed the pull of the future to work—and to propel them far beyond the limits and boundaries of the past. Their wave of the future acts like a radio receiver; they tune into the world around them and connect with anything that fits their vision. The past is not pushing them; *they allow the powerful reality of Future Pull to work*.

The principle of Future Pull poses critical questions for each of us entering a third phase world. What is pulling me? What is my purpose? What is pulling my organization? Success and deep personal fulfillment come when one is fully open to connecting with those individuals, circumstances, and events that will lead to the fulfillment of one's purpose. The challenge is to put the future in the driver's seat by harnessing the energy of life to the power of Future Pull.

MASTERING THE FUTURE

These principles are a stunning contrast to what has long been accepted as reality. The entire framework that forms the basis of the logical-causal model of reality has been proven to be, at best, only a small slice of a much greater reality.

The trick to mastering the future is to base our new thinking solidly on these three cornerstones: Creativity, Connecting, and Future Pull. *If any one of them is missing, the whole edifice will totter and fall.* If a person or organization applies Creativity, but is not pulled to a clear future vision, potential cannot be fulfilled. Even applying Creativity and Future Pull without being open to the possible Connections around us will severely limit our potential.

If you let some element of the old belief system creep in, your best efforts will be sabotaged. If you believe the past drives the future or that people are not creative or you just can't connect with certain racial, ethnic, or religious groups, it will be impossible to shift to the third phase.

In total contrast to prevailing views, we believe that the deep forces of nature can and must be understood in a better way. Otherwise, we cannot support our own and other's growth, we will not know how to respond to Breakpoint change, and we will not know what new rules to apply to guide the creative growth of our organizations. Through looking closely at the new knowledge of nature's deepest and most powerful processes, however, the facts of our natural, if invisible, human condition emerge.

We are creative partners with nature in bringing into being what never existed before. Everything exists in two simultaneous states, our *being* and our conscious creative act and choice of *becoming*. The only risk we take with the future is not to take the risk of recreating it.

Our reality is defined by how we choose to connect and relate with everything and everybody around us. We create ourselves by our curiosity, interest, and ability to make interdependent connections. Each of us is inextricably pulled to the future. The reality of the future is expressed in our potential to envision a different future.

We are not bound to the illusionary second phase causal worldview that limits us as mere extensions of the past. We can master the future if we take personal responsibility of joining in the recreation of our world. With the natural powers of creativity, connecting, and future pull, we can take the tensions and crises along with uncertainty and complexity as the exciting opportunity to recreate our planet.

As we have seen, we are all involved in a continual creative process. As anything moves through the three phases of growth, the phenomena that are often labeled disorder and randomness actually operate to provide necessary opportunities to create new, deeper, and broader connections among things, ideas, and people. They allow nature—including us—to create giant, unpredictable, nonlinear leaps of evolution and creativity.

If we and nature are truly enjoined in a natural and wondrous creative process, then how can we express our potential at the highest level in our lives and in our organizations? How do we move beyond our circumstances and collect our natural inheritance of creativity? This requires concretely applying these new understandings in ways that will successfully guide us as individuals and as a species in a turbulently changing world.

PART TWO
MASTERING THE FUTURE

6: PARTING WITH THE PAST

> Only through a radical shift in our thinking can we succeed in this new era. It calls for nothing but a complete break with the tradition-bound ways of the business leaders and managers of the industrial age.
>
> John Sculley
> Chairman and CEO, Apple Computer

"The poor will always be with us." So the saying goes—and we nod, well aware that our society lives on with this enduring problem, accepting that somehow its causes and cures continue to elude us. A second phase worldview imagines that the ever-present problems of humanity will go on forever. Thus, the reality of the future is determined.

But imagine a world where people think differently. Picture billions of individuals making a decision to recreate themselves and the world, taking the risk of believing that opportunities for fulfillment could come to everyone, shifting to a Creative Worldview. "Just nonsense," some will say. "Get real, stop daydreaming. Be practical. Don't you see human nature for what it is—and always will be? Look at history."

This is the same response one of the authors received from an elder in a desert nomadic tribe. "Tell us the truth about your tribe," he said after hearing some of the author's comments about the United States. He couldn't visualize a tribe that lived in houses, protected from the cold nights and blistering sun. He couldn't conjure up an image of plentiful food or of living much beyond two decades. His imagination was shackled to his experience and history.

How many of us, just a few years ago, could have imagined owning a personal FAX or copying machine or having a powerful personal computer or being instantly linked to vast networks of knowledge or making telephone calls where our voice traveled 22,000 miles in space and back in seconds? Could we have envisioned microwave ovens, laser surgery, genetic engineering, microcomputers, telephones in our cars, hundreds of satellite TV channels, or the world's commerce of over $750 billion a day being transferred through invisible electrons, with no money changing hands? Some people could see, could imagine, could dream of possibilities beyond anything we have ever known—and they happened!

This is the phenomenal promise of a third phase world.

We have used knowledge about nature's invisible power to cross the technological Breakpoint. Now, the greatest frontier yet known to humanity is to recreate *ourselves* according to those same deep and invisible forces of nature.

This frontier is the most demanding, creative, and exciting challenge known to humankind—the frontier of changing our minds about what reality means, pushing past the bonds of the past, and creating a totally new kind of future.

If we ever wanted a hero's or heroine's journey, we have it today. The new world awaits. The glorious challenge is to create a world populated by human beings who have consciously decided to embrace their own and others' creativity, who connect in ways that promote cooperation and trust, and who allow themselves to be pulled to an extraordinarily different future.

FROM TECHNOLOGY TO HUMANOLOGY

The great creative opportunities in this era are far beyond the technological, they are within the personal and social domains. And they are on the move. Could we have foreseen the fall of the Iron Curtain, the unification of Europe, or the surge of democratization moving across the globe? Even the true beginnings of integration of minorities and women into the workplace is a trail-blazing phenomenon taking place right before our eyes. Human society is recreating itself!

The first step for individuals to take is the resculpting of their own lives—the highest pursuit of creativity. It begins by learning the art of changing one's mind. This is the most formidable task. After we have put together a new frame of mind, we then can rebuild our society by reinventing our organizations.

If we are going to turn this second Breakpoint of civilization from its breakdown into its breakthrough, we must devise the means to change our minds about what is real: from a belief in the limits of a rational, past-driven world to belief in the limitless potential of a creative world. The third phase of creative growth and change provides the opportunity to let go of restrictive boundaries and explore unexamined potentials. Once the restrictive boundaries are removed and the new and different begin to come together toward a common vision, it becomes possible to create what never existed before.

The three foundational principles of Creativity, Connecting, and Future Pull allow us to use the Creative Worldview lens to understand and use the natural forces driving our age. First, let's look at each of the foundational principles of the third phase and then survey how people are unconsciously and intuitively both opposing and embracing third phase change in organizations and in today's society.

CREATIVITY

In phase three, the creative growth process focuses on achieving the unrealized potentials of the system. Processes shift from logical and straightforward to innovative and discontinuous. The basic human strategy moves from "solving problems," by attacking them piecemeal and getting back to normal, to formulating broad and original opportunities. Attitudes shift from finding and applying the "right," tried-and-true, traditional answers to energizing the production of unique advances: major breaks with the past. The system moves to creating the impossible; not just doing things differently, but *doing different things*.

CONNECTING

Third phase breakthroughs occur because of the connection and integration of the new and different. Second phase connections based on similarity and likeness shift to include all parts of the system, no matter how disparate. Humans, separated by mutual fear and distrust, unite by forging bonds based on openness, friendship, trust, genuine respect, and love. Previously separated parts of the system are brought together, creating unanticipated levels of success and hybrid vitality. The third phase thrives on social vibrancy and dynamism; the interdependent whole honors diversity as the whole becomes much greater than the sum of the separate parts.

FUTURE PULL

Individuals and all of civilization can now move from the push and bondage of past patterns to the pull of future possibilities. Strategies can focus on a vision of ideal potentials, rather than on practical constraints and traditional limits. In any organization, including the family, the most practical, bottom-line principle is the power of individuals committing to and sharing a common purpose.

The pull of the future is now not only interconnecting organizations, but it is pulling all parts of the world into an integrated whole. Space satellites now make the most remote areas of the globe accessible. What happens anywhere, now happens everywhere. We are an interconnected world. To think otherwise is an illusion.

NEW RULES

To be successful in this third phase world, we must adopt operating rules that converge with and take advantage of the massive changes surrounding us. Applying the foundational principles of the Creative Worldview will move us beyond this Breakpoint in our evolutionary journey.

1. Unleashing our creative capacity.

- Encouraging creative thinking to augment and expand rational thinking

- Recognizing that every individual is both being and becoming simultaneously, continually growing and changing

- Incorporating flexible procedures, rules, and standards, as well as versatile personal roles

- Basing contributions on the unique way each person can make the organization and the world a better place

2. Connecting all parts of the system.

- Integrating the new and different, embracing the enrichment of diversity

- Empowering individual responsibility and self fulfillment of all people

- Basing social systems on our being interconnected and interdependent

- Replacing conflict and competition with trust and cooperation

- Unifying previously separated activities, roles, and functions

3. Replacing the anchor of the past with the pull of the future.

- Creating a shared and compelling vision of an ideal future

- Making day-to-day decisions based on that vision, not on the past

- Assuring that all people have the opportunity to contribute to the vision

THE THIRD PHASE CREATIVE WORLDVIEW

When we compare the three phases of civilization, we can see the dramatic differences in the way the operating principles of each phase are applied.

Civilization's Journey

WORLDVIEW→ ↓	Phase 1 SPIRIT Survival	Phase II LOGICAL Growth	Phase III CREATIVE Fulfillment
THOUGHT PATTERN	Intuitive/spontaneous Past, present and future part of unified continuum	Rational Past Leads to Present and Future	Creative Future Vision Drives Present and Future
POWER	Assumed by Skilled Members as Needed	Physical Force Hierarchical Power Structure Inherited Power	Shared Responsibility
RELIGION	Worship of Infinite spirits and nature	Gods Organized Religion Merged With Temporal Rulers	Individual Spirituality
TIME PROCEDURES	Unstructured emphasis on seasonal cycles	Rigid Schedules Mechanical	Flexible Versatile
RELATIONSHIP WITH NATURE	Humans Dominated by and in awe of nature's mysteries	Humans Conquer Nature	Ecological view
SOCIAL SYSTEM	Ability dictates roles Community-based	Specific roles Unequal status	Empowerment of All
WORK & PLAY	No Separation	Divided and Different	Joyful Work and Play
HUMAN MEMBERSHIP	In Clan by Birth	Extended by Commonality	Enriched through Shared Differentness
RELATIONSHIPS	By Necessity Dominated by Nature	Dependent Independent Competitive	Interdependent Cooperative

P.D. Ouspensky and G.I. Gurdjieff said "Ideas by themselves cannot produce change of being; your effort must go in the right direction and one must correspond to the other." Today, in the postindustrial world, we find the occurrence of two distinctly different kinds of activities. On one side, we have the emergence and application of natural third phase operating rules, on the other we observe futile attempts to fan the dying embers of the second phase. Let's look at some examples of both creating and resisting this massive Breakpoint in civilization's journey.

Shifting from Logical Thinking to Creating What's Never Existed

RESISTING As late as October of 1989, the Association of California School Administrators, operating from a viewpoint of second phase thinking, announced, "The purpose of the school system is not to provide students with an education." Individual education is "a means to the true end of education, which is to create a viable social order." Here the leaders of one of the largest school systems in the world have declared that students can enter the twenty first century supported by schools that do not have education as their central purpose!

The educational crisis of recent decades has spurred building more schools, developing new curricula, and improving testing. Emphasis has been on more of the same: more teachers, smaller classes, tighter discipline, longer hours, and more homework. These strategies will help students acquire existing knowledge and logical, linear thinking skills. Such learning strategies work only in cultures in which future problems can be anticipated and solutions preformulated. Hardly the environment that exists today, when all the knowledge ever accumulated doubles every four years and new kinds of work spring up daily. Knowing the right answers must be replaced with learning how to learn and how to create new solutions.

In industry, the same sort of siege mentality often sets in. Many large, traditional companies have instituted Back to Basics strategies. Cost cutting, incremental improvements, eliminating innovative ideas, and centralizing control are seen as the way to survive and profit.

In a world in which the future cannot be predicted based on the past, the current approaches in both business and education have extremely limited utility. A third phase worldview recognizes the need for developing exceedingly uncommon capacities and skills: how to connect with emerging information from many diverse sources, how to assimilate information rapidly, how to think creatively and adapt that knowledge to new situations, how to work cooperatively with others. Clearly, second phase strategies of limited access to information, rote training, routinized jobs, and separated functions are not relevant in a third phase world.

CREATING   Many schools like the Minneapolis-based Tesseract experimental schools have adopted innovative approaches that develop their students' creative potential. Open schools, discovery, cooperative learning, and the ability to recognize that each child is uniquely gifted reflect the system moving into the third phase of learning.

Italy's entire Reggio Emilia Province supported the establishment of preschools for toddlers that were based on building self-esteem and supporting the individual creativity of each child. This bold experiment utilizing art as a means for children to express themselves is incredibly successful and is being emulated by other schools around the world.

In Amherst, Massachusetts, a consortium of private and public colleges and universities broke out of the old mold of competition to permit students enrolled in any of their institutions to take classes in any of the others. Smith, Mount Holyoke, Amherst College, Hampshire College, and the University of Massachusetts put age-old differences aside to forge a unique cooperative enterprise that serves the unique needs of students.

Branch Bank in North Carolina energetically taps into the creative potential of its employees and customers. The bank's mission, "to help customers achieve their economic goals," can, the bank believes, always be fulfilled at an ever-higher level. It continually seeks new insights to make its services better with creative and frequent community meetings in every town it serves. Branch's phenomenal success dramatically shows that people and their ideas make a difference and that their contribution is vital.

The Body Shop, which is more than a business, originated in England and has expanded across the globe. It incorporates not only natural, biodegradable products and refillable containers to support the environment but aggressively and imaginatively pursues campaigns against everything from the killing of whales to the repression of political dissidents. The Body Shop is motivated by forces traditional management techniques simply miss. It attracts employees that want something more out of work than a paycheck. Anita Roddick and her husband Gordon have realized a dream that both humanizes work and produces a profit.

Creative organizations continue forging an amazing future. The opportunity for everyone to make a *creative* contribution includes frontline workers as major contributors. Organizations can do what companies like North American Tool and Die did. NATD's president Tom Melohn's approach was to share responsibility, authority, and creativity with the total team actually doing the work. "Let them create, let them grow" is his practical third phase philosophy. It creates such miracles as the routine production of the highest quality products in the industry.

Connecting—Integrating the Different

Opening up the boundaries and allowing in those people and ideas previously excluded provides the dynamic that will renew organizations and nations. This requires the ability to connect broadly with diverse people, ideas, resources, values, and beliefs.

Throughout the world there are innumerable groups and millions of individuals willing to connect broadly with a wide array of diversity. And yet at the same time millions resist the challenge to move beyond this massive Breakpoint in civilization's journey by holding onto outworn ways of thinking and interacting.

RESISTING   The exclusion of minorities and women from all-male organizations was accepted as a normal practice for centuries. In the wake of the civil rights and women's movements, the Junior Chamber of Commerce, Lion's, Rotary, Elks, and prestigious all-male clubs came under increasing attack for their discriminatory practices. Yet, the International Lion's Club and the Junior Chamber of Commerce fought in the courts for years to keep women out. They ultimately lost their fight, but only under court order did they open up their membership.

Since 1960, we have seen an unprecedented number of women entering the work force. Today, 57 percent of all women work outside the home. Rather than anticipating and experiencing the unique differences brought to the workplace by women, most organizations have expected women to conform to the standard patterns of their male counterparts, from the way they dress to how they behave. The differences, the distinctive contributions that women could add to enrich the system, have been denied.

CREATING   Outside the mainstream, however, we see the hybrid vigor of integrating differences. Small businesses are creating the majority of new jobs in the United States economy. Hispanic owned businesses increased by 81 percent in the 1980s, five times the growth rate of all other United States companies in the same period. Black owned businesses increased by 20 percent. In 1987, 31.56 percent of all businesses in the country were owned by women, up from 7 percent in 1977. If this pace continues, by the year 2000, one half of all new businesses will be owned by women. They are leaving traditional second phase institutional organizations in order to create cultures that allow them to fulfill their unique potential. Mary Kay Ash, president of Mary Kay Cosmetics; Jean Nidetch, the founder of Weight Watchers; Debbie Fields, creator of the famous cookies that carry her name, stand out as models of third phase success.

RESISTING   The Vatican, in a twenty-three page document, said that increased attempts to fuse Eastern and Catholic meditations pose "dangers and errors." It said these efforts, "need to have their contents and methods ever subjected to a thorough going examination so as to avoid the danger of falling into Syncretism"— the merging of different religious practices.

CREATING   The Ecumenical movement is growing; the Methodist Church has selected six vital churches from around the United States as examples of blending religious practices to meet the needs of a complex population. The Church of Religious Science, and the Unity Faith, along with various other denominations, welcome people from all traditions into their congregations. Their orientation is to make room for diversity.

Creating an Interconnected and Interdependent World

CREATING   Civilization's connecting journey has already created an interdependent "global village." Consumers may start the day with a cup of Colombian coffee, Mexican strawberries, and Florida orange juice. They might wear a suit made from sheep shorn in Ireland, cloth woven in Brazil, tailored in Hong Kong, and purchased in Peoria. In the time it takes to get to the office in their Japanese car, powered by Arabian Gulf oil, they find that the money they have saved for years has either grown or devalued, sometimes dramatically, depending on what has happened on the Tokyo or London stock exchange. Our regular day-to-day life would come to a halt without the dominant reality of today's international connections in information, goods, currencies, and stocks. Choices made by individual consumers, not by powerful nations or corporations, have instigated this global intermingling.

Our awareness of the ecological interdependency and interconnectedness of the planet grows daily. The air we breathe, the food we eat, and the weather we experience are inextricably linked. Mount St. Helens erupted, and her ashes affected weather patterns around the world. Chernobyl exploded and showered nuclear fallout across Europe. The oil fields burning in Kuwait are causing black snow in the Himalayas. Air quality, acid rain, and ocean pollution are no respecters of the artificial national boundaries separating people. Around the planet, we are beginning to recognize that we all share significant benefits and dangers. Our world is interconnected. To think otherwise is an impractical illusion.

Initiatives for international understanding now break the old rules and happen regularly outside the traditional channels of diplomacy. Reciprocal efforts by artists, physicians, musicians, and housewives are breaking through national barriers to build ingenious and vibrant people-to-people bridges between longstanding enemies. Multinational corporations are evolving into transnational enterprises in which a variety of national participants act as valued partners with unique contributions. The differences between people are germinating planetary hybrid vigor.

The future of all nations demands a vision of our planet as interlinked, interdependent, and creatively evolving. We can create not merely "peace" but the excitement and rewards of a *cocreative purposeful peace*. Acknowledging our connections one with another throughout the globe and the great potentials that can emerge from combining our diversity serves as a prelude to building a great vision of global unity.

The kaleidoscope of diversity of the various races, cultures, and ethnic groups of the world can be seen as the planet's greatest future strength. This diversity can serve to competitively divide or creatively synergize our world. When we look at the 189 sovereign nations cohabitating this sphere through the lens of the creative process of growth and change, we can identify vast differences in where these countries are in their own development. The different phases of growth and change overlap one another and exist simultaneously. Margaret Mead pointed out, "We live in a unique era when every possible level of cultural development is still alive, often living side-by-side."

All over the globe, regions and nations seek to find appropriate expression of their own natural phases of growth. Often, they encounter staggering confusion as other nations, in other phases of growth, try to impose ill-suited and ill-timed expectations. By trying to force fit cultures to one another, we ignore a very basic principle of nature: *Evolution cannot skip a step*.

A culture cannot leap from the first phase to the third phase; it must develop its own successful independence before it can become interdependent. Developed nations such as the United States, must work with others in ways that are most appropriate to their unique growth needs. We cannot continue to apply the second phase technique of attempting to make them be like us. Phase differences in national development lead to extreme barriers in communication and understanding and often result in conflict.

RESISTING   War and defense are still seen as the way for nations to achieve their ends and assure their security. Since 1700, wars have claimed more than 100 million lives worldwide, and more than 90 percent of these deaths occurred in the twentieth century. According to Ruth Sivard's study, the ratio of civilians to combatants in the death toll has also increased steadily. Historically, about 50 percent of war-related deaths were civilian. By the 1980s, the figure had risen to 85 percent.

Antiquated beliefs prevail that "winning" is possible, despite the clear evidence that with contemporary armaments, both sides invariably lose, even with so-called conventional war. Iraq, Vietnam, Nicaragua, Afghanistan, and the disaster in Kuwait and Iraq stemming from the Gulf War are stark reminders not only of the futility of warfare but of how the lack of understanding of phase differences in cultural development aggravates attempts to join in mutual planetary growth.

The Force of Future Pull

To move beyond this social Breakpoint necessitates believing that the future can be different from the past. Let's look at some examples of both creating and resisting the inevitable pull of the future.

RESISTING   The concentration on quarterly reports within the most well-managed organizations keeps the business focus on short-term objectives. The measurements of profits and loss for a ninety-day period that determine management competency and rewards, simply pushes the past continually into the future— making it impossible to create a tomorrow different from yesterday. This is why so many traditionally well-managed organizations find themselves being replaced by businesses with far less resources.

In the public sector, for thirty years, schools throughout the United States have tried a myriad of techniques, programs, and incentives to reform schools and meet the needs of a nation caught up in the whirling winds of change. Yet the national report, "A Nation at Risk," recommended tightening graduation standards, assigning more homework, requiring more academic rigor. State after state passed legislation intended to get Back to Basics. The result: continuing decline. The public schools cannot be reformed, they must be transformed. An entirely new vision of why schools exist is required. Only then will the schools be pulled to a dynamically different future.

Increasing costs, long lines, insufferable waiting periods, and irate citizens do not seem to reverse the paralysis within many government bureaucracies. No amount of cajoling or criticism by citizens or elected officials seems to shift bureaucratic attitudes about how to be of service. Only by creatively involving these people in the development of the overall vision of how government can best serve its constituents will third phase change occur.

CREATING   Former Mayor of San Antonio Henry Cisneros had a vision that partnerships could be created with government, the business community, and disenfranchised minority communities. His incredible ability to bring all parties to the table to hammer out their differences and to forge new bonds based on mutual understanding paved the way to the vitality that has emerged in San Antonio. Jean Nidetch, the founder of Weight Watchers, saw a vision in which she was "teaching people how to eat for the rest of their lives." Merck & Company's vision means "victory against disease and help to humankind." MicroAge saw the potential of kit microcomputers to fulfill its vision of "creating a business to change the way the world works."

Organizations such as Weight Watchers, Merck, and MicroAge are pulled by compelling visions of the future. They are then able to join fully in the drive of nature to connect their people, customers, and suppliers at deeper and broader levels. Through those connections they can continually innovate. They vividly embody the way organizations will contribute to bettering life on the planet. In their essential nature, they differ from second phase organizations that depend on following well-defined and limited paths hewn in the past. Third phase organizations are driven by a future vision that builds on the past and also escapes its bondage! From limits and expectations, they move to possibilities and potentials. They lift their sights from confining boundaries to horizons that continually expand.

The vision of the European Economic Community was predicted by hosts of experts to fail. Of course, it was plagued with countless setbacks. Taking on and overcoming centuries of distrust, animosities, and deep suspicions was formidable. But a new climate is being created that is bringing the nations of Europe together. Under a common economic banner these fourteen nations will enjoy a powerful future together.

Visionary leaders have frequently been thought of as extraordinary, somehow possessing powers beyond the normal human. Understanding the Creative Worldview permits us to see that visionary leaders intuitively break the accepted cultural rules and allow the incalculable forces of natural processes to assist them. When organizations fail to develop a compelling vision as their primary source of vitality and step back into a "managed" second phase system, they eventually falter and break down.

Our work over the years with superbly successful organizations shows consistently that they are propelled and impelled by the pull of a future vision. Countless books and articles researched and written by such luminaries as RosaBeth Moss Kanter, Tom Peters, and Peter Drucker attest to this fact.

Developing the ability to create a compelling vision requires overcoming the pressure to return to the way it used to be before the onslaught of massive Breakpoint change.

BREAKPOINT PRESSURES

The daily newspaper presents a surfeit of growing crises. Entire nations are resisting the major changes required at civilization's second to third phase Breakpoint. Their concentration on protection, maintenance, and conservation of past status, conventions, and customs is entirely natural. Leaders believe that improving what they already know how to do is the answer to their problems. While this approach has worked throughout the long reign of the second phase, in the third phase it leads inevitably to confusion and chaos. Legions of unanticipated and seemingly insoluble problems rise up to overthrow the best laid plans.

In 1888, the French chemist Henri Le Chatelier first discovered the natural principle that applies in the Breakpoint crisis. He found that every stable system will respond to change in such a way as to attempt restoration of its original condition. As we have seen, systems in their second phase create an envelope for perpetuating pattern-limited growth, erecting barriers to resist change. They do this for what appears to be the best possible logical reason: to grow most efficiently by repeating and improving a successful pattern.

This second phase replication principle only becomes a problem when a system, like civilization, extends itself far into its environment, becomes fragmented and complex and reaches diminishing returns in the use of its natural resources. Civilization simultaneously generates such a volume of garbage pollution and industrial, chemical, and nuclear wastes that the effective use of the remaining assets is impaired. The rule is, nothing fails like success. At the end of the second phase, a system must shift to new processes and goals or enter the path to obsolescence and extinction.

A good example of this growth paradox is the phenomenon of large modern cities as diverse as Mexico City, Cairo, Phoenix, or New York. Since World War II, unprecedented growth has characterized metropolitan development. People and organizations flocked to Phoenix to enjoy the wonderful climate, clean air, low crime rate, and easygoing Southwestern quality of life. By 1988, Phoenix was confronted with traffic congestion, water shortages, one of the worst air quality standards in the United States, and a lifestyle beset with typical urban pressures and hassles.

So, people strive to solve the mounting problems with tried and true solutions: clean up the air, the water, improve the flow of traffic, increase police protection; get back to the things that made Phoenix attractive in the beginning. The catch is that fixing things, reinstating the traditional pattern, will attract even more people—and could end up multiplying the problems beyond redemption. Successful second phase growth naturally leads to the subversion of the very qualities that attracted growth in the first place.

Just so, New York City attempted to solve its problems of poverty and housing. Welfare benefits were increased and subsidized housing was constructed. In the good old days, before cheap long-distance telephone calls, easy transportation, and the information networks of radio and television, the poor from the rest of the country would not have known what was happening in New York, nor would they have cared. Powerful community linkages kept people at home. However, by the time New York implemented its answer to the housing and poverty problem, the solution served only to compound the problem. The result was a gigantic magnet that attracted the poor from throughout the South and Puerto Rico—many of whom would remain locked into a cycle of government dependence that keeps repeating the past with each generation.

On the scale of global problem solving in Third World countries, foreign aid programs have often backfired. The most disturbing example is the dramatic public health initiative that leads to famine when the population soars beyond the people's capacity to feed themselves. The less obvious and longer-range issues—lack of connections, insufficient organization, education, transportation, and communication—were put aside in favor of "quick fix" methods. After a long history of failed projects, a recent World

Bank study sadly concluded: "Many forms of development erode the environmental resources upon which they must be based."

This Back to Basics Bump focuses on solving isolated problems. It results in short-term improvements and growth of the established pattern, but defeats sustained growth that elevates the quality of life. If perpetuated long enough, Back to Basics solutions result in deep decline of the entire system and potentially its ultimate demise. Attempting to create the future by first getting Back to Basics does just that, moves everything backwards.

Along the way, in the United States we find ourselves deep in the Back to Basics mentality, struggling to resurrect the American dream. Paul Simon sings, "We came in the age's most uncertain hours and sing an American tune." That American tune was lustrous for nearly 200 years, guiding not only the United States, but all nations of the world to create a new future. It becomes dimmer as the United States, snared by its own economic materialism, attempts to recapture the past. With such obsessive commitment to a rearview perspective, the United States drifts further into the backwaters and away from the inspiring leadership that must be offered in this vital planetary third phase.

A third phase approach would not attempt to solve problems in fragments nor would it attempt to restore things to the way they used to be. It would look at the whole, to the long-range future, and involve a broad representation of its citizens in creatively envisioning the ideal quality of life. It would then work backwards from that great vision, including all the different sectors of the economy and the participation of many different people, in developing unique steps toward the future—boldly and creatively breaking with the past.

The Soviet Union finally broke apart after a failed coup against President Gorbachev, who promised an open society under glasnost. His rhetoric, from the beginning, had all the right words: "We want our decisions to be prepared with the involvement of the whole society." Gorbachev promised a major break with the past without recognizing that it would require a 180-degree shift in the rules. The old guard was unable to see the magnitude of the shift that was required of them. The old rules will not take us to the future. The dynamic creative process of growth and change inevitably moves forward despite temporary setbacks.

Attracting previously excluded people into a system without entering into joint creative process with them guarantees problems. Imposing a "vision" from above denies the power of shared commitment. Strategies that extrapolate past trends automatically limit potential performance; success cannot exceed the plan. The way popular "fixes" of our era are being applied is much like trying to force jigsaw pieces into the wrong puzzle; they belong to and can only fit within the old and obsolete pattern.

CONSCIOUS TRANSFORMATION

To move beyond the limited mentality of rational problem solving requires the conscious decision to adopt a Creative Worldview. We must fully recognize and rethink the limited reality assumed within a logical, cause and effect belief system. Like the Greeks, we have the opportunity to become conscious of a new way of living and relating to one another. When we embrace the Creative Worldview an unprecedented era of creativity will emerge that will far exceed the Golden Age of Greece.

Eileen Caddy suggests, "Life is full and overflowing with the new. But it is necessary to empty out the old to make room for the new to enter."

The way of thinking and attitudes that work in the second phase are quite different from those of the third phase. The thinking methods we can choose to integrate foreshadow the changes ahead.

We can move:

FROM	TO
THINKING METHODS	
Logical/rational	Creative/imaginative
Linear/continuous	Nonlinear/discontinuous
Analyzing	Synthesizing/integrating
Knowing	Learning/exploring
Deductive	Inductive
Conscious/calculating	Intuitive
ATTITUDE	
Certain	Curious
Judging	Choices based on vision

Responding/reacting	Initiating/anticipating
Comparing with the past	Experiencing the present
Monotonous	Wonder/awe/enthusiasm
Egoist	Healthy ego
Competitive	Cooperative
Co-dependent	Interdependent
Discordant	Harmonious
Cynical	Optimistic

Values and beliefs that correspond with a Creative Worldview undergo even more radical transition as we grow in our ability to choose new behavior:

FROM	TO

VALUES

Fondness	Loving
Guilty	Self-accepting
Pleasure for its own sake	Joy
Secretive/guarded	Open/honest/forthright
Competitive	Cooperative
Problem-centered	Opportunity-centered
Owning/getting	Sharing
Gain/loss	Win/win
Holding on	Letting go
Protective/defensive	Open/visible
Safe/secure	Adventuresome

BELIEFS

Fear/dread/anxiety	Trust/wonder/reverence
Suspicion	Trust
Judging/blame/fault	Acceptance
Scarcity	Abundance
Limits	Potentials
Sexism/racism	Accepting differentness
Good/bad/right/wrong	Nonjudgmental
Conservative/traditional	Evolutionary
Repeating old patterns	Exploring new ideas
Protecting the past	Creating the future

We recognize that the world changes only when individuals shift to living with a new set of values, beliefs, attitudes, and assumptions. Each of us is capable of changing our thinking patterns, of using our untapped mental power to create a very different world.

Our experience with hundreds of organizations, over a period exceeding thirty years, has led to the conclusion that *organizations and nations don't change—only individuals change*. When enough individuals believe and live the Creative Worldview, organizations and nations will also. Our focus now moves to how individuals can make the leap beyond Breakpoint.

7: CHANGING OUR MINDS

> If we believe in the rebirth of our civilization...then clearly this renaissance must begin in the chambers of our own hearts....We cannot wait for society to change, or for our institutions and organizations to be renewed. We, as individuals, must assume responsibility for our own personal transformation.
>
> Georg Feuerstein

Everyone living today is an eyewitness to the powerful joining of immense evolutionary forces. The Breakpoint changes cascading through our civilization, our organizations, and our individual lives are coming together simultaneously. Science and technology have unlocked amazing secrets of nature, social and political changes are reshaping the globe, and the dismantling of past prohibitions is bringing about new possibilities for enormous freedom and self-realization for individuals. All these forces have brought us to this third phase Breakpoint. Startling possibilities grow out of this dramatic confluence. The opportunity for people to have lives that are rich with meaning, to reinvent the organizations that are the building blocks of society, and for both individuals and organizations to live according to a new worldview lies within our immediate grasp.

The shift from one worldview to another begins when a few individuals question the prevailing values and beliefs undergirding a society. These daring pioneers who lead the way are usually unheralded. In his extensive research on major social changes, Dr. Everett Rogers of the University of Southern California concludes that 5 percent of a population needs to change before the established leaders begin to take notice that something new is happening. Once that intrepid 5 percent convinces another 15 percent, then a rapid and unstoppable momentum shifts the other 80 percent.

Marilyn Ferguson, in her landmark work *The Aquarian Conspiracy*, observes that a leaderless but incredibly powerful network is carving out a new human agenda, particularly in the United States. The shift overtaking us is "not a new political, religious, or philosophical system. It is a new mind—the ascendance of a startling worldview that gathers into its framework breakthrough science and insights from earliest recorded thought."

As we look at the natural processes uncovered in the Creative Worldview, we discover another fact: the foundational ideas leading to this shift in consciousness were actually laid over countless centuries by scores of great thinkers and religious leaders. Like the deep layers of earth that crystallize to form precious stones, these ideas have shaped themselves into great jewels of wisdom. Until science's recent penetration of nature's deeper secrets, however, these ideas have been considered to be vague ideals, never to be fully attained by mortals.

Often, enlightened thinkers were so far ahead of their time that they were either martyred or spent most of their lives in seclusion. Howard Gardner, one of the preeminent thinkers about creativity in the United States, observed that "most cultures throughout human history have not liked creative individuals. They ignored them or they killed them. It was a very effective way of stopping creativity." At this momentous Breakpoint, society and organizations cannot build an alternate or better future without encouraging and supporting the creative evolution of individuals.

Individuals who are moving to live the Creative Worldview can now merge their personal ideals and principles with the wisdom of great thinkers and with the momentous scientific discoveries of the twentieth century. The coming together of these natural truths now forms a solid foundation for those willing to change their minds about how our world fits together and works.

CHANGING OUR MINDS

FROM IDEAL TO REAL

There is a roadmap that we've found to be of tremendous help in making the conscious shift to a Creative Worldview. It provides a way to become a part of the 20 percent who will make the shift in worldviews unstoppable. Together we can and will shape a different future.

Let's return to the three foundational cornerstones supporting the Creative Worldview:

- Each of us is inherently creative and perpetually engaged in a dynamic *Creative Process* of growth and change.

- We create ourselves on the basis of how we *Connect* with people, resources, information, circumstances, and events around us.

- *Future Pull* operates as a driving force in each of our lives. We align with this powerful process when we develop a compelling vision and commit to achieving it.

NATURAL COMPETENCE

When we observe the shared qualities of people living not only successful but deeply fulfilled lives, we find they intuitively transcend the accepted truths that the world operates in a logical, limited, past-driven way. They align with nature's wisdom by opening to their own creativity, removing obstacles to connect with the people, ideas, resources, and material assistance they need and allow themselves to be pulled to a great vision. The combination of these foundational principles provides the means to enjoy a life with great meaning and phenomenal success. The big difference between outstanding creative people and people who can produce creative ideas, products, inventions, or even art is simply that the former have chosen to not merely think creatively but to live creatively!

The greatest creative act is the sculpting of one's life. The attention, diligence, and care of those consciously expressing their creativity in all of their daily interactions, relationships, and experiences require great commitment. The creative results—the products, the innovations, and inventions—the art—follow naturally.

Ted Turner, the cable television pioneer, went through a metamorphosis in his mid-forties. Even Turner characterized himself once as "a little right of Attila the Hun." His transformation into an individual with global influence in solving international problems is a stunning contrast to the ultraconservative, competitive sailor and the flamboyant owner of the Atlanta Braves. His change in attitude came about in the early 1980s as he saw the competitive arms race leading inevitably to war. Today he urges cooperation instead of conflict by promoting cultural exchanges between the Soviet Union and the United States. Turner's revolutionary vision for a new kind of world is reflected in the influence of CNN and his commitment to develop television programs on vital world issues through the Better World Society.

Wayne Townsend, a training manager at General Motors, decided he just couldn't go on with the usual games of distrust and suspicion accepted by people around him. He committed himself to the goal of completely changing the way people in his division related to each other and to their customers. He went far out on a limb and put his managers through a new kind of high intensity outdoor training in which telling the truth and trusting one another were essential to survive. Not only did he create a very different kind of culture, one that led to exceptional performance and profitability, but he moved on to lead an effort to transform the entire corporation, starting at the General Motors Saturn plant in Tennessee.

John Eisle discovered after eighteen years with IBM that his career was stalled. He was just plodding along, going through the motions and was deeply bored. Together, he and his wife Barbara admitted that their marriage had also grown stale. They took the big leap to participate in a truth-telling marriage encounter program with their church group one weekend. It was life changing. It took time, but together they abandoned old, easy patterns and recognized entirely new possibilities. They completely revitalized their marriage. In time, both became volunteer directors in the marriage encounter movement within their church, each changed careers, and today they are still growing.

Breakthrough stories like these abound. Ted Turner, Wayne Townsend, John and Barbara Eisle began asking, "Who am I really? What are my values? Why am I on the planet at this time? What do I really want in my life?" These deeply personal and significant questions moved them to the essence of who they are—and allowed them to tap into their own internal knowledge of nature's wisdom.

These pathfinders broke with their past. They could no longer grow where they were. Their second phase environments of successful independence had been exhausted. They wanted to create and relate in completely new ways. They made a conscious decision to transcend the mighty barriers of the second phase worldview, willing to experience life anew. They allowed themselves to move beyond the invisible Breakpoint barrier to experience a greater flowering of their potential.

- They committed to a purpose greater than themselves.

- They believed they could bring into being something that never before existed.

- They opened their minds and hearts broadly to connect creatively with the great diversity of people, ideas, and circumstances around them.

By tapping into the deeper forces driving the universe, they exemplified unconscious competence. They simply turned themselves over to their most compelling instincts—and had the courage to go against the conventional tide. Each of them experienced what it felt like to transcend the accepted truths of the limited logical worldview.

Today, they are joined by millions of others who are the true vanguard of the future. They are in the company of those individuals who loom as towering figures in manifesting what appears to be beyond normal abilities. In our own time, leaders and thinkers as different as Mother Teresa, Anwar Sadat, Betty Friedan, John Sculley, Robert Schuller, Lester Brown, and others before them like Albert Einstein, Amelia Earhart, Martin Luther King, Jr., John Kennedy, Mahatma Gandhi, and Thomas Edison instinctively called upon the extraordinary powers of these three universal and natural creative processes.

THE CREATIVE YOU

When we move to the individual level and consider the instinctive creative thinking approach, we see that creative people discover their purpose by first exploring many alternatives, winnowing these down to a few choices and integrating them into the most exciting possibility. If we examine the essential keys to how creativity works, we spot the invisible dynamics underlying the power of the Creative Worldview.

First, *they had unshakable commitment to a vision as the beginning point.* Creative people know intuitively that to be drawn by a vision or dream that is larger than themselves is vital. John Kennedy's vision of landing a man on the moon within a decade pulled all of the opponents and proponents of such a grandiose idea around one common purpose. Martin Luther King, Jr. didn't know the details of how equality for black people would manifest itself, but he had a "dream."

Second, *they believed they could bring into being what never existed before and couldn't have been predicted based on the past.* Lester Brown, founder of Worldwatch, expected to be a farmer like his parents. Never surrounded by books or well-educated parents, two events changed his life. First, a teacher introduced him to the biographies of Abraham Lincoln, Thomas Jefferson, and others who had made a difference in the world. He began to realize the power of a single individual committed to a significant purpose. The other event was a trip to India that left him with an overwhelming concern about poverty and world food problems.

Brown freed himself from the assumption that the past and present would determine his future. Neither of his parents had a grade school education. This did not deter him; he took his interest in farming and expanded it to gain a wide perspective about agriculture, poverty, and the interlocking factors that have an impact on world conditions. His vision of understanding how the world reached a state where widespread poverty was so prevalent led him to integrate this knowledge into something that would have great impact. With funding from the Rockefeller brothers, he established Worldwatch, a totally unique concept. Today, Brown and his group of researchers at Worldwatch publish an annual assessment of the state of the world that goes to over 120 countries, along with hundreds of separate articles and comprehensive research reports. These reports have an impact on world opinion and provide a foundation for thinking about how a society where food, water, shelter, and an adequate income is available to all the earth's people. Brown's dedication to a sustainable society pushes against the status quo and leads him far beyond the limits of what others believe possible. Lester Brown followed his vision and created what never could have been predicted based on his past.

Third, *they opened themselves to connect with the resources, ideas, people, and possibilities that would lead them to achieve a great vision.* The fetters of a logical worldview are put aside by visionaries who connect with circumstances, people, and resources in a nonjudgmental, imaginative, creative way. Creativity research has shown time and again that nonjudgment is the key to generating ideas. In this way our minds can operate without governors. This has been seen, however, as "deferred judgment" or "brainstorming," something one turns on only when generating ideas to solve a problem. In a creative life, this way of approaching nonjudgment does not work very well.

If people spend 90 percent of their time going through their regular life invoking nonjudgment only when they want to be imaginative about a problem, they miss 90 percent of the new possibilities that await them in the rest of their world. Judgment invokes perceptual filters that screen out much, if not most, of the information and connections—the possibilities—around us that could be useful in shaping a different kind of future.

Being open to all the possibilities, however, can be very confusing. If a person is not using judgment, how in the world can he or she make decisions? This is the catch. Without a purpose to pull us to the future, to guide our choices, we are forced to fall back on judgments. The critical thing to remember is that the basis of all judgments lies in the past. Judgments are always made against some expectation. The result is that choices are made that replicate the limits of our old, and often outmoded, knowledge and experience. Making choices based on alignment with purpose allows us to do the natural thing—create what never has been.

There are certainly critics of the notion that you can eliminate judgment. They argue that it is impossible because one has to make choices. There's a substantial difference between judging something and choosing. You don't have to judge as bad, inferior, or lacking in some quality those things you set aside as not helping you to fulfill your purpose. They may have value, you just don't choose to incorporate them into your life because they won't help you to get where you are going.

The training manager who had the great vision of changing the culture of one of the largest companies in the world had no idea how it would be accomplished. He was open to connect with all the people, resources, ideas, and material support available to help him achieve his vision. He considered all the possibilities—even outlandish ones such as survival training—without judgment and was able to make choices that were appropriate to his vision. Lester Brown moved beyond linear thinking to integrated thinking. He accepted the essential truth: "everything is connected with everything else." Both Wayne Townsend and Lester Brown were constantly open to the dynamics of creativity: exploring all possibilities and then selecting those alternatives that would best achieve their vision.

THE SAFE RISK

A recent *New Yorker* cartoon portrayed a man in a business suit with a briefcase, standing on a street corner. The caption read simply, "Born in captivity." It captured the essence of the creative dilemma. Submitting to past practices and tradition relieves us of doubts, from the need to make new decisions. It promises safety and security. When you step away from accepted and proven rules and guidelines, the unknown awaits. Why take a chance with an untested relationship or idea? Why risk incurring the wrath of other people? Why break old and comfortable habits? Upsetting the old order can be a messy, ambiguous, and emotion-filled process. As the old saying goes, "Better safe than sorry."

At the same time that we are tormented by the possible rearrangements we might have to make to accomplish something new, we also can imagine the other possibilities of joy, satisfaction, and fulfillment. The Ted Turners, the Lester Browns, the Betty

Friedans of the world inspire us, but we also remember that for every success like theirs, there are also hundreds, if not thousands of failures. How can we enter the world of creative life successfully? How can we take the big risk—safely?

What the discoveries of science and the Creative Worldview show is that the processes embraced by naturally creative people are like the proverbial three-legged stool. It falls over if any one leg is missing.

Operating with a great vision requires making a multitude of new and different connections. You can imagine a distant dream but if connections with people and ideas are screened by old standards of good and bad, right and wrong, the resources, people, and new possibilities will fail to materialize. You are left with extending and enhancing the boundaries of the past.

Or, try connecting broadly without judgment but bereft of purpose. This produces total confusion—productive decisions are all but impossible. A person in this state jumps from idea to idea, from project to project but without real progress.

Then imagine people who have a wonderful purpose and also connect widely but don't believe that they and the world are creative. They automatically are stuck with whatever works first. They don't go on to build a better and different future.

Take the great costume designer who produces original breakthrough costuming for show after show, but leads a lonely and isolated life because of his biting comments and deep personal prejudices. Or, a collection of people who continually try to improve the quality of life for their special group, yet contend there is little, if any, good in those who don't believe as they do. Or take the multitude of knowledgeable people who cannot absorb new information because it does not agree with what they have already come to accept as the truth. Any one of the cornerstones is not enough. Successful creative people and organizations mirror what science tells us about successful natural change. They intuitively know that if any element of the natural process of change is absent, any activity, any ideal, can become mired down. Without all three—Creativity, Connecting, and Future Pull—any effort becomes ill-fated.

From the most pragmatic viewpoint, why would anyone want to brave the forces of tradition and live in a creative way? We believe that the main reason could well be that creative people, be they baker or diplomat, teacher or welder, shape their lives with a profound sense of personal meaning. They are not manipulated by circumstances. They are responsible, free, and fulfilled. They love and enjoy their lives, their work, and the people around them. They are energized by their purpose. They continually discover new resources and possibilities. They feel great satisfaction and peace of mind flowing from the contributions they make in shaping a better life and world.

DISCOVERING WHAT YOU ALREADY KNOW

The most heartening news is that each of us already knows intuitively what being creative feels like and what are the necessary qualities of an environment where we can work creatively.

For a moment, let's look at the qualities that permeate a work environment where creativity can take hold and grow. Imagine a time when you were your creative best, when you expressed your natural abilities at the highest level. Maybe it occurred when working on a project; maybe you were part of a team. If this has never happened for you, then conjure up what it would be like.

List the qualities permeating the work environment when you were your creative best. Maybe some of the ideas that we have heard from others will stimulate your thinking:

- I worked with a group that had a common purpose as to what we wanted to accomplish.

- We had respect for each other and continually offered one another support.

- The environment we were working in was free of judgment.

- We trusted each other.

- We really accepted one another.

- Sure we made mistakes, but we learned, and we didn't fear being punished.

■ It might seem a bit strange but actually there was a feeling of love.

See if you can add other qualities that have been present when you performed creatively.

We've been asking these questions of individuals around the world over the last four years and the results have been startling. In setting up this scenario and asking what qualities are found in a creative environment, we have found the answers are basically the same; it doesn't matter whether a person grew up in Europe, North America, Japan, the near East, the Middle East, or Africa. Here is a sampler of what individuals and groups have told us about the qualities the environment must have in order for them to contribute at a high level of creativity.

■ We respected and supported one another.

■ We had clear communication.

■ Everyday, we learned from one another and looked for what was possible. We didn't follow the rule book.

■ I had the freedom to make mistakes and take risks without fear of punishment.

■ I felt fulfilled because I had a chance to grow.

■ Each of us was equal.

■ We were open to new ideas.

■ Our team had a commitment to a common purpose that gave us a sense of direction and unity.

■ We knew we were creating something worthwhile.

■ More than anything, we had a beginner's mind.

■ We learned how to be creative. It was a conscious decision to engage our creative mind in what we were doing.

■ What we did was bigger than "me." Our focus was on how "we" were going to do it.

■ There was a sense of playfulness and fun.

- I can't remember judging anyone.

- We were flexible and highly motivated.

- I remember that I was always being stimulated to think differently and take initiative.

- It was exciting to go to work, and we had enthusiasm and passion for what we were doing.

- We were open with each other and told the truth.

- For the first time I was really encouraged to give all that I could, and I got honest feedback.

- We trusted each other.

- There was a very interesting balance between the group achieving and the individual contributions of each person.

- We couldn't have done it without our willingness to work cooperatively together. Competition was eliminated.

- We cared deeply about each other; in fact a sense of genuine love emerged.

- It was great to know you were doing something important. We felt inspired.

- Everyone took responsibility.

- We felt empowered.

- Our focus was on the long-term, rather than short-term results.

- We were patient in our work with each other and achieving our goals.

Is your list similar?

Now let's move on. Think of the qualities that dominate most normal work environments where you either presently work or have worked in the past. Take time to think about your own situation.

What prevailing qualities permeate the normal environment where you now work or have worked?

Again, whenever we ask this question, a list of qualities that are quite similar emerges no matter where we may be in the world. We list the most common qualities that people mention and ask you to compare it with the list you have made.

- We have the right answers.

- New ideas are discouraged.

- Our company is locked into analysis paralysis.

- We are competitive with one another and also with other departments and divisions.

- The atmosphere is adversarial.

- Mistakes are punished. The best advice is to cover your backside so no one finds out you made a mistake.

- There are fixed beliefs, rules, procedures that you just don't buck.

- It is a fear-based organization.

- We have a closed environment.

- It just isn't a fun place to work.

- Having control is important.

- This organization is self-serving.

- Organizational structure squelches growth.

- We have short time horizons.

- The attitude prevails that the cup is "half-empty."

- "Not my job" mentality.

- Organization is hierarchical—the people at the top have the power to stop things from happening, and they do.

- Numbers drive the organization.

- We don't have a vision of where we're going.

- "Wasn't invented here" syndrome.

- Internal competition for resources.

- Praise and encouragement are almost nonexistent.

- No matter how much I do, I'm expected to do more.

- Little appreciation for the job I do.

- When something goes wrong, there is always someone to blame.

One of the most striking aspects of this exercise is that human beings know instinctively what qualities will either suppress or support a third phase creative atmosphere. Our difficulty lies in accepting that each of us is naturally creative and then fostering an atmosphere where we allow that inborn creativity to blossom.

Exploring how to consciously adopt a Creative Worldview and make this uncharted domain a part of our lives is our focus. Our commitment is to provide specific principles of how to live creatively, how to remove the barriers to connect at the highest possible level, and how to align with the pull of the future.

THE NAVIGATION MODEL

We invite you to consider a metaphor drawn from navigation as the internal guidance system to understand and apply the Creative Worldview. Any responsible ship's captain determines the seaworthiness of the ship before setting sail. This requires an inventory of the vessel's capability. Ascertaining the condition of your own personal vessel requires you to answer the question, who am I?

From the Creative Worldview perspective, this is not defined as a collection of limitations based on past experiences. The past is of concern only in how it contributed to your present situation. Navigators don't carry rearview mirrors in their tool kits. It is irrelevant that there was a terrible storm yesterday or that you were becalmed the day before. What is important is the knowledge that you are a creative being capable of bringing into existence something totally original elicited from your unique gifts and talents.

In order to do this, ask yourself what is pulling you. What is your purpose? What vision do you have for your life?

That destination, even though it may be fuzzy or unclear, is vital. You must be absolutely certain that you have a worthwhile destination.

Since winds and waves, storms and lulls are unpredictable, the final requirement is acute awareness in transit, so as to make the proper course corrections. The excellent navigator pays attention to everything without judging it. The last vital capability is to be open, receptive, and sensitive to your environment. Ask yourself if you are learning as you go, connecting with all the possible resources, ideas, information, experiences, and people that might move you powerfully and creatively toward your purpose.

We were sharing this simple and straightforward metaphor for navigating through life at a presentation when one of the participants with great enthusiasm shared her story of how this technique helped her. "I know just how the principle of navigation works. When I was in Japan recently, I was driving a rental car and found myself completely lost—without the ability to speak or read the language.

"I went into a small store and the clerk was able to help me locate where I was on the map. He quickly removed the crumpled map from my hand and spread it out on the counter. Somehow, with sign language, he then made me understand that what he needed to know was where I was going. I knew my destination and even the proper Japanese pronunciation, and I was able to blurt it out. He then pointed to the place on the map where I was headed, and took a marker and colored in the route on the map. I left that store with the essential tools you just explained. These were the tools to navigate through a complex, foreign city. I had a fully functioning car, I knew where I was, where I was going and also, in bright florescent yellow, I now had a guide to the connections I needed to make it through the streets of Tokyo to get to my destination."

Just like the tourist in Tokyo, you can apply the powerful metaphor of navigation and let these simple rules guide you in embracing the processes and principles of a Creative Worldview. We will focus in the next three chapters on how to become clear about who and where you are in your own creative growth and development, where your organization is and how you and your organization can engage the power of Future Pull to reach your destination, and how to employ the tremendous capabilities of connecting at the highest possible level on your journey. You will find that you can easily apply the methods of navigation to your own life journey as you commit to living creatively.

These three cornerstone foundations of the Creative World-view apply equally as well in family relationships as they do in your own personal development. They also can be powerfully utilized in your organization, with volunteer groups, and within your community.

8: THE CREATIVE DRIVE

The creative individual not only respects the irrational in himself, but courts it as the most promising source of novelty in his own thought. The creative person is both more primitive and more cultured, more destructive and more constructive, crazier and saner, than the average person. It follows that the creative environment is one that encourages this dichotomy through freedom of expression and movement, lack of fear of dissent and contradiction, a willingness to break with custom, a spirit of play as well as of dedication to work, and purpose on a grand scale.

Frank Barron, Professor
University of California, Berkeley

When we ask our clients if they consider themselves creative most respond with an unequivocal "no." Most individuals truly believe they are not creative. They let their greatest asset go undeveloped because of the combined messages received from family, friends, schools, church, or the people at work. Not only do you inherit the gift of creativity, as a part of your nature, but also the benefits of actively participating in a dynamic creative world.

By creative, we mean bringing something original and unique into being.

In the long tradition of the Second Phase, most people in Western cultures inherited a belief system that subscribes to the notion that the Creator resides outside of them. This results in not accepting the fact that they are inherently creative. At the very best, it leads to the belief that only a few people have creative capacity, that very few people are empowered, and even fewer are capable of taking their life and molding something exceptional out of it.

It becomes quite obvious how deeply we have accepted this belief system when we look at the way our organizations are structured. Naturally, the person at the top has more authority, power, and influence. After all, people at the top have better ideas and are more creative. This is the person responsible and empowered to cause things to happen. As you descend the organizational chart, people become less powerful and important. The mass of people on the bottom of the pyramid have little opportunity, they believe, to see themselves as responsible, empowered, or creative. In fact, it would be more accurate to say they are treated like pawns, often see themselves as pawns, and in many cases act like pawns.

These beliefs run directly counter to what is needed today. As Rollo May said, "We are living at a time when one age is dying and the new age is not yet born." What is so desperately needed are creative people who don't want to live in the world as it is today, but who want to create a different and better world.

Tom Melohn at North American Tool and Die is giving birth to this new world with his philosophy; "There is no correlation between creativity and job title.... A guy who takes a chunk of steel and makes a part that is accurate to one-fourth the thickness of human hair is enormously creative." Mehlon believes workers are just as creative as executives, "it just takes a different form."

Accepting your unique creativity is the critical first step in living the Creative Worldview. The five other principles of creativity will enable you to experience the power of opening to your distinct creative voice.

THE CREATIVE DRIVE

CREATIVE PRINCIPLE NUMBER 1: ACCEPT YOUR INHERENT CREATIVITY

Dr. Calvin Taylor at the University of Utah, one of the great pioneers in education for the gifted and talented, found some great surprises in his research. He found that all children are gifted and creative! Some are creative in their speech, some in their body movements, some in drawing or writing. Others are gifted in the way they relate to others or in the way they organize things. He discovered a vast panoply of talents, many that had never before been recognized. The challenge for the teacher becomes finding those unique talents and helping children to express them naturally. He provided a new direction for education.

Our research on creativity reveals that the vast majority of small children are actually creative geniuses. One of the authors gave eight tests of divergent creative thinking to 1600 children in the early days of the Headstart program. He gave the same tests to these children over several years. The first tests were given when the children were between three and five years of age. Ninety-eight percent of the children scored in the genius category. When these same children took identical tests five years later, only 32 percent scored that high. Five years later it was down to 10 percent. Two hundred thousand adults over the age of twenty-five have taken the same tests. Only 2 percent scored at the genius level. What happens? One thing we know is that the brain doesn't disappear. All of us can guess the answer.

The socialization process restricts the natural creativity of our thinking potential by automatically assigning value judgments such as good, bad, right, wrong, proper, improper, ugly, beautiful. Small children have no conception of these values and interact without these limitations. Our proficiency in expressing our creativity gradually drops off as we learn to accept others' opinions, evaluations, and beliefs. What we have seen in our work with adults is that the five-year-old creative genius is still lurking inside—just waiting to break free.

If you visit any kindergarten you find little four- and five-year-old children expressing their creativity in countless ways. They use the word *yes* virtually all the time. Ask kindergartners if they want to sing, and the answer is "Yes!" and they start singing...

not one of them, but the entire class. They say yes to dancing, playing tag, painting, skipping, flying kites, cart-wheeling, and exploring. Ask a graduate student if they would like to sing. What do you hear? "Oh, no, I don't think so, I haven't sung in years." Would you like to dance? "No, I never learned how to dance." Inside every adult is a five-year-old creative genius waiting to say yes.

Retaining or recapturing the simple playfulness of a child opens a person up to creative possibilities. This is when wonderful things start happening, when you move outside the boundaries and different possibilities emerge. Listen to music, fingerpaint, wear a crazy hat, make a face, dance, monkey around, talk to yourself, fiddle, scream, yell at the moon. Recapture your childlike nature.

Two mature adults who hadn't lost their sense of play had just started eating hot fudge sundaes. He looked at her holding that spoonful of ice cream dripping with hot fudge and noticed a glistening in her eyes. Alex said, "Don't even think about it." But as the words left his lips the ice cream landed across his nose. No way was she going to get away with that. He landed a volley below her right eye. They drenched each other in vanilla ice cream and hot fudge. Undoubtedly a few cherries exchanged rounds.

N.C. Wyeth, the great American artist, nurtured the creative spirit of his family with a passion and fervor. Now the fourth generation of Wyeths all have this childlike quality. One of his grandchildren claims that "Grandpa started it, created this world—witches, goblins, and fairies—and I've brought my children up that way." Today N.C. Wyeth's children and grandchildren continue their profound impact on the arts because of their ability to cultivate their childlike nature. It's our inner child that opens up the world of our deepest creativity. This inner world of our fantasies, dreams, intuition, imagination, and deep yearnings usually is sealed off by adulthood. The logical, reasonable path has seized most adults, and they have yet to explore these invisible recesses of the mind. It's here we search for hidden treasures of creativity.

The World of Invisibles

It is from the depths of the unconscious that the truly original ideas spring forth, where our wave of becoming resides. This is the place where you really have to dig. And the mystery is that we know so little about it, and in many cases we're afraid to look deeper.

Abraham Maslow called this place *primary creativeness*. It comes out of the unconscious, and is the "source of new discovery, of real novelty which departs from what exists." This kind of creativity is our heritage as human beings, yet few have unleashed their primary creativeness because of the repression our society erects around what it means to be a mature adult. The adult world, according to the prevailing worldview, requires one to be realistic, possess common sense, display good logic, be mature, take on responsibility, and keep emotions under control.

In many people the result is a sharp split between what they know about themselves and what lies concealed in their unconscious. The quest for safety, security, and comfort where there is orderliness, predictability, control, and mastery leads to a general unwillingness to explore the unconscious world. Being afraid of one's emotions or instinctual urges can lead to tightness and rigidity and cuts us off from the very resources we need to find new solutions in a third phase world. These patterns are not conducive to discovering the unconscious realm and the deep reservoir of creative potential.

Walling oneself off from the unconscious realm happens at a great cost. This is where the abilities to play, fantasize, imagine, dream, laugh, and be spontaneous and crazy actually live. This is where the really great ideas are located. It's been said that every great idea looks crazy at first.

Giving up our primary creativeness means giving up our artistic nature, giving up our poetry, drowning our childlike nature. Oliver Wendell Holmes put it well, "Alas for those who never sing but die with all their music inside of them." Not developing this area means giving up a huge portion of our deeper selves.

Turning our backs on our deepest selves allows us to avoid what might threaten us. What many haven't realized, however, is that what threatens us is softness, tenderness, emotion, lack of realism, illogic, and being out of control.

Many men and women prefer the more down to earth tools of rationality and common sense that seem to move them ahead in the working world. The fact is that color, fantasy, poetry, romance, imagination, intuition, music, emotion, irrationality, tenderness, and relaxation are the most powerful aspects of the effective and productive creative life. Up until now, explorations in these areas have been thought to be a sign of weakness. What we are learning is that these aren't weaknesses at all, but it requires opening to new possibilities.

T.S. Eliot expresses why the creative journey to the invisible wave of potential takes courage.

In order to arrive at what you do not know

You must go by a way which is the way of ignorance

In order to possess what you do not possess

You must go by way of dispossession

In order to arrive at what you are not

You must go through the way in which you are not.

The pathway into this realm can best be found through the world of children. Children are accepting. They don't understand mutual exclusions or opposites. They aren't aware of taboos, inhibitions, order, or planning. A child doesn't calculate impossibilities or possibilities. Lewis Carroll captured this spirit when Alice said to the Queen, "There's no use trying, one can't believe impossible things." "I dare say you haven't had much practice," said the Queen. "When I was your age, I always did it for half-an-hour a day. Why, sometimes I've believed as many as six impossible things before breakfast."

Opening to the area of self knowledge requires going into a world of invisibles beyond the conscious mind—where our imagination, intuition, and dream world give us access to our inner wisdom. Here is where 90 percent of our potential lies. This is where we connect with our wave of possibilities. Over half of who we could become is in this domain.

CREATIVE PRINCIPLE NUMBER 2: CONNECT WITH THE INVISIBLE WAVE OF POTENTIAL

A starting point in exploring the invisible sphere begins by realizing that dreams carry powerful messages from the unconscious realm. Your dreams belong to you alone and within this world resides a storehouse of information. It requires learning how to interpret the symbols of the dream realm. Carl Jung spent a lifetime exploring this area. He diligently kept dream journals and his most potent dreams were written up in his special red book of dreams. Many of these dreams powerfully influenced his work and were credited by him as the source for many of the great contributions he made in his lifetime.

Dreams have unlimited potential. They give clues about the beliefs you hold about relationships, where the best ideas can be found, and how to expand your creativity. Alan Huang of Bell Labs invented the first working optical computer, the most important breakthrough in computer science since the microchip, because of what happened to him while asleep. For months he dreamed about armies carrying pails of data and sometimes colliding with one another. In his last dream, the armies marched right into each other with no collision. The dream made Huang realize that laser beams could pass through one another unchanged—like the opposing armies in his dream. This led to the breakthrough for his invention.

Dreams reveal where certain patterns of behavior originate and how to overcome limiting beliefs. They can introduce you to the reason why you have such difficulty staying on a diet, keeping commitments, or following through on projects. This unconscious realm often sabotages your best efforts. It is tremendously helpful to learn what the unconscious really believes. Then you can meet the challenge of changing patterns that no longer serve you.

Sigmund Freud and Carl Jung dared to explore new territory. Fifty years ago there was little, if anything, known about the unconscious realm. These two pioneers ventured where no one had gone before, expanding the possibilities of what it means to be human. Both of them faced great trepidation as they charted unexplored paths. But they had the courage. Rollo May has called it the "courage to create." This is the kind of courage needed today.

To expand your creativity requires collapsing the walls around what has been unexplored. Ask yourself what you think you should do, and do the opposite. Do you dare to get rid of those "shoulds" and "oughts" that constrict your life? Are you willing to chart new territory by going places you've always wanted to go but never tried? Are you willing to make waves?

The underlying message in a second phase organization is don't rock the boat. Don't make waves. The very opposite quality is needed. Making waves is not for the sake of rebellion, but to wildly explore all possibilities in creating a different future, connecting with your deepest self in fulfilling your purpose. Make waves! Make waves as big as you possibly can. This requires going into uncharted waters.

In order for this to occur in the lives of millions of people, the world of the unconscious and the world of reality must be brought together. Every human being is both child and adult, both masculine and feminine, both sensible and crazy, both logical and illogical. The idea of *both...and* is critical to make the successful crossing to a new worldview. The fully evolved human is both rational and irrational, both playful and serious, both poet and engineer. *The notion of either...or, of dichotomies, of duality thinking cuts us off from our full wave of potential and ultimately from our full creativity.*

What do we really mean when we say each person has the inherent capacity to be fully creative? First of all it means you have given yourself permission to be you. This is who you are, free from the boundaries and expectations of parents, religious restrictions, or the career path someone else thought you should take, but the one you've never really liked.

Often the expectations of others lead people into a situation in which they work for years in an occupation unsuited to them. When Harold came back from Korea, he went to work in his father's very successful printing business. It was what everyone expected of him. He dutifully fulfilled his responsibilities until the day his father died. Within a month, he astonished everyone by abandoning the business and enrolling in medical school. He was forty years old! In Korea, he had served in the medical corps and learned the joy he received from healing. Now, every day Harold approaches his work with excitement and happiness—and he has become one of the most sought after medical doctors in his state.

His new life was directly related to his knowing who he was and then finding the courage to become that person.

Even though it was thousands of years ago that Plato said, "The unexamined life is not worth living," one of our greatest challenges is to truly know who we are. Lester Brown has been honored for his creative contribution at Worldwatch and knows well the power of knowing himself. As a young boy he asked himself why he was afraid of certain situations, how much risk he was willing to take, and how he felt about competition. Brown was able to move to a vantage point where he could observe himself and integrate what he discovered. This critical skill required development and a determined commitment.

CREATIVE PRINCIPLE NUMBER 3: KNOW WHO YOU ARE

Making a creative contribution necessitates knowing who you are, what you really care about, what you love, and what you want to commit your life to accomplishing. This is how you find the source of what will motivate you to make an exceptional creative contribution. Wayne and Donita Parker knew they enjoyed getting in their car and driving, particularly into unusual and magnificent natural settings. They loved meeting people when they traveled. They wondered how to combine their unique interests into making a significant contribution. Finally, it came to them: offer travel tours to the Grand Canyon, Sedona, and other beautiful scenic spots from the resort hotels in Arizona. Wayne and Donita quit their old jobs and now have a thriving business. They tapped into their creativity by offering thousands of people their unique blend of enthusiasm, expertise, and sense of wonder about nature's grandeur.

Ellen Stewart, once a fashion designer now operating LaMamas in New York City where countless aspiring playwrights get their start, received a coveted MacArthur Award for her own creativity. In a wide-ranging interview with Denise Shekerjian who was studying the uncommon genius of forty MacArthur recipients, Stewart expressed her deep feelings about the importance of loving what you do. In her unique style she said, "Trust me now because I know what I'm talkin' 'bout—you got a love for what you're doin' and everythin' else, all the rest of this cree-a-tivity stuff you're wonderin' 'bout, it just comes."

When you know what you care about, what you love, what you have passion about, you have discovered the deep truth about who you are and can fashion these gifts into something original. As a shaper and builder, our emphasis has been to recognize only the external manifestations of creativity, such as extraordinary paintings, great literary works, or startling discoveries. The greatest creative challenge is not only to do something different, but to be something different. The most creative act is the molding of your own life. Very little credit has been given to those who are deeply engrossed in shaping their own lives.

People have the capacity to express their unique skills and talents in their own individual way. Have you made an inventory of your own uniqueness and determined in what ways you find the greatest pleasure in expressing yourself? If not, begin now! Those people who experience the greatest joy offer to the world their distinctiveness. It was the eighteenth century poet Edward Young who asked, "Born originals, how comes it to pass that we die copies?" It takes great resolve to live according to our own inner wisdom, yet the seed is planted within all of us. The challenge is to nurture that seed—even within conforming work environments—allowing it to grow and express itself in wonderfully unpredictable ways.

Each of us is gifted with unique skills and talents. When expressed, they allow us to manifest our creative potential at ever-higher levels. Our potential is always in the process of unfolding. Our wave of potential expands as we express our creative gifts.

A sixty-year-old engineer retired from his firm after thirty years of service. He immediately moved from his hometown, bought a place on the ocean and set out to experiment with a new art form. Using his expertise as an engineer and his knowledge of how to create special angles, he began creating some extraordinary forms. He has now exhibited his unique sculptures and is being hailed by critics as a profoundly creative talent. He's expressing his gifts and talents as an artist in a different way than he did as an engineer. He found a way to incorporate *both* his engineering *and* his art.

We have had the opportunity to work with many people in expanding their creativity who were in their sixties and seventies.

Time and again they have said, "Don't wait till you're my age to realize that you never did what you really wanted to do."

Creative Risk Taking

Some people would claim that truly creative people are irreverent and also iconoclasts. At the very least, creative people are risk takers.

Wally "Famous" Amos, the successful entrepreneur who created the great cookies, put it this way: "There are many kinds of risks in life: emotional, intellectual, and physical. The important ones are those that help you grow and express your values. To laugh is to risk appearing foolish. To weep is to risk appearing sentimental. To reach out for another is to risk involvement. To expose feelings is to risk exposing your true self. To place your ideas and dreams before the crowd is to risk loss. To love is to risk not being loved in return. To live is to risk dying. To hope is to risk despair. To try at all is to risk failure. But risk we must because the greatest hazard is to risk nothing at all."

A creative person risks loving life, laughing often, and unabashedly showing enthusiasm and involves himself or herself in the human drama, caring deeply for others by showing compassion and concern.

Michael Ray, professor at the Stanford Business School, believes that compassion is the most important part of creativity. He's not talking abut compassion that is the "mushiness of do-gooders." What he refers to is a "deep inner trait that we all have (but almost never recognize or act upon) that bestows loving kindness first on ourselves and then on others." Dr. Ray believes it is that part of us that acknowledges the unlimited creative potential in ourselves and in others.

When individuals give themselves permission to be who they really are, they are often the ones who "make trouble" in an organization. They tend to break the bureaucratic china by their unconventional, undisciplined and, some would say, even irresponsible behavior. Besides that they are often emotional about what they want to create. How can those individuals who are creatively alive and dynamic stay within the organization and make a contribution? This will be the major hurdle for organizations moving to the Creative Worldview. A real service can be offered by those who learn how to identify these people, but most importantly, who figure out how to hold on to them in the organizational setting.

As John Sculley suggests, "The traditional management gospel only thwarts us in trying to understand creativity. Management and creativity might even be considered antithetical states. While management demands consensus, control, certainty, and the status quo, creativity thrives on the opposite: instinct, uncertainty, freedom, and iconoclasm." Apple computer started with a significant advantage in that it didn't have to overcome the embedded investment of a well-managed second phase organization.

Creativity in organizations thrives when certain factors are present.

■ *Nonhierarchical organization.* Let the extended hierarchies and organizational charts disappear along with layers of management that control rather than support teams.

■ *Teams working together on creative solutions that champion diversity.* Bring people together from across disciplines with a real focus on cultural, gender, race, and age diversity.

■ *Passionate commitment to purposeful change.* As Tom Peters suggests, "Evaluate everyone on his or her love of change." This is change with a direction. Purposeful change toward fulfilling the vision of the organization leads the way to creative solutions. Passionate commitment to find creative solutions has an edge to it. You don't know how it will be accomplished, yet you're willing to put yourself and the team on the line.

■ *Safety and security in the midst of great risk.* This paradox is absolutely fundamental to fostering creativity. People must know they are safe to go out on the edge where creative solutions await. They can't think they're going to be fired tomorrow for not meeting someone's bottom line expectation. Creative people make mistakes, in fact they learn to love mistake making because this is where new information and learning occurs. Creativity is a risky, messy business requiring an atmosphere of security in order to thrive.

- *Complete faith in the function of ambiguity, chaos, and disorder.* "No surprise is the best surprise" dominates the thinking of well-managed second phase organizations. Understanding the purpose of disorder is critical for creative success. Disorder in pursuit of a meaningful purpose always leads to higher levels of connections, both within organizations and with outside suppliers, vendors, and customers. You cannot love change and creativity unless you know this is how natural creativity works. You have to have complete faith—not blind faith, but informed faith about the function of ambiguity, change, uncertainty, and chaos. You must truly believe that chaos is beneficial. Embrace it, understand it, use it!

- *Atmosphere of trust, honesty, and open communication.* Our clients worldwide agree that without fundamental trust and honesty creativity cannot flourish. People working together must know they can count on one another, can tell the truth, and can expect to hear the truth from their colleagues.

This isn't meant to be an exhaustive nor a prescriptive list but operates within the framework of the Creative Worldview. Believing in the inherent creativity of all people, being pulled to a great vision, and a connecting with the people, resources, and ideas to maximize the creative capacity of an organization are fundamental.

Waking up to our creative capacities by moving to a new level of thinking is a very exciting process—very much like overwriting an old program in the computer. This will happen as we give up our old models and begin to consider some new possibilities.

Creative Curiosity and Creative Failing

Central to all expressions of creativity is incessant curiosity. You ask questions. The natural curiosity of children leads them to ask around 125 questions a day, where an average adult living with a logical worldview asks only about six questions a day.

The times mandate curiosity. To create anything new requires first questioning the old. Why are we doing it this way? Is this the very best way? Have you tried this? Why does this work like this? Why? Why? Why? Challenge old assumptions, question the status quo, ask for new solutions. This is one way to hasten the movement past the Breakpoint barrier of the second phase.

Curiosity brings with it a passion for learning and experimenting and a commitment to look at mistakes as opportunities for growth. Failure is an opportunity to begin again more intelligently. Letting go of the old ways, the rote learning models, the classic classroom, the teacher-student division, and the process of competition and building an environment where people can engage in creative thinking processes and continually begin again more intelligently is a solution to effective learning.

CREATIVE PRINCIPLE NUMBER 4: ESCAPE THE LIMITS OF THE PAST THROUGH CREATIVE LEARNING

The tremendous challenges faced by society today demand new approaches to learning. In the third phase, unique information, knowledge, and understanding emerge. How can anyone escape the trap of knowing how to become a creative learner? The Creative Worldview supplies the answer. The logical worldview sees change as a linear process, the result of past causes. The deep assumption is that the present was caused by the past and will affect the future. With this orthodox sense of the world, with each new experience the past becomes the automatic reference point. It becomes easy to take the knowledge of the past and project it into the future.

Chris Argyris, the eminent researcher of learning at Harvard, calls this type of second phase thinking *single loop learning*. It generates a closed circle of knowledge that tends to either stay fixed or get smaller. This type of learning constantly attempts to bring new events into line with what one remembers and can rely on. You see someone walking down the street. Recalling she was rude to you yesterday, you cross the street to avoid her. A logical decision. Yet, since yesterday two things have happened: She has changed and you have changed. Your past-centered prejudgment and choices stand in the way of your meeting—and learning. We make ourselves victims of history.

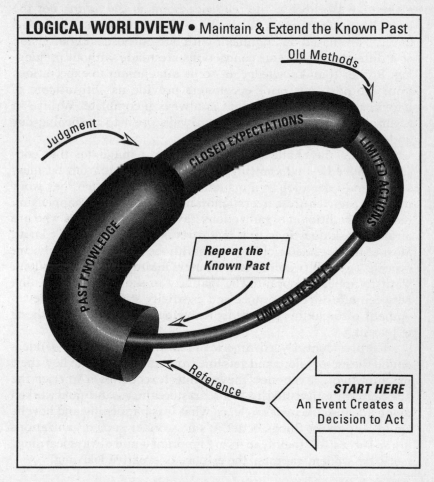

LOGICAL WORLDVIEW • Maintain & Extend the Known Past

Old Methods

Judgment

CLOSED EXPECTATIONS

LIMITED ACTIONS

PAST KNOWLEDGE

Repeat the Known Past

LIMITED RESULTS

Reference

START HERE
An Event Creates a
Decision to Act

The great philosopher Martin Buber once observed, "All living is meeting." We meet with people, with information, with ideas, with circumstances. When we routinely reference the past, we bias our experience and, most often, reexperience the past. We miss the meeting—with life. With this habitual viewpoint, we cannot possibly fulfill our potentials in a rapidly and tumultuously changing third phase world. As Dennis told Joey in a Dennis the Menace cartoon recently, "You can't live in the past, that was this *morning*!"

The world is continually and creatively changing. To take advantage of those changes requires a new kind of learning. With a Creative Worldview, the reference point is the *future*, not the past. We don't need to fall back on the past for our decisions. Choices are based on alignment with our purpose and our vision of a different world. Our connections are made without prejudging. Rather than knowledge, or some attachment to expectations from the past, our prior encounters provide us with a store of information—information that is always incomplete. We live in a state of "informed ignorance," always open to deepening our understanding.

Meeting the challenge of today's world mandates that education move beyond *knowing*. Managers graduate from business school and take a job in a manufacturing plant. Often they work through their entire careers ignorant of what really happens on the line. Traditional organizations have many executives who are afraid to ask questions that might reveal what they don't know. Most of the presidents of large corporations we work with who are over the age of fifty don't use computers mainly because they don't want to appear ignorant. The inability to see the profound link between informed ignorance and creativity stifles the very development of breakthrough ideas. Knowing becomes the antithesis of learning.

The president of North American Tool and Die regularly wanders out on the factory floor and gets line workers to teach him how their machines work. Even one of the wealthiest executives in America, the late Sam Walton, visited his Wal-Mart stores incessantly and worked alongside his colleagues to learn what was happening and how he could help make things better. It's no wonder such organizations are so successful; their leaders are ignorant—and always learning.

Rilke's poem captures the essence of creative learning:

Live the questions now

And perhaps without knowing it

You will live along some day into the answers.

The commitment to learning is a vital component in bringing forth the kind of unique creativity needed today. Third phase

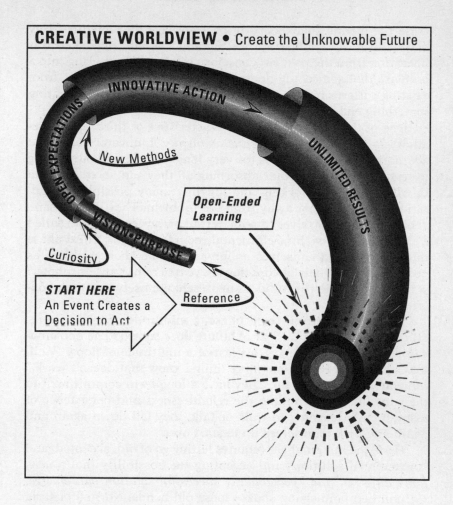

CREATIVE WORLDVIEW • Create the Unknowable Future

INNOVATIVE ACTION

OPEN EXPECTATIONS

New Methods

UNLIMITED RESULTS

VISION·PURPOSE

Open-Ended Learning

Curiosity

START HERE
An Event Creates a
Decision to Act

Reference

creativity calls on us to stretch our minds and consider the impossible; to reach far beyond the boundaries of what has been
considered normal, logical, or reasonable. It invites us to create
what has never existed before.

CREATIVE PRINCIPLE NUMBER 5: OPEN TO
CREATE WHAT NEVER EXISTED BEFORE

The great artistic inventor, Picasso, noted that, "Every act of creation is first of all an act of destruction." The inventor is able to

erase the mental blackboard of past answers and imaginatively play with novel configurations. Sigmund Freud referred to this liberation from the past as "conscious self-deceit," entering into a pretense that something doesn't exist. This illusory escape from existing patterns restores the mystery opening the door to creating something entirely new.

One of the most dominant characteristics of third phase creativity is *the capacity to tolerate ambiguity*. Innovators can hold a situation in mental chaos for very long periods without having to reach a resolution. After absorbing all they can about the area in which they are working and juggling many possible configurations, they then get away from the problem. They play, dream, and immerse themselves in nonrelevant activities. Einstein sailed a small boat to give himself mental room for insight. Third phase thinkers stretch themselves as far away from their problem as possible, letting their unconscious have free rein; they "incubate," waiting very patiently for ideas to present themselves to their consciousness.

Within any natural third phase, a multitude of trials are required. To an innovator, fear of failure does not exist. As one innovator put it after suffering his last of a multitude of flops, "Well, that's progress. Here's one more thing I know that doesn't work." Innovators won't give up. They have a long-term commitment to their dream. They emulate the relentlessness and persistence of a small child learning to walk or talk; they fall down again and again and pick themselves up to start over.

Here, the imaginal act requires letting go of old, accepted, and conventional solutions and accepting the possibility that a *new, quite different, and spectacularly successful solution can emerge*. Uninhibited fantasizing shakes loose old bonds. Normal criteria such as good and bad, right and wrong go by the wayside. Third phase creativity decrees that innovators introduce a maximum of tension into the thinking process, unifying concepts that often appear to be opposed, solving problems that appear impossible.

Third phase solutions embrace contradictions and put dissimilar elements together. As a result, creative ideas emerge such as earthquake-proof buildings that do not resist the earth's shaking but flex with its movement or dynamic human relationships that incorporate rather than avoid conflicts. The noted psychiatrist Albert Rothenberg calls this kind of creative thinking "Janusian," referring to the Greek god who looks both ways. Innovators make the strange familiar and the familiar strange. Their working method includes *both . . . and*.

In literature, the device of the oxymoron, a paradoxical metaphor, introduces this third phase creative, Janusian strain. A phrase such as *tender strength* or *good wickedness* calls on us to conjure up a different impression beyond the words themselves. Innovators use such conflict producing methods to stimulate thinking.

Faced with the immense problem of soaring teacher salaries and declining learning, the paradoxical concept of teacherless students might initially raise the image of total disorder. Yet, the novel concept of joining those contrary elements in cooperative learning creates a new opportunity; teachers work with teams of students who teach each other; the result—learning soars and costs drop dramatically.

This illustrates a fundamental third phase creative concept—inclusion of what was left out. Every second phase pattern rejects elements that were present in its first phase. *These come back and are integrated in the third phase*. Women played a vital leadership role in early first phase societies; after millennia of exclusion, they are once again being integrated. Profound interconnections with nature dominated first phase cultures. Now the concern about nature has found its way back into our society through the ecological movement.

Implementing solutions to the diverse challenges in our world today can be greatly facilitated by learning how to learn by adopting the uniqueness of third phase creativity. Any of this will be greatly enhanced if we are capable of co-creating with others.

CREATIVE PRINCIPLE NUMBER 6: JOIN WITH OTHERS IN CO-CREATING A POSITIVE FUTURE

A new future awaits only if we can bring diverse points of view together and create something totally new. Co-creating with one another requires a willingness to move from discussing our separate points of view to engaging in a dialogue with one another. David Bohm, the well-known physicist, offers a distinction between discussion and dialogue. Discussion is associated with defending a point of view. Dialogue happens when information and meaning flows through people. No one is trying to make a point.

A dialogue requires the willingness to hold in front of us varying viewpoints without believing in any of them. In order to engage in a dialogue, you must have the willingness to suspend your beliefs and to really listen to what another person has to say with the intention of truly grasping his or her perspective.

The first barrier to true dialogue is our opinions, and our tendency to defend them. What would a conversation without opinions be like? Let yourself imagine your mind completely free of any thoughts. What would happen if you approached what others had to say with intense curiosity and interest, suspending any thoughts, holding no beliefs, expectations, or judgments while they shared their ideas?

This happened when long time computer rivals, IBM and Apple, forged a stunning agreement of cooperation. The unthinkable became thinkable because these two companies were able to suspend their biases and judgments about each another long enough to create a potentially incredible partnership.

Having the capacity to engage in a dialogue and co-create requires moving beyond your position on any given subject or issue. Some might ask, but what about ethical and moral considerations? Aren't there any parameters to my willingness to engage in a dialogue? A dialogue is a deliberate intention to consider another possibility, to suspend your opinions, to enter a conversation without prejudice or bias.

Let's take the Jewish-Arab conflict in the Middle East. Both sides refuse to meet because each is prisoner to its point of view or position. Drug gangs in the inner cities are denounced, arrested, threatened with extinction, and the problem worsens. Is it possible that these gang members have something to tell us, something to teach us? Corporations spend countless millions on lawsuits and only meet their adversary in court. If the actual participants learned the art of dialogue and had the skill to suspend their opinions long enough to find out the viewpoint of the other party, disagreements might be resolved without litigation.

Each of us has the opportunity to begin thinking beyond our independent point of view. If you find yourself holding your personal position as the only truth, then another person cannot co-create with you. It becomes impossible to create with another when that person is inflexible. A good way to see if you identify too completely with your position is to determine if you can hold the opposite position as a possibility.

The greatest barrier is the ego. If you are unable to consider another possibility, then it is conceivable, even probable, that your position "owns you." You have become a prisoner of your opinion. If you are willing to suspend your opinion, then it becomes possible to create what might have first seemed impossible and unbelievable. Wouldn't it be likely that if you were willing to engage in a dialogue that your participation would be different? Wouldn't it be likely that people would talk freely with the purpose of inquiry and learning? Out of such a dialogue might come vast movement in an entirely new direction. A true dialogue leads to exciting creative possibilities. "The liberation from the bondage of the self constitutes the only way towards a more satisfactory human society."

Colliding frames of reference produce the unexpected twist. When people are so tightly wedded to their point of view that they are unwilling to even listen to one another, co-creation proves impossible. Bringing together a diverse set of talents to work out a problem from varying perspectives is how we will get creative solutions.

THE DYNAMIC PRINCIPLES OF CREATIVITY

To open the vast storehouse of your own creativity and take the beginning steps in living the Creative Worldview, our experience confirms that these six creative principles will prove extremely helpful.

- Accept your inherent creativity
- Connect with the invisible wave of potential
- Know who you are

■ Escape the limits of the past through creative learning

■ Open to create what never existed before

■ Join with others in co-creating a positive future

As the Creative Worldview ignites the unlimited creative capacity within us, we will, one by one, awaken more and more of our possibilities. We will change the context of what we believe about ourselves and about others. It requires taking action to escape the tyranny of the past; this will only happen when we allow ourselves to be pulled to a different future.

9: THE POWER OF FUTURE PULL

The purposiveness of all vital processes, the strategy of the genes and
the power of the exploratory drive in
animal and man, all seem to indicate
that the pull of the future is as real as
the pressure of the past.

Arthur Koestler

The prime catalyst impelling any growing organism to move
creatively through the three phases of natural growth and
change is the force of Future Pull. If we explore inside nature's
majestic evolutionary process, we can see how this force manifests
itself.

Evolutionary growth and change move like a great river. The
headwaters of any mighty river originate within small springs
and rivulets that come together to form tiny creeks and channels.
Over time, they carve their own converging paths leading to an
ever larger river, all headed in one direction...toward the sea.
The springs don't push the river toward its goal. Gravity pulls the
river to its future. Were this not so, tributaries would dissipate in
countless directions.

The wonders in living things show the same irresistible mag-
netism and energizing vitality of the future. Plant a garden with
peas, beans, zucchini, and summer squash, and watch each of
those seeds germinate and grow. The cells in every plant some-

how know how to form the necessary roots and leaves, flowers and fruit. Each plant receives nutrition, water, and light. As they run into obstacles or snags, the different parts of the plant find unique ways to cooperate and change. Given even the barest necessities, in the end the plant will express its inherent purpose. Every seed that is planted, every tree that is growing, every cell on the planet is pulled by an internal vision of its future whole.

A human life begins as a solitary cell. However, that cell has within its nuclear DNA a molecular blueprint not only of itself, but of the whole human body. As that beginning cell multiplies, it gradually forms an incredibly complex human being. According to the closest estimates, the human body has between 600 and 700 trillion cells! Imagine trying to "manage" this endeavor. How can it be that this colossal multitude of cells knows how to work, grow, and undergo great change together?

The secret is the same as that of the river. Since every cell can reference its common internal vision of the future whole, it can contribute its part to maintaining the emerging integrity of the entire system without getting off track. If a cell couldn't get in touch with its nucleus, where the picture of the whole developing organism is stored, it would go awry. Because each cell is working from a common blueprint, as the human body encounters unexpected challenges, every cell can support the whole system in its own special way as they all grow and focus their energy together.

New findings in biology reveal that complex systems are not controlled or limited by their past. Nobel prize winning biologist Gerald Edelman says about recent findings, "What they have found is truly startling . . . when you are born, you have all the information in your antibody system that you will ever need in your whole life to recognize anything you may ever encounter, including things that don't exist!" It turns out that natural systems are self-creating.

This revolutionary new discovery, uncovered by molecular biologists, is known as *autopoiesis,* meaning self-organizing or self-creating. The ability for natural systems to grow and change in extremely flexible, versatile, and creative ways occurs because no matter what the circumstance, every part of the system shares the same blueprint of the future whole. Through the natural guidance of autopoiesis, complex organisms can thrive in rapidly changing and turbulent environments.

The human brain functions using autopoiesis. This accounts for how a virtuoso violinist plays with such brilliance when every scientific measurement substantiates that the nervous system is incapable of carrying messages at such speed. Some years ago, one of the authors asked Pablo Casals, "How are you able to play the cello with such magnificence?" He replied, "I hear it before I play it." At the time, that statement didn't make much sense. But Mozart said basically the same thing. He could "hear" the piece in his mind before he played it. Later it became clear that both men had an internal picture of the finished piece of music. The process of autopoiesis—of Future Pull—allows artists such as Casals or Mozart to compose and perform with a splendor that has left audiences spellbound.

In recent years, we have seen exactly the same Future Pull phenomenon operating in the field of athletics. Visualizing the ultimate outcome and allowing the mind and body to operate automatically produces astounding results as pole-vaulting champion John Uelses testifies. He relies on a vivid image of winning to spur his performance. Jack Nicklaus says that vision" ... gives me a line to the cup just as clearly as if it's been tattooed on my brain. With that feeling, all I have to do is swing the clubs and let nature take its course." In fact, as a number of outstanding athletes have discovered, if you can get your opponent to concentrate on how they are doing—rather than the overall result—their game goes to pieces.

New discoveries in biology and psychology join with those that caused so much consternation in physics. They underscore how we—and every other part of nature—are being *pulled to the future*. The reference point for real growth, the power to impel success, cannot be found within the confines of the past. As Thoreau advised, it lies in the direction of our hopes. "I have learned this at least by my experiments: that if one advances confidently in the direction of his dreams, and endeavors to live the life which he has imagined, he will meet with a success unexpected in common hours."

Integrating the pull of the future into your life can be accelerated by integrating the four principles of Future Pull:

■ Know your purpose and vision
■ Commit to achieve your purpose and vision

- Experience abundance as nature's natural state
- Make the world a better place by living according to shared values

FUTURE PULL PRINCIPLE NUMBER 1: KNOW YOUR PURPOSE AND VISION

We define purpose as how an individual or organization makes the world a better place. The vision is a compelling image or picture once the purpose has been achieved. Landing a man on the moon in a decade was the vision John Kennedy held out to the United States as the compelling image of space exploration—a symbol of his New Frontier. The purpose for landing a man on the moon was to develop the technological capability for "manned" space flights.

Purpose and vision are as important for nations and organizations as they are for individuals. John Mahoney did what others expected him to do for thirty-seven years; he was miserable. Then one day he realized things could be different. He doesn't know where his excessive drinking and self-destructive bitterness would have taken him, but at the age of forty-eight he finally decided to follow his childhood dream of acting.

At age eleven, he fell in love with acting. He got involved in community theater doing Gilbert and Sullivan in summer festivals around England. He clearly knew then that acting was what he wanted to do with his life. He even quit high school to commit himself full time to acting. That's when the problems started. His parents protested with screaming and weeping. "At least finish high school," they said. "That's all we ask. Then you can do what you want to do with your life."

It took thirty-seven years but John Mahoney finally recognized the importance of committing to his unique purpose. And, the very act of doing it aligned him with the power of Future Pull. Mahoney realized his life couldn't work if he stayed wedded to the past. He acknowledged and developed his unique talents and skills and today has one of the busiest careers in Hollywood. "I'm finally doing what I want with my life."

In our culture, we believe that goal setting, hard work, and discipline all join together to achieve anything worthwhile. We give little thought to the power of doing what you love to do. Once you have found your natural creative gifts, the accomplishment of great goals becomes much easier. When discipline, will power, and painstaking effort surround you, you can rest assured that whatever you are doing isn't the pathway to your own creativity. Like John Mahoney, you can extend the phenomenal force of Future Pull into your life by asking where you are going. What is your purpose? What vision do you have for your life?

You are the only one who can decide what makes you happy. If you don't know what makes you happy, then you really have to stop and ask yourself why. What stands in the way of your knowing yourself well enough to know what really makes your heart sing?

A compelling purpose energizes life. It is the force that activates our "wave of becomingness." It brings forth happiness and joy. Without a compelling purpose we live life as a fairly haphazard experience, being easily swayed by the latest fad, temporary pressures, or the most recent advice on what others think we ought to be doing with our lives.

George Bernard Shaw believed the true joy in life was "being used for a purpose recognized by yourself as a mighty one; the being thoroughly worn out before you are thrown on the scrap heap; the being a force of nature instead of a feverish selfish little clod of ailments and grievances complaining that the world will not devote itself to making you happy."

Having a purpose allows us to be creatively pulled to the future. We are able to build on the past while escaping its bondage! From limits and expectations, we move to possibilities and potentials.

FUTURE PULL PRINCIPLE NUMBER 2: COMMIT TO ACHIEVE YOUR PURPOSE AND VISION

Outstanding leaders have known the potent force of an inspiring vision. Deep commitment to a great purpose joins the organization and each individual within it to the vitality and energy of the natural pull of the future.

- Jan Carlzon, the president of Scandinavian Airlines, has a vision that 50,000 "moments of truth" occur every day, whenever an SAS employee delivers a service to one of its customers.

- Theodore Vail of AT&T dreamed of "universal service," a world where anyone could reach anyone instantly via telephone.

- Mary Kay Ash knew she could make cosmetics that women would love, make a profit, and treat the people who sold her products with respect and concern.

- Steve Wozniak and Steve Jobs, founders of Apple Computer, imagined changing the world by giving the average person access to the world's knowledge through personal computers.

- James Rouse, the great urban planner, had a vision to improve urban life along with giving his people gratification for the quality of their work. Faneuil Hall Marketplace in Boston, South Street Seaport in New York City, Baltimore's Harborplace, and the Arizona Center in Phoenix completely altered these urban environments for the better and attest to his compelling vision.

Tom Watson Jr. of IBM commented on why its competition didn't keep up, "No one at the top had my father's vision." And Tom Jr. kept it alive and strong. Jack Welch of G.E. adds that great managers are, "People who develop a vision of what they want their business to be . . . gain through sharing—listening and talking—an acceptance of that vision."

Legions of outstanding successes in business demonstrate the seemingly extraordinary force of Future Pull. Even in huge enterprises the natural power and central thrust of a compelling vision bring all of the different aspects of the corporation into a coherent, vital, and energized whole.

Most organizations have no vision. Complex multimillion dollar enterprises operate with a limited mission statement as their compass to the future. "Our mission is to return maximum profitability to our shareholders." "Our mission is the long-term increase of shareholder equity." "Our mission is to achieve 15 percent profit before taxes." Is it any wonder that most people within these organizations are uninspired? There is no forceful purpose, no picture of the future whole, no internal DNA for self-creation or even to provide a reference point for decisions. Most of all, the loss of the real and powerful natural force of Future Pull occurs when a compelling vision is never created or shared within the organization.

A fifty-seven-year-old chief operating officer of a huge military industrial company called together 300 of his top managers. Sighting lagging profits and high costs, he told them, "The only purpose of this company is to make a top return on the capital invested. We're not around to build the best products." Little did he know that many of his top managers would leave within a year and that poor morale would sink even lower.

The former president of Notre Dame, Father Hesburg, feels "The very essence of leadership is you have to have a vision. It's got to be a vision you articulate clearly and forcefully on every occasion. You can't blow an uncertain trumpet."

The skill required to create a shared vision within an organization is something that must be developed. Today few companies have any visioning "muscle." Tormod Bjork, the managing director of the Karmoy plant, a divison of Hydro Aluminum, which is Europe's largest producer of aluminium, involved all of his 1,500 employees. He learned how to develop his own muscles around visioning by working with an outside consultant experienced and dedicated to teaching visioning skills. He hired an artist to make a picture of his vision of the Karmoy plant, and then he set out to involve everyone. It took two years and the results were stunning. The Karmoy plant was revitalized. Higher productivity, reduced emissions, lower energy consumption and higher electricity yield are areas in which records are broken every month. Operating profit soared from 1.59 million kroner to 1.089 billion kroner in three years.

Individual Purpose

Individuals face the same challenge as organizations. They must find what they deeply care about, what gives their life passionate meaning and then harness those things to a compelling purpose. Each of us has been gifted with our own remarkable way of expressing our humanity. Recognizing this is our challenge.

Great accomplishments are preceded by a compelling purpose. Debbie Meier is trying to do nothing less than create a new system of public education, and she's doing it in the most unlikely place—Harlem, New York. She took on this impossible task of creating a new school in Harlem to try out her theories of education. "Largely my ideas about teaching and learning focus on democratic values, by which I mean a respect for diversity, a respect for the possibilities of what every person is capable of, a respect for another person's point of view, a respect for considerable intellectual rigor."

Debbie Meier truly cares that young people become critical thinkers and creative problem solvers. She wouldn't take the job of superintendent unless they gave her kindergarten through high school because she knew it required time to build these skills. She built her schools based on the notions of self-respect, rigorous thinking, challenging old assumptions, and learning creatively.

The results are impressive. In the first year, a 5 percent turnover rate in her schools was one-tenth the citywide average. The dropout rate dropped dramatically and district-wide test scores improved significantly.

Debbie Meier's creative ideas seem to have no bounds. She's always coming up with a better way. Brimming with ideas, Meier doesn't worry about the risks she's taking. Pulled by her compelling vision, she challenges the status quo, goes beyond the boundaries, breaks the rules.

Anita Roddick had a $6,000 bank loan and an idea she loved, a business that would sell body care products and that would care deeply about nature, about employees, and about customers. She founded The Body Shop. Fifteen years later, with no advertising, with an organization with sales over $150 million, her electricity and passion still infuse the enterprise. She says of the people she works with, "You want them to feel that they're doing something important, that they're not a lone voice, that they are the most powerful, potent people on the planet." Her commitment runs deep. Customer service, employee education, and concern for the environment matter—success and profits naturally follow.

Your purpose not only inspires and gives meaning to your life but makes nature your silent partner in the evolutionary journey. The most powerful purpose comes out of giving your unique skills and talents to make the world a better place. From teacher to carpenter, from manager to musician, we all have special gifts to give. To uncover your own purpose, focus on those unique qualities that describe who you are, and then look at the ways you enjoy expressing them. What do you love to do? What makes you happy? What is it you dream of becoming? These are the questions that will lead you to your purpose.

Joseph Campbell calls the commitment to a purpose following your bliss. "If you follow your bliss, you put yourself on a kind of track that has been there all the while, waiting for you, and the life that you ought to be living is the one you are living. Wherever you are—if you are following your bliss, you are enjoying the refreshment, that lies within you, all the time."

Most of our cultural conditioning tells us we can't do what we love to do. Conventional wisdom says work is work and fun is fun and you can't combine them. Making a living is a serious business. Recently, we overheard a conversation in which a teaching chef talked about how very earnest he is with his students. "I tell my students, who think they can just have fun at this endeavor, that they better get serious because being a chef is primarily hard work, followed by more hard work. They can't be led to believe they are just going to have fun, that's not how you make a living."

Today, it is estimated that of all the people that go to college only 15 percent ever work in the field of their major. And, within that huge college population, only 2 percent of them will do what they really love to do with their lives.

Because money has become the badge of success, particularly in the United States, the brightest young people move away from their primary creativeness. This reality was brought home to us as we watched two fine young men make their career choices. One loved filmmaking, the other was an accomplished musician and was gifted at playing a myriad of musical instruments. They were both in college and their parents insisted that if they pursued their dreams of doing with their lives what they loved to do, they wouldn't ever be able to make a living. Today, both of these young men are headed for law school. One still plays his music as a hobby and the filmmaker has quashed his dream. Now, what kind of lawyers are they going to make?

Selecting a life's path based on secure employment and the money it will garner is hardly going to lead to finding what one loves, one's real identity, or what one can truly pursue with passion. These early choices lead many to end up miserable and unhappy, without pride in their work, without the drive to excel—because they aren't doing what they love to do.

FUTURE PULL PRINCIPLE NUMBER 3: ABUNDANCE IS NATURE'S NATURAL STATE

We quite frankly believe that abundance and following one's unique path go together. Abundance comes to those who have the courage to follow their dreams, to consecrate their lives to doing what they passionately love to do. This brings not only material abundance but connection with the profusion of resources, opportunities, and assistance vital to the full expression of one's talents.

Today thousands of people are doing what they love to do in the most unlikely occupations and making an excellent living. There is a natural tendency for us to want to support people who are doing what they care about and value. It doesn't matter if the person is pursuing cooking, gardening, homemaking, or an obscure art form; creating a new type of music; or following a traditional occupation. Consider the Reverend Robert Schuller, who started the Crystal Cathedral in an unused drive-in theater and now inspires millions every week with his gospel of love. One woman we know loved making unusual sounds with a variety of percussion instruments that she invented. Strange as these sounds were to many nonmusicians, she has now introduced her percussion sounds into symphonic music. Her travels now take her worldwide playing with various international orchestras.

Alan Hald of MicroAge held on to his dream: "I wanted to be part of an endeavor that would help change the world toward a more positive vision of the future." One day he saw an ad for "Kit Computers" and he remembers, "Everything fell into place." He shared his excitement with Jeff McKeever, a business associate, and discovered they had a similar vision. Together they committed to create a business to "change the way the world works." In just a few short years their fledgling enterprise grew into the nation's largest microcomputer distributor with profitability and a significant return on investment.

Individuals who express what they love to do in their work automatically commit to providing quality to their customers. Think of trading with auto mechanics who take pride in their work. The public is so pleased to find a repair shop with that commitment, the mechanics can't meet the demand for their services. People will even pay more to receive quality products from people who love what they are doing. This we see every day in the marketplace.

A small minority of people shapes world opinion, creates the inventions, and develops new ideas that set the pattern for others. When we release the creative potential of a large population, massive shifts will take place in which former "problems" will become great opportunities for change.

The multitalented author and computer guru, Jerry Pournelle, expressed the great power of Future Pull. "Who chooses the future? Those who dream the future choose the future. You can't predict the future, but you can invent it."

Inventing the future requires *giving up control*. No one with a compelling purpose and a great vision knows how it will be achieved. One has to be willing to follow an unknown path, allowing the road to take you where it will. Surprise, serendipity, uncertainty, and the unexpected are guaranteed on the way to the future.

In 1985, we had the exciting opportunity to participate in a totally new kind of learning experience that is contributing to fostering profound individual and organizational change. It was at Larry Wilson's Pecos River Learning Center. The creation of this wonderful place is an amazing story, the outcome of Larry Wilson's unique vision.

It was in 1965 that Larry, a frustrated high school teacher who had left teaching to successfully sell insurance, created his true dream—about a special place where people could really learn, not in a boring classroom but where they could get involved, excited, and energized. A place where they could stretch their minds and spirits. He dreamed that real learning could be great fun. He tenaciously followed his dream, creating not only Wilson Learning Corporation, one of the largest and most successful training organizations in the world, but also carving this wonderful Pecos Learning Center out of the mesquite covered mountains near Santa Fe. People from all over the world now come to Pecos to stretch in ways they could never have imagined.

And what an incredible learning experience the authors had there! Who would have thought we would have been willing to jump from a 40-foot pole, leaping to catch an elusive trapeze— or to jump from a 150-foot cliff heading down a zip line over the Pecos River, holding onto nothing but a pulley? Certainly, we didn't think we would ever bargain for such an adventure, but somehow we did it. We saw mature corporate executives learning things that are impossible in a "normal" teaching setting, overcoming their deepest fears, working together in astonishingly productive ways, ready to creatively face a future filled with unknowns.

At the end of one day's events, we had dinner with Phil Bryson, the young man who had designed and conducted the extraordinary outdoor events we had just experienced. We asked how he ever got into such an unusual business and found that the creation of these events came directly out of "following his bliss."

"I was only 13 when I started rock climbing and once I was into it a lot of my buddies wanted to go with me because they knew I was really having fun. Within time, I realized that this kind of experience had some real power in changing people's lives, primarily because it changed mine. I started offering rock climbing events to more of my friends. I realized here was a way I could spend time doing what I loved to do... and positively impact other people's lives. My family, particularly my Dad, kept asking me when I was going to give it up. He thought I needed to learn to make a living. Well, I just couldn't give it up. I tried my best to continue with school and combine my real love. It took me a lot longer to get through college than my Dad would have liked.

"By the time I was through college, I recognized that my real life's work somehow had to be in sharing what I had experienced in my rock climbing. I was committed to offering people the excitement of realizing they could break through their self-imposed limitations to be more than they ever dreamed possible. I had absolutely no idea how I could make a living doing it but I decided to go for it.

"It wasn't until about five years ago that I really felt complete about the contribution I was making. That happened when my Dad finally accepted my invitation to take one of my courses. At the end, he told the group of business executives who had gone through the ropes course with him, 'I want all of you to know how proud I am of Phil, who stuck with his dream and willingly broke new ground to assist all of us here and thousands of others in living more fulfilled lives.'"

Phil's company, On the Edge Productions, is now thirteen years old and over 100,000 people have participated in these life changing ropes courses. Phil Bryson, as well as Larry Wilson and countless other individuals, had the courage to pursue his dreams, doing what he loved to do. They all had a vision, but didn't have any idea how it would be fulfilled. They gave up trying to control the how by connecting with the people and resources that enabled the vision to unfold.

Abundance naturally followed for Robert Schuller, Alan Hald, and Jeff McKeever at MicroAge, Larry Wilson and Phil Bryson. This doesn't mean just financial prosperity, but the abundance of a life worth living. All of these individuals had untold support that they never would have envisioned once they committed to their purpose.

Goethe says it well:

Until one is committed

there is hesitancy, the chance to draw back,

always ineffectiveness.

Concerning all acts of initiative (and creation),

there is one elementary truth,

the ignorance of which kills countless ideas

and splendid plans:

that the moment one definitely commits oneself,

then Providence moves too.

> All sorts of things occur to help one
>
> that would never otherwise have occurred.
>
> A whole stream of events issues from the decision,
>
> raising in one's favour all manner
>
> of unforeseen incidents and meetings
>
> and material assistance,
>
> which no man could have dreamt
>
> would have come his way.
>
> Whatever you can do, or dream you can, begin it.
>
> Boldness has genius, power, and magic in it.

Great purpose and vision must be closely connected to making a worthwhile contribution. There have been world leaders with great vision who wreaked havoc on their own people and millions of others because they gave no thought to the last vital principle essential to align with the pull of the future.

FUTURE PULL PRINCIPLE NUMBER 4: MAKE THE WORLD A BETTER PLACE BY LIVING ACCORDING TO SHARED VALUES

Our experience confirms that scant emphasis is placed on the belief that one can make the world a better place. This is as true for individuals as for organizations. Many believe the purpose of a business or their life is making money. Actually, money is the by-product of making a significant contribution. Creating an outstanding life or building a great organization begins with the question, how do I and how does my organization make the world a better place? The answer goes directly to the underlying purpose and values that motivate an individual and drive an organization.

Levi Strauss and Co. had a long tradition of both strong financial success and a commitment to social values. Levi's jeans became an icon of the pop culture during the postwar era assuring year after year of financial prosperity. By the 1980s an uncertain economic climate greeted the new chairman and CEO. Robert Haas and his management team had to "rethink every facet of the business—including its underlying values." Robert Haas believes that "a company's values—what it stands for, what its people believe—are crucial to its competitive success."

Values have been thought of as the soft stuff of the organization, something that goes on a bronze plaque in the front corridor. Somehow the values get separated from how the business really runs. Inevitably employees and customers know it. Haas believes that "values provide the common language for aligning a company's leadership and its people."

Ivan Blostone, former president of Leaseways Worldwide Leasing Operations took a newly formed company in 1960 and achieved close to $1 billion in sales by 1970 because he hired people with common values who were committed to telling the truth in meeting their customers' needs. Instead of selecting employees primarily because of their technical competence and appearance, he added two critical components—shared values and behavior. By organizing work groups around self-managed teams with common values, their contribution to making the world a better place was dramatically increased.

Robert B. Horton, chairman of British Petroleum Company is committed to changing his company to meet the challenges of the 1990s. He's convinced that building on a shared vision and common values is necessary to develop the internal trust and co-operation to give customers the best service, to liberate people to think creatively, and to maximize the contribution the company can make to its community.

The authors' own company, Leadership 2000, believes the level of commitment all of us have to our values provides the single most powerful foundation for our organization. Our group knows that whatever we say isn't nearly as significant or important as how we live. The shared values each of us has committed to guide our actions.

The most successful companies and individuals "walk their talk." Over the years Levi Stauss had developed a reputation for treating employees fairly, providing for their welfare, and actively supporting the community, but according to Haas, "What really mattered was getting pants out the door." He felt that if that continued employees would stop believing in the company. An organization faces serious problems when the people working there lose faith that the company is going to do what it says it values. Levi was willing to make major changes to bring the aspirations and values into alignment with its actions both within Levi and outside with vendors, customers, and the community.

The purpose and values are the heart of forming the vision that will pull the organization to its future. These ingredients provide the essential elements of successful self-creation: the picture of that future whole. It is the internal guidance system, the DNA that allows everything to work together. The purpose, values, and vision furnish the internal reference point for making choices and connections in a complex and rapidly changing world. They endow the individual and the organization with direction to be pulled to the future.

THE POWERFUL PRINCIPLES OF FUTURE PULL

The principles that build great meaning in your life, that put you in alignment with the natural power of Future Pull are:

- Know your purpose and vision
- Commit to achieve your purpose and vision
- Experience abundance as nature's natural state
- Make the world a better place by living according to shared values

Being pulled to the future to accomplish a great purpose requires the integration of the Force of Connecting. Living the Creative Worldview requires the ability to express the powerful principles of connecting at the highest possible level.

10: THE FORCE OF CONNECTING

Growth, change, and ultimately evolution occur as individuals, organizations, and society increase the depth
of their relationships by continually
broadening and strengthening their
interdependent connections.

Beth Jarman & George Land

The vital last cornerstone of the Creative Worldview provides the greatest challenge for both individuals and organizations. People define themselves based on their relationships with themselves, with others, and the full range of resources in their environment. This is the ability to connect. How do you connect? How do you build and sustain your relationships and your interactions with others, and how do you connect with information, ideas, resources, and opportunities?

If you are willing to change the way you connect, you will not only do something different, but, much more importantly, you will be something different. The only way to move beyond this Breakpoint in history is to be different. This will happen when we alter the way we connect—the way we relate and interact with one another. Then it will be possible to create a different future.

The way every growing organism makes broader, deeper, and more interpenetrating connections has been shown to be nature's most powerful method in moving beyond a Breakpoint. As individuals and organizations take advantage of this natural phenomenon, it will lead to broadening and enhancing their connections in ever more creative ways. In shifting our context to embrace the notion that we are creative beings, being pulled to the future, interconnected with one another, the vital skill to master is the ability to connect.

The great mythologist, Joseph Campbell, who died in 1986 at the age of eighty-six, knew intuitively that central to the creative process is the Force of Connecting. Campbell continually connected with the resources and people who could help him achieve his great vision of learning everything he could about the mythology of every culture on earth. If Campbell had let setbacks or criticism from others stand in his way, he would have never connected with the diversity, myths, cultures, people, and assistance that allowed him to make his profound contribution.

He paid attention to everything that appeared in his environment that might contribute to his vision. Any person who wants to maximize his or her connections must pay attention. The authors of *Creativity in Business* suggest you pay attention "to what you are feeling, what you are sensing, and what you are thinking; to the sounds around you, the opening bud, the color of the autumn leaf; to the wind, the shrug of a shoulder, the taste and texture of your food. This kind of paying attention immerses you in life in a new way." Pay attention by connecting with everything—inner feelings, knowledge, and outer circumstances.

The Nature Conservancy had no idea in 1951 how they would connect with the resources and people to fulfill their vision of preserving natural diversity or to fulfill their global mission of finding, protecting, and maintaining the earth's rare species and natural communities. However, in only three decades it connected with over half a million members and today protects upwards of fifty-five million acres. The director, Pat Noonan, implemented a strategy of cooperation rather than confrontation. He was convinced that corporations had an interest in conservation and believed that working with them rather than against them would lead to mutual benefit. It worked. Today, The Nature Conservancy maintains over 1,200 natural preserves—the largest private system of land management in the world. It did this by opening to connect in ways that were new and different. Their critics maintained that litigation, not deal making, was the correct posture to take with corporations who weren't conservation minded. Noonan responded to his critics by saying, "You say it's tainted money? I say t'aint enough."

There simply is no straight line to a destination in a future that is unpredictable. In researching the flight patterns of airplanes, we found that they are actually off course nearly 90 percent of the time. Third phase living requires constant course correction. Learning as you go, maintaining flexibility, adaptability, and not giving up are each essential.

By integrating the seven principles of connecting into your life it becomes possible to construct a new roadmap to the future in this era of unprecedented change:

- See the potentials and possibilities in everyone

- Offer mutual support

- Extend equality to all people

- Bring about the circumstances in which everyone can win

- Recognize that whatever you focus on expands

- Eliminate judgments

- Trust and love one another

CONNECTING PRINCIPLE NUMBER 1: SEE THE POTENTIALS AND POSSIBILITIES IN EVERYONE

As we have already discovered, the findings of nature reveal that everything exists in two simultaneous states: as a particle and as a wave. As we connect with our particle state, our beingness, and the potential of our wave state, our ultimate becomingness, we uncover the Force of Connecting.

Our willingness to recognize that all of us have potentials that are in the process of manifesting themselves provides us with a frame of reference to enhance our connections. By looking at our own and everyone else's present state of being as well as our own and everyone's becomingness, we shift the context of how we connect with ourselves and others.

At one time, you may say, "It's absolutely impossible for me to understand computers." When I hear you say that, I may agree with you—and at the same time think you have the capacity to be absolutely terrific working with computers. This is living the reality of wholeness—seeing the being and becoming of every person and circumstance.

Day to day we manifest so little of our ultimate capabilities that limiting anyone on the basis of what they think about themselves or what we have seen of them keeps them locked into a very narrow range of past-bound possibilities.

No one knows this better than parents as they rear their children. Parents intuitively see both the present reality of their children and their future becomingness. They have the ability to unconditionally accept their children exactly as they are and at the same time offer tremendous encouragement to their unfolding. For one of the authors, this experience of identifying with her son's becomingness was significant in getting through a very difficult time.

Sitting with my son at a parent-teacher conference when he was fourteen provided a great realization for me of how I identified with both who he was and who was emerging. His ninth grade English teacher could only see a gangly, skinny, unmotivated kid who was abrupt, argumentative, and unhappy. All she wanted him to do was complete the assignments, sit up tall in his chair, and stop arguing with her.

I saw a young man who had grown six inches in the last year, who had moved to a new school in a big city, after living for fourteen years in a small town where he knew nearly everyone. Here was my teenage son adjusting to his parents being separated and contemplating a divorce and feeling helpless to alter the course of events. As his mother, I could unconditionally accept his present mental state, although at the same time I knew who he was struggling to become. This ability to see beyond the moment to connect with the possibilities unfolding within our children seems to be a natural creative quality of most parents.

In retrospect, had I then embraced the principles of the Creative Worldview, I would have been able to also see his teacher's being and becomingness. What I then saw was a teacher who seemed very critical of my son. What I can now see was a woman trying desperately to do her job in the best way possible, a teacher

facing the frustrations of a heavy load of students, dwindling resources, and a community that wouldn't support the real growing
needs she had in her school.

Today I would ask, "How can we *all* get what we want?" The
three of us could work out a new and different solution. Perhaps
the teacher would provide some special materials—that she didn't
have time to use—and I would find several hours a week that I
could tutor not only my own son but two other teenagers who
were having similar difficulties.

Seeing What Others Cannot See

This ability to connect with another person's unfolding potential was a natural quality of a German lawyer from Oregon who
envisioned building the finest small hotel in the world. He began
his dream when he built Las Mañanitas in Cuernavaca, Mexico
over three decades ago. His biggest challenge in those early days
was training a new staff to operate a hotel with the kind of care
and attention that would assure each guest had experienced the
pre-eminent hotel in the world.

He hired local people with the intention of training them himself. One of these young men was Ruben Cerda. "I remember when
I saw Mr. Strauss the first time. He had hundreds of young Mexican Indian boys lined up for interviews...standing in the hot sun
in front of his new hotel. My mother brought me so I could get
some money to help her buy food for me and my brothers. Since
my father had disappeared, we had so little money.

"Somehow I got the job. As soon as I started working, Mr.
Strauss insisted I learn all the different jobs that needed doing
in the hotel. I was only fourteen when I started. I cleaned the
kitchen, helped the chef, watered the lawn, tended the flowers,
helped the waiters, cleaned the rooms, and even fed the animals.
All the time, Mr. Strauss encouraged me and told me what a good
job I was doing.

"I didn't even know Spanish. Our family spoke native Indian
and so it was hard for me at first. Little by little my Spanish
improved, and I kept getting more jobs to do. When I was eighteen, Mr. Strauss brought me into his office and said, 'Ruben, I'm
sending you to Germany and France to study to be a chef and then
to enroll you in the best hotel management program in Europe.'
'What! I still don't even speak Spanish very well.' 'Never mind,

you speak well enough, and you're quick. I've watched you for four years; you learn languages easily.' 'Mr. Strauss, you know I can't go to Europe or anywhere else. How would my mother take care of my brothers?' 'Don't worry about your mother or your brothers. I'll see that they receive exactly the same amount they receive now. I'll talk to your mother and she can just come by on Fridays and pick up the money you would have given her if you had been here.' "

With much persuasion Ruben Cerda went to Europe for four years. When he came back, he was a different man.

From the very beginning, Mr. Strauss saw in Ruben what he couldn't see in himself. Mr. Strauss connected with Ruben's present state of being and his becomingness—his wave of potential. Actually, Mr. Strauss could see in Ruben Cerda his successor.

For the next twenty-two years, Mr. Strauss entrusted him with every detail of the business, but more importantly he gave him his love and confidence. Several years ago Mr. Strauss's health rapidly deteriorated. Ruben tells the story of sitting by Mr. Strauss's bedside when he told Ruben that he was giving Las Mañanitas to him. Ruben with great sadness said, "And I will continue to run it just like you have for all these..." Mr. Strauss angrily interrupted him in mid-sentence, "Young man, that is impossible! No one can run Las Mañanitas like I did. What I want you to do is run it like Ruben Cerda would."

Even in his final hours Mr. Strauss connected with the uniqueness that Ruben was not able to see in himself. He wanted Ruben to be his unique creative self. Ruben Cerda today personifies the creative dream of potential . . . the becomingness of every one of us . . . the other half of our reality.

Guillaume Apollinaire could be describing Mr. Strauss's treatment of Ruben:

Come to the edge, he said.

They said: We are afraid.

Come to the edge, he said.

They came.

He pushed them . . . and they flew.

THE FORCE OF CONNECTING

If we are going to allow possibilities to surface and potentials to be unleashed in our own lives, we must make room for the unexplored, the unknown, the dawning. The latent potential existing in each of us finds expression and life becomes more exciting, alive, and vibrant. As it presently stands, we have erected blinders to who we really are—and can be. Blinders are a good idea for horses moving along a steep trail. For humans, the challenge is to put our old blinders aside to connect with the glorious—and very real—possibilities we haven't yet permitted ourselves to discover.

The dynamic relationship between Mr. Strauss and Ruben Cerda uncovers another of nature's connecting principles.

CONNECTING PRINCIPLE NUMBER 2: OFFER MUTUAL SUPPORT

By offering mutual support and giving and receiving from each other, we will experience our connectedness. Nature operates as a mutual support system. Our old interpretation of nature teaches us just the opposite. We have been told that nature operates in the context of survival of the fittest, that nature is ruthless, uncaring, and harsh. We invite you to join the new ecological perspective and see that everything is interrelated and that we bask in the abundant support of a beneficent universe. The earth rotating on its axis, the sun offering its constant warmth, the mutual support of one organ of our body to the other goes on most of the time without our acknowledgment.

Mr. Strauss's inspired notion of creative shared leadership gave Ruben a gift of mutual support. Ruben can only repay him by giving to others. Today, Ruben has opened another hotel, not because he needs the money or because he doesn't have enough to do, but because he wants other Mexican Indian boys like himself to receive the support he received from Mr. Strauss. Giving and receiving are all part of one process. Opening ourselves to receive opens us to give.

We are reminded very powerfully of the mutual support system built into nature when we visit Bio-sphere II near Tucson, Arizona, where scientists are attempting to replicate the earth's climate zones. The Bio-sphere is a human-designed replica of the earth. In determining what birds to include inside the Bio-sphere, the scientists decided to try a hummingbird. They found that a hummingbird needs at least 1,000 flowers a day to support it. This kind of mutual support found everywhere in nature isn't often appreciated. We tend to take it for granted.

Our interconnections manifest themselves constantly. Drug problems have an impact on every taxpayer, as does the cycle of poverty or the number of drive-by shootings by street gangs. Child rearing practices in individual homes ultimately have a collective impact. The condition of our water, the stand of timber in our forests, the amount of pollutants in the atmosphere all merge together as part of the planetary condition. We are one, and the sooner we move beyond the belief that we are separate, the sooner we will recognize that the way to solve our problems is to mutually support one another in creative and caring ways.

CONNECTING PRINCIPLE NUMBER 3: EXTEND EQUALITY TO EVERYONE

One of the greatest barriers that stands between us and the opportunity to truly connect with one another is our unwillingness to see everyone as equal. For countless centuries, we have been in the business of erecting elaborate structures based on the notions of inequality. Since the establishment in Jericho of the world's first city some 8,000 years ago, unequal relationships have prevailed.

Even in a nation like the United States, which began with the declaration, "All men are created equal and endowed by their creator with certain unalienable rights," unequal relationships fester. In the late 1700s there were a million citizens along with a million slaves. Inequalities still plague the United States. They constitute the major weakness in achieving real democracy—creative democracy. Our experience tells us that all people want to be treated with dignity and respect and to feel that their lives truly have meaning.

Probably the greatest barrier to seeing each other as equal comes from our focusing on and assigning values to the differences that manifest themselves from one person to another and from one group to another. It is interesting to speculate on what kind of a world we would have if nature operated this way. Carbon atoms would hang out in exclusive private clubs, oxygen and hydrogen wouldn't get together to form water, and the countless strange alliances that would have to come together to make up a living cell would be barred by class lines. As we discover the ecological ethos, we uncover the vast and unseen web of relationships that support and enhance the evolution of life. In nature, all parts are essential.

Perhaps our greatest task will be to move beyond vested self-interest, to connect with each person by seeing that person as part of ourselves. This shift in consciousness can only occur, one person at a time, by extending our love and mutual support to each other.

J. Allen Boone in his book *Kinship with All Life*, suggests, "We are members of a vast cosmic orchestra in which each living instrument is essential to the complementary and harmonious playing of the whole." If we were able to integrate this into our everyday lives we would create circumstances in which everyone wins.

The great challenge for organizations is to move beyond exclusive and elaborate special privileges for a few. In the 1990s only 15 percent of the new entrants to the work force will be white males, compared to 47 percent in 1988. The diversity of the growing work force will be unlike anything corporate America has ever seen—with vastly different ethnic minorities, women, and the elderly. True equality, understanding, and opportunity are the path to the future.

These entrants to the work force will bring unique and diverse viewpoints that provide the ideas and concepts for building a different tomorrow. Encouraging their uncommon and unusual approaches will generate a situation in which more people feel included. It will lead to making the fourth principle of connecting an actuality.

CONNECTING PRINCIPLE NUMBER 4: BRING ABOUT THE CIRCUMSTANCES IN WHICH EVERYONE CAN WIN

The assumption that when one wins another must lose is not just a distasteful part of the second phase exclusion process, but a foundational assumption of how individuals and groups interact.

Our present worldview maintains that competition and winning at the expense of someone else is the way life unfolds.

The Creative Worldview maintains that this old view is counterproductive. As nature teaches us, we are all part of the whole. The one way we can move beyond our separateness is to recognize that the notion of win-lose only leaves us with lose-lose. We have so accepted the idea that competition is essential, in fact vital, that we haven't honestly assessed the consequences.

What seems to be happening in the workplace is an evolution of values. D. Quinn Mill of the Harvard Business School found that the most effective groups, according to young managers he interviewed, were creative, cooperative, had a clear sense of mission, and fostered open communication. They wanted to be involved when they were participants—and preferably partners—in making decisions.

This kind of partnering between labor and management is beginning to happen. An entire town saved itself when the workers at Weirton Steel in the Ohio Valley voted to buy the dying company. The new owners, instead of fighting for survival, started running a company. Now, nearly a decade later, they listen to customers and the people who do the work; they take on all competitors and have eliminated the adversarial relationship between labor and management. They have a total commitment to be the best in the industry. People working together not only saved their jobs, but revitalized their company and restored their community.

In most industries and institutions the opposite situation prevails. Our prison system, criminal justice system, drug problems, educational challenges, political turmoil, and widespread business upheaval reflect our commitment to the second phase win-lose belief system. It's easier to declare a "war on drugs" than commit to create the conditions in which drug dealing isn't desirable, tolerated, or supported. Competition, adversarial relationships, and playing tough are mindsets that will no longer serve us. The environment has been exhausted and there is no more room for growth using the win-lose model.

By using a second phase approach to attacking the problems that we've created, we wander down a blind alley. The way to approach problems is from a creative perspective. The following method provides a way to move beyond the constraints of the win-lose mindset.

Create a Profound Win

Select any conflict in your life. Make a 100 percent commitment to approach it from a creative context. See yourself as a creative being, totally connected with everyone who is involved in the conflict. Recognize that no one can win unless everyone wins. Your commitment is to figure out, in the most creative way possible, how everyone who is a party to the conflict can experience a profound win. You are able to accept everyone exactly as they are—while also seeing that they have unlimited possibilities waiting to unfold.

The first thing is to truly believe you can *co-create* whatever you want in the situation. Being co-creative means you are open to everyone winning at a profound level. You listen, you actively value the viewpoints of others and co-create with them to reach a solution none of you could have created alone. Our experience verifies that the collective wisdom of the participants in any situation results in far better solutions than if an authority figure imposes a solution by force.

The four key questions to ask yourself are:

- What is it I really want?

- What would it look like if I got what I really want?

- What would I be willing to do to get what I want?

- When am I going to do it?

Of necessity you have to search diligently underneath each of these questions to find the creative answers. You have to be a sleuth, a virtual Sherlock Holmes, to get to the depth of what you really want. The answers go right to the core of what you value most in any given circumstance. What is it you hope for? What would make the situation work out best for everyone involved?

In the mid-1970s, a significant community crisis was solved when one of the authors asked these questions. The Iowa Beef Packers went on strike in Sioux City, Iowa. The strike spread to the construction trades and on to some of the smaller unions. Within time Sioux City was in economic distress. The city experienced as much labor conflict as any city in the United States at the time. The economy was in trouble, it was difficult to get workers, and many people were packing up and moving to take jobs elsewhere.

Frank Griffith, the president of Iowa Public Service, now Mid-West Resources, decided to invite thirty executives together to discuss the situation. A creative strategic thinking session was facilitated by one of the authors whereby these executives could find out what was really underneath this conflict between labor and management. They spent three days together and came away with the priorities they felt needed to be addressed to create a great community. They didn't talk about the labor conflict. They talked about what they wanted to create in Sioux City.

After their meeting, Frank Griffith thought perhaps the union leadership would respond favorably to a similar type of meeting. He called the head of the postal union, who then talked to other union leaders. In a short time, the unions brought thirty union people together for a similar three-day meeting. They didn't talk about their gripes and complaints about management, instead they talked about what kind of community they wanted to create.

"The two leaders then decided to invite fifteen individuals from each side to a combined meeting. By this time, they had developed some trust in me as an outside facilitator who didn't have any biases one way or the other.

"When the combined labor and management group met, I imposed some new rules. They couldn't talk about the conflict. What I insisted on was their looking at the results of what each of their separate groups had decided were critical needs to create a great community. What was shocking to everyone was that both groups had similar priorities. At first neither side believed they could possibly have common goals. There were some tense moments at first—they were convinced I had set them up. It took some doing, but within time both groups realized that what they really wanted were good schools to educate young people, jobs so families wouldn't have to leave to find work, excellent health care, and a good community in which to retire."

After an additional three days together, what both groups decided, despite their long three-year strike and the turmoil it had caused, was that they had far more in common than their diverse points of view might have suggested. In the afternoon, the two groups even played golf together. When it was pointed out to them that they were playing golf with one another and enjoying themselves, both sides agreed they would have never predicted that possibility. Perhaps golf is the great equalizer.

Even though neither group had the intention of walking out with an agreement, they did leave with a decision to set up a joint labor and management organization funded by both groups with an executive director to work on the solutions to create a better community. Within three weeks the Iowa Beef Packers strike ended, and for many years now this community has suffered no significant labor problems. Today this same labor and management organization continues into its twentieth year.

A significant shift occurred in this situation. The union and management teams were asked, "How might you create the kind of community you want in Sioux City?" The entire discussion moved from the apparent conflict to what both teams really wanted for their future. What did they hope for? What did they want to create? This allowed the focus to shift from conflict to creating. The labor-management group went on to implement the strategies they identified as critical to their community.

Focusing on how you connect with the circumstances in your life in the most positive way enhances the possibility that you will create something meaningful out of the experience. If you focus on all the things that are problems, that are negative, difficult, and impossible to accept, you build up resistance to ever connecting with the actual circumstances in a creative way. You concentrate your energy on resistance rather than on taking advantage of the opportunity to learn something about yourself or the other people involved. Concentrating on the positive aspects of any given situation allows you to connect with the circumstances in the most co-creative way possible.

CONNECTING PRINCIPLE NUMBER 5: RECOGNIZE THAT WHATEVER YOU FOCUS ON EXPANDS

This powerful principle has tremendous force in our lives. It can be a guiding principle of greatness. Those who use it in any given field focus their attention on those things that expand their capabilities. The people we know who integrate this principle experience a profound shift in the quality of their lives.

Jean Nidetch was at one time overweight—in fact her weight was over 200 pounds. She wanted to be thin, beautiful, and energetic rather than complaining all the time about her looks. She found herself being negative, constantly talking and worrying about her weight. She found a New York City Board of Health diet, and knew what she really needed was support if she was going to lose the weight and keep it off. She thought other struggling dieters might need the same kind of support so she invited them to the basement of her apartment building. Her focus was on the positive aspects of becoming thin. Anyone who joined her initial meetings was told to bring a folding chair because Jean didn't have enough seating space. Some women, along with their chairs, even drove up in limousines. So much interest was generated that Jean finally rented a hall along with fifty chairs.

At the first Weight Watchers public meeting 400 people showed up. Jean didn't even know how much to charge, but noticed the movie theater downstairs charged $2.00, so she said, "$2.00." Ten years later in 1978 over 17,000 people gathered in Madison Square Garden to celebrate the founding of Weight Watchers. Jean Nidetch focused on the positive. In so doing she helped countless people and created a profound success in her own life.

By focusing on the positive, millions of people who have changed their behavior have learned forcefully that what one *focuses on expands*. This happens whether it's modifying behavior or dealing with people.

Rather than just seeing people as they presently appear, one can also focus on who they are becoming. This viewpoint provides a powerful shift in the way we connect, by expanding our attention to see the potential of each individual. In his book, *The Vital Balance*, Dr. Karl Menninger talked about what really works, "It is the assertion of hope, of faith in every individual's potential for growth and development and self-transcendence. It is a declaration of love for and of belief in one's fellow creatures."

To truly move to a belief in one another, our most significant act would be the elimination of judgments—judgments of every kind and description, good or bad, right or wrong, ugly or beautiful, superior or inferior, proper or improper, perfect or imperfect.

CONNECTING PRINCIPLE NUMBER 6:
ELIMINATE JUDGMENTS

Perhaps our most binding limitation is our tendency to judge based on preconceived beliefs or thoughts. The list of our learned discriminations extends without bounds. The inculcation of the second phase logical worldview places emphasis on the ability to judge, analyze, and evaluate. Nearly everything that appears in our daily lives is judged on the basis of some expectation from the past. The fact is that second phase society keeps its commonality protected through the awesome limiting power of judgment. It stands as the largest single barrier to connecting with what is really going on—all the glorious events, circumstances, and people that could bring new potentials into our lives.

Students at Stanford University enrolled in the tremendously popular Creativity in Business class, nicknamed their Voice of Judgment the VOJ. The VOJ is activated continually as we judge others, judge ourselves, judge the collective society as a whole, and even judge the judgment. It haunts our interaction with others. And, most profoundly, our constant judgments about ourselves stand as the single largest barrier to developing our creative potential.

The groups we work with imagine what it would feel like and what it would look like if they lived in a world without judgment. Here are some of their ideas:

- I'd feel free to be me.

- I could express who I really am.

- I would be accepted and loved.

- I wouldn't have a fear of failure. There would be permission to experiment and learn.

- I would stop denying my feelings and my sense of repression would end.

- I'd have broader freedom of choice. There wouldn't be large categories of "oughts" and "shoulds" and "rights" and "wrongs."

- My life would be richer because I would feel free to connect with a whole range of people whom I now judge.

- Prejudice and discrimination would fall away.

- Everyone could stop worrying about doing anything wrong.

- We could stop living life based on fear.

- I'd be capable of seeing things I now cannot see because most filters would be down.

- There would be far less energy going into resistance.

- My uniqueness would be celebrated.

- I wouldn't feel so confined within limits and expectations.

- We would eliminate the triple threat of blame, shame, and guilt.

- I could eliminate obligations and do things because I wanted to, not because I had to.

- Everyone would have more energy to participate in life because walls and boundaries would be removed.

- It would simplify life enormously. Choices would revolve around not wrongs and rights but how I can achieve my purpose.

Begin your own process by noticing how often your mind automatically turns to the act of judging. This manifests itself in such popular concepts as "constructive criticism"—a self-cancelling act. *Any criticism* disconnects us from others. It raises resistance and defense. The trick is to replace every criticism with a thought that allows you to *unconditionally* accept and connect with the person or circumstance you are judging. We replace the "no" or "but" with "yes, and . . . ," building connections, rather than breaking them.

Being aware of the tendency to judge takes constant attention. It doesn't require you to think you'll never have a judgmental thought again. Both authors are constantly engaged in identifying when they are being judgmental, and they work on recognizing how their own judgments invariably cause them to disconnect from people, circumstances, and events. Judgments trap us in our belief systems, and since these beliefs stem from the past, we cannot be fully present to what is happening around us.

By eliminating judgments, we allow ourselves to let go of fear, distrust, and suspicions. Once we eliminate judgments, we can shift to the most positive and affirming manifestation of connecting, and that requires action by opening our heart to our infinite capacity to love.

In a very basic sense, when we pay attention without judging we can actually hear what others are saying. We listen to understand, not to evaluate, we don't offer advice unless it's sought, and we stop thinking we know what the other person *means*. Gerald G. Jampolsky has this to say about not judging others: "Not judging is another way of letting go of fear and experiencing Love. When we learn not to judge others—and totally accept them and not want to change them—we can simultaneously learn to accept ourselves."

CONNECTING PRINCIPLE NUMBER 7: TRUST AND LOVE ONE ANOTHER

To connect with others, the most important thing we can do is to trust and love one another. Oh, how well we know the trepidation of using the "L word." Love is hardly the word you would expect to find in the world of organizations. In fact, both authors have been asked by some corporate executives to not use the word *love*.

How can love have anything to do with running a successful organization? What we're finding out, along with a good many other people, is that it has a great deal to do with success, in fact it might be the greatest secret to success.

James M. Kouzes interviewed Major General John H. Stanford who said, "I have the secret to success in life. The secret is to stay in love.... I don't know any other fire, any other thing in life that is more exhilarating and is more positive a feeling than love is." Jan Carlzon, president of Scandinavian Airlines System, built one of the most successful airlines in the world by managing people with love. "People are not willing to take risks when they feel afraid or threatened. But if you manage people by love—that is, if you show them respect and trust—they start to perform up to their real capabilities." Even an executive within the competitive world of automakers has dared to use the word love. Joe Kordick, head of Ford's parts and services division, supervises 7,600 employees and has as his guiding principles "trust and love."

Peter Grace, CEO of W.R. Grace and Company believes, "The whole thing comes down to truth and love, and in every walk of life, those are the only two important values." What we're talking about is not people hugging one another in the corporate corridors or the halls of academe or the teachers' lounge or government offices. What we mean by love is genuine caring, developing a deep feeling of trust, mutual respect, and honesty. Robert Townsend, former chief of Avis Rent-A-Car, put it this way: "The real essence of leadership is to care about your people." Tom Melohn at North America Tool and Die says, "It boils down to the innate goodness of people. They're really good human beings, and if you treat them like that, you'll be stunned with the results you get."

What is clearly evident from American workers is that there is a great deal of stress in the workplace. In a study conducted by Northwestern National Life Insurance Company in 1991, seven in ten workers said job stress caused frequent health problems. 46 percent said their jobs are highly stressful. Lower productivity, employee turnover, higher health care costs have an impact on the bottom line. A recent *Industry Week* survey revealed that 86 percent of those surveyed said they believe workers today are less loyal to their companies than they were just five years ago—and 75 percent said their companies were less loyal to them. Perhaps the most enlightened executives will realize that creating a humane and, we would even suggest, a loving environment might be the most cost effective strategy for any organization.

It is impossible for anyone to reach out farther than they can reach within. The degree to which we truly love and accept ourselves is the extent to which we can love another. If we begin with ourselves, unconditionally accepting and connecting with who we are, with every part of us, then we can move forward to impart or express the kind of connectedness we now know is expressed at the very foundations of nature.

Shifting our context comes about only when we see the invisible reality of each other as inseparably connected. This new creative vision reaches us by way of our hearts as we recognize our profound links with nature and our common humanity. We simply can't see our potential unfolding or our connectedness unless we open our hearts to one another. In a restricted second phase world, we have held the belief that only a few special people have the capacity to open their hearts to their infinite capacity to love. In most cases in the past, we made saints or martyrs of these people and went on about our daily business thinking it impossible to treat ourselves or anyone else in a continually loving way. It was Gandhi who maintained he was not a special person or a saint, as many claimed. "I am engaged in trying to show I am as frail a mortal as any of us. I own that I have an unconsumable passion for truth and love."

Contrary to conventional wisdom, love is not limited to the emotional connection between two individuals, but can encompass all of our interactions. The great scientist, Louis de Broglie, who opened the door to the new world of physics, concluded: "If we wish to give philosophic expression to the profound connection between thought and action in all fields of human endeavor, particularly in science, we shall undoubtedly seek its sources in the human soul. Perhaps philosophers might call it 'love' in a very general sense—that force which directs all our actions, which is the source of all our delights and all our pursuits. Indissolubly linked with thought and action, love is the common mainspring and, hence, their common bond."

Love gives profound meaning to our lives. Love is the high point. Healing ourselves, our relationships, and our society will occur only when we open our hearts to ourselves and to one another.

THE BENEFITS IN CHANGING THE WAY WE CONNECT

Samuel Oliner had many reasons to believe the worst of humankind. Oliner's family and friends were victims of the Nazi atrocities. He has now gathered 600 stories of people who helped rescue Jews from the Nazis. He and his research staff have interviewed over 200 people who did nothing to help. His findings cast light on how compassion surfaces in human nature and whether goodness can be taught.

He found that those who helped were more empathetic and caring and had a greater sense of responsibility. These people had become more compassionate in part by "living around people who were not of their faith or background; they had learned to see others as fellow human beings." The most important influences came from the way parents disciplined their children. The non-helping bystanders were much more likely to have been beaten and abused as children by their parents. Rescuers had parents who used reason as the primary form of discipline, instilling values as well as compassion. "Kind caring parents were the model for kind, caring children."

We have the opportunity to significantly change our minds about how we relate and connect with one another. Our suggestion is to shift immediately to the belief that we are all interconnected. If we accept this reality, we will shift the way we communicate with one another, and that will have an impact on the way we treat each other. We have the potential to interact in a spirit of trust, openness, and honesty. And perhaps with an ecology of the human spirit we will move to true interdependence throughout this magnificent planet where we reside.

These principles certainly run counter to the accumulated advice from those who maintain that, "You better be careful in a dog-eat-dog world." "You better watch out for number one." "You really can't trust anyone." Allen H. Neuharth, former CEO of Gannett, the communication giant, entitled his biography *Confessions of an S.O.B.*, and it contained pithy advice on corporate infighting, how to use devious calculations to get ahead, along with nasty stories he employed to get the job done. Many believe that anger, mistrust, and aggression are the common characteristics of those who make it in high-powered positions whether it be in government or business.

Max DePree, the chairman of Herman Miller, runs one of the most respected companies in America and believes corporations should be communities, not battlefields. At their heart lie "covenants" between executives and employees that rest on "shared commitment" to ideas, to issues, to values, to goals. "Words such as love, warmth, personal chemistry are certainly pertinent." What distinguishes Hewlett Packard, the $12 billion giant with over 90,000 people? Pete Peterson, VP for Human Resources at Hewlett Packard, explains that the success and creativity of HP is its fundamental belief in people; giving them the maximum amount of freedom to get the job done. He is glad the "HP way" is built around trust, "if a company has the attitude that it needs to control employees and that we don't trust you, that will be self-fulfilling...."

How can you implement the principles of connecting in an organization? Our experience is that it's very easy to say and very hard to do. Begin by believing in your people. Follow Max

DePree's advice, treat each employee as a meaningful participant in a shared enterprise. At Herman Miller every full-time employee becomes a stockholder within the first year of service. Teams of workers receive bonuses on a quarterly basis based on the ideas they contribute. DePree believes "Everyone has the right and duty to influence decisionmaking and to understand the results."

The beliefs of many people run directly opposite to what we're advocating. We know that once you make the decision, your interactions and relationships with others immediately change. If you are trustworthy, you'll be trusted. If you connect based on trying to create a profound win for everyone, others sense the shift. This natural way of connecting with people has profound consequences for good. Try it! And stay with it. Find out for yourself.

We can then join together and co-create solutions that transcend our old and outdated second phase formulas. We are inextricably linked and the sooner we acknowledge that fact, the quicker we will get on with building a far different future, not only for ourselves, but for our loved ones, our organizations, and the world.

Teillard de Chardin expresses this powerfully:

Someday, after we have mastered the winds, the waves, the

tides and gravity, we shall harness for God the energies of love.

Then for the second time in the history of the world, man will

have discovered fire.

THE POWERFUL PRINCIPLES OF CONNECTING

The principles of connecting that will vastly improve your relationships and the quality of your life are:

- See the potentials and possibilities in everyone
- Offer mutual support
- Extend equality to all people

- Bring about the circumstances in which everyone can win
- Recognize that whatever you focus on expands
- Eliminate judgments
- Trust and love one another

The combined principles of Creativity, Connecting, and Future Pull provide the natural foundations whereby you can live the Creative Worldview. It provides a beginning point for anyone willing to make the crossing to a new way of living, relating, and being with one's self and with others. We now turn to strengthening this solid bridge to the future so that you can integrate the powerful principles of the Creative Worldview into your life.

11: A SOLID BRIDGE TO THE FUTURE

> Of all the creatures of earth, only human beings can change their patterns. Man alone is the architect of his destiny.... Human beings, by changing the inner attitudes of their minds, can change the outer aspects of their lives.
>
> William James

When we look around at a world in the midst of great turmoil—from the dismemberment of the traditional family to vast geopolitical shifts, one is tempted to ask: "What's the matter?" The more appropriate question, in a world feeling the effects of the giant invisible forces of a planetary Breakpoint, is, "What is matter?" Unfortunately, decisions about how to deal with our changing world are still made on the basis of a solid matter-based logical world—that's the matter.

For hundreds of centuries humanity based the reality of nature's laws on what could be seen and felt; the solid visible world. The way objects bang against one another, the way reaction follows action created a logic founded on the structure and behavior of material objects. At the turn of the century Marconi sent invisible radio waves through the air, and W.C. Roentgen sent invisible waves right through solid objects—or what had always appeared to be solid objects. The exclusive notion of solid material reality evaporated.

The results of a host of thinkers and doers adopting the new Breakpoint rules have been profound. As we have seen, at the turn of the century they dug in and rebuilt the foundations that once supported a matter-based logical belief system. The new reality of particles with invisible waves triggered an onslaught of new technologies. Ordinary logic quickly discounted these strange new discoveries; they were thought to belong only in the realm of obscure science. However, these nonlogical approaches have produced many of the massive Breakpoint changes that shape today's world for every one of us. As George Gilder puts it, "The global network of telecommunications carries more valuable goods than all the world's supertankers." And the invisible forces that brought about radios, telephones, TVs, VCRs, microwaves, computers, and satellite communications demonstrate convincingly that these odd ideas work pretty reliably—and make possible a world undreamed of a scant fifty years ago.

It's time to abandon pure logic and the limits of physical reality and start reconstructing the foundations of our personal and organizational lives based on deeper and more powerful understandings. Logic and reason have certainly served us, but they are not the only methods of thinking our brains are capable of undertaking. Until we tap into a deeper reality, using our intuition, inner wisdom, playful childlike nature, and other realms beyond the limits of logic, we will never be able to express the true greatness within us.

However, accessing the vast realms of the psyche and living within the expansive context of the Creative Worldview require a steadfast committment. Looking back over the basic themes and foundational principles we have discussed, it's easy to accept the idea that it is useful in an organization to have a vision, it's practical to be connected in teams, it's probably even a good thing to come up with some creative ideas. Innumerable programs have been adopted in countless organizations along these lines and many self-help techniques follow this same thread of thought. Some good results have followed. It's not enough. It's too easy to slide back into old ways.

Our experience with hundreds of organizations and hundreds of thousands of individuals over the past thirty years shows that all of us (the authors included) cling tenaciously to our outmoded beliefs. Programs and techniques consistently bog down in the quicksand of orthodox thought. Shifting the deep foundations of a belief system is difficult at best. Yet, that is the only way the real magic of nature's dynamic creative rules of change and growth can be experienced—continuously. And, it's clearly the passage to take us beyond this Breakpoint in history.

Taking an alternate path to the future requires a commitment to not only do things differently but change our underlying assumptions. The Creative Worldview will only happen when individuals become different. Only when individuals change their minds will organizations and nations shift to a new worldview. Underlying organizational change is the ability of individuals to take the same steps scientists took at the turn of the century and redefine reality.

The powerful natural forces of Creativity, Connecting and Future Pull provide the solid ground to erect a new bridge to the future. They give new meaning to our organizational and personal lives. They also challenge us to commit to learning and integrating these principles on a daily basis.

A CREATIVE CONTEXT

Adopting a Creative Worldview requires creating a *different context* for interpreting what occurs in our lives. Context differs from content. The contents of our lives are the specific circumstances that occur. The context is the worldview, the mindset, the backdrop, or frame of reference from which we interpret the meaning of the circumstances that occur in our lives. In order to embrace a Creative Worldview we must shift our context.

Each of us, as the creators of our life experience, has two distinct domains from which we create our lives.

- *We create our viewpoint about whatever happens to us.* This is how we make meaning out of our life experiences. It provides our orientation. A person is not so much hurt by what happens but by his or her interpretation of life's events.

- *We also create the form of our participation.* We determine how we are going to connect with the people, ideas, and events that occur.

A case in point. A plane carrying 300 passengers arrives at its destination. The luggage is delayed and finally after thirty minutes, the customer service representative announces that some baggage won't arrive until tomorrow. Each passenger creates his or her own orientation or viewpoint and determines how to connect with the news about the delay.

One young woman traveling with a group tour, starts yelling at the airline representative: "I think you are an incompetent fool for letting us stand around for the last thirty minutes waiting for our luggage when you knew it wasn't coming. I'll tell you one thing, I'll never use your airline again." A young couple traveling with the same group, upon hearing the news say, "No problem, we'll pick up all our gear tomorrow, or if you deliver, we'll give you our address."

In what mood will the young woman or the couple experience the rest of the day? How will they connect with the other experiences that lie in wait for them? These three people were confronted with the same circumstance, and they decided to interpret it based on their mindset, frame of reference, or worldview. In addition, all three determined how they would connect with the experience.

The same situation occurs every day in the organizations where we work. If people have the viewpoint that they aren't responsible or empowered for what happens, then when something goes wrong, they most often find someone else to blame. However, if one's frame of reference is based on a deep commitment and love of one's job, then circumstances occur and the individual responds as a full participant taking responsibility for the results.

These principles also apply to emotional issues that have an impact on one's daily life. Take the following situation for example: A young woman who has been physically and verbally abused by her parents is now living on her own. Her attitudes about herself and the world have been greatly influenced by the way she was treated as a child and a young woman. It is easy to see this woman as a victim, yet within the murky waters of abuse, she has choice. She can choose to remain a victim, which will most likely result in low self-esteem, unfocused anger, a variety of misplaced emotions, and very probably, a repetition of the pattern of abuse with her own spouse and children.

Another choice is to take responsibility for how she will relate to her experiences of abuse. The child who was abused was not responsible for what happened to her, yet it can be transformative, as the adult looking back on those experiences, to take responsibility, at least for one's own perception of them. As the young woman becomes accountable to herself for her experience, she can use this strength to create an intention for how she wants to relate to the pain. The emotion involved is healthy when expressed with a powerful intention in mind. If she wants to be more loving in her relationships with other people, or to release the pain she has within her own heart, she has the vision needed to pull her through the dark corners of her own memories.

By making the choice to take responsibility for the situation, this young woman accepts her own strength and begins to make decisions based on her own desires, not in response to her anger about her childhood. She will have taken a profound step into breaking the patterns of the past and making space for a more loving and accepting future to emerge.

These principles apply equally in the everyday events of life. We are constantly presented with choices of how we will interact with people and circumstances depending on how we perceive the world. Not only do each of us create our perceptions about the situations and relationships in our lives, we get to say who we are relative to those circumstances. If it rains and we say, "I hate rain," we have committed to resisting deriving any pleasure from a rainy day. We have consciously chosen our orientation.

If your context for life comes out of the belief that it is a constant struggle, or if you subscribe to Murphy's Law—that if anything can go wrong it will—then your interpretation of getting rear-ended on the freeway will be oriented from this belief. You will create your connection and participation with the circumstances and will figure out what it means based on that context. It's easy to imagine the events, feelings, and consequences that will follow such a collision.

In order to operate from the context of a Creative Worldview, three things are vital:

■ Accept that you and everyone else are creative beings. By behaving towards others creatively, you can continually participate in co-creating what never existed before. Each of us can choose to be empowered by taking responsibility for shaping a positive, creative present and future.

■ Commit to fully participate in life by connecting with people and circumstances exactly as they are and exactly as things happen, without judging or preconditioning your thinking about them. Connect with the present state of what is happening and with the unlimited possibilities that are unfolding—the becomingness.

■ Live as if your life makes a difference. Offer your unique talents to realize the future purpose and possibilities of making the world a better place—in every situation.

WHAT IS YOUR ORIENTATION

From what viewpoint are you looking when you interpret the everyday events of your life, whether it be at work or with your family and friends? Take a look at the following scenario:

Scene: a large city at midday. Three people are descending in an elevator in a tall downtown building. The elevator has stopped between floors and the lights have gone out.

FIRST PERSON: "Well, wouldn't you know it. Nothing in this lousy city ever works. The garbage, the police, the ..."

SECOND PERSON: "You think you've got problems! I'm going to be late for lunch with my biggest client! This is all I need. I'll probably lose the account."

THIRD PERSON: That's you. You've decided to see this experience out of the context of a creative worldview. How do you interact from a creative context? How would you connect with the people involved?

Maybe this provides a time to sit down in the elevator and just relax. At least you could introduce yourself and find out if any of your elevator mates have the expertise to get you out of this predicament. Maybe one of you is a singer, another a mechanical engineer, and another an advertising executive. You might figure out how together you can make the elevator experience at least memorable.

A Creative Worldview orientation would see this situation as an opportunity—not as a problem. You accept each person in the elevator as a creative being and commit to fully connecting with each of them just exactly as they show up, without judging or evaluating their behavior as good or bad, right or wrong. You also hold the possibility that they have the ability to respond to the circumstance in other ways. You draw on each person's unique contribution as you co-create how best to experience being in the elevator together.

For each person in the elevator, what he or she believes is what is made real. If your context comes out of a mindset that says this is just another bad thing in a difficult world, that will be your orientation to the situation. In this, as in any and all other circumstances, what anyone looks for determines the form of what appears. If one looks for problems, it's easy to find problems. If your orientation is to look for opportunities, that's exactly what you'll find.

One of the legends at IBM is the story of Mr. Watson finding out that one of his managers had made a series of decisons resulting in a substantial loss of money to the company. The manager assumed he would be fired, cleared out his desk, and was to have a final meeting with Mr. Watson. When the manager came into Mr. Watson's office feeling the heavy burden of impending doom, he was given the opportunity to tell his side of the story. After they talked through the situation and the manager acknowledged he knew he was going to be fired, Mr. Watson looked at him and said something to the effect, "We can't afford to fire you, we've invested too much in your education!" Mr. Watson was able to move beyond the problem into creating a new possibility, and out of it came the opportunity for this young manager to make a profound contribution to IBM—far beyond the amount of money he lost.

Circumstances always happen against some backdrop. If a person's context comes from the viewpoint that life seems like a successive chain of problems where things just don't work out, that backdrop powerfully influences what happens. The catch is that our beliefs allow us to live in such a way as to continually perpetuate them. Epictetus said, "Men are disturbed not by things that happen, but by their opinion of the things that happen."

In a conversation with Bill Moyers, Joseph Campbell suggests, "It was Freud who told us to blame our parents and Marx who told us to blame the upper class. Actually the only person you can ever hold responsible is yourself."

Moyers in pondering this idea asks: "But what about chance? A drunken driver turns the corner and hits you. That isn't your fault. You haven't done that to yourself."

Campbell responds by saying, "Chance, or what might seem to be chance, is the means through which life is realized. The problem is not to blame or explain but to handle the life that arises. . . . The best advice is to take it all as if it had been of your intention—with that, you evoke the participation of your will."

Campbell is referring to what we now see as the being and becoming of reality, the particle and the wave. Chance presents us with the being—what we do with the other side, the invisible half of reality, the becoming—is ours to create. It's scientifically accurate to say, you don't make life, but you do make what you create of it. The meaning of the events in your life are based on your interpretation of them.

MEANING-MAKING AND INTENTION

We make meaning out of our lives by our intention. In order for us to embrace the possibilities of a Creative Worldview, we must have the intention of interpreting circumstances and events out of a creative context. It is our intention and willingness to act that makes meaning. Meaning-making encompasses both the present moment and future possibilities—both halves of reality. Our intention creates the meaning of present circumstances and events as well as the invisible future possibilities.

Understanding the meaning of the Creative Worldview is only one half of reality. The other half is your intention to take action to integrate this way of being as the cornerstone or context for how you interpret your life experiences. Understanding the ideas and principles uncovered in these pages must be followed with the commitment to express and work with them continuously in order to integrate them into your daily life and within the organization where you work.

The creative dynamic of nature proves we live in a creative world—events, experiences, ideas, and people are constantly changing and producing results that never before existed and could not have been predicted by the past. Each of us can accept our role as nature's greatest evolutionary agent and take on the challenge of changing our life in order to move beyond this Breakpoint in the human journey.

We Are All Responsible for Our Lives and Empowered to Change Them Whenever We Choose

Transcending where we are can occur when we recognize that we are infinitely able to empower ourselves to change when it is appropriate. Changing our conscious belief to one of self-empowerment will be the doorway to changing everything else. As individuals shift, so too will organizations and the larger society.

In his early twenties William James fought relentlessly with severe bouts of depression. At the age of twenty-five, he contemplated suicide, knowing he could never make the contribution his brother Henry was making to the world. He decided to challenge himself for thirty days, "To act as if what I do makes a difference." With that simple commitment, he created a totally new kind of life. James, who became one of America's great psychologists and philosophers, taught at Harvard University and found his life far too short to do justice to his proliferating ideas. Toward the end of his life, James offered this advice:

To change one's life:

Start immediately

Do it flamboyantly

No exceptions (no excuses)

Betty Friedan, founder of the modern feminist movement is not reluctant to change. She now advocates moving beyond radical feminism. In her book, *The Second Stage*, she offers her viewpoint on why men and women working together is critical to create a society that supports life by working cooperatively to transform all of society's institutions. Friedan changed her orientation even though she was denounced by countless feminists who saw her as a traitor to the cause.

And you don't have to be William James or Betty Friedan to change.

A twenty-three-year-old heroin addict, divorced mother of three, weighing 326 pounds and on welfare, hated herself enough to prostitute her own body to get money for dope. She went to her first meeting of Overeaters Anonymous believing "none of it. 'These people are crazy,' I thought. 'I'm a fat, ugly junkie, and they're telling me I can get thin, and regain my self-respect if I want to.' 'No way,' I told them, right out loud. They didn't throw me out. A beautiful, middle-aged man put his arm around my shoulder and said, 'Come back and listen. Try us for thirty days.'

"I didn't believe him, but I went back and back and back. Today, I've lost 121 pounds, and I'm still losing. I'm drug free, and I have a responsible job and the love and respect of my children and people who believed in me when I didn't believe in myself."

Not only are individuals making profound changes, but organizations are forging partnerships with former competitors. General Motors, Ford, and Chrysler have all developed working relationships with Japanese car manufacturers they once regarded with disdain. Even groups as militant as the Black Muslims, who not long ago preached bombings and revolution, have shifted course. They now welcome white cooperation, and emphasize self-help projects instead of violence. The burying of long-held distrust and fear between the United States and the Soviet Union is replacing conflict with cooperation. Perhaps a planetary "declaration of interdependence" will one day emerge.

As creative beings, we—individually and collectively—have within us the power to choose to be whatever we really want to be. With that choice, we open up the future to unlimited possibilities. It was Gandhi who knew, "We must become the change we seek in the world."

In order to adopt the Creative Worldview as the foundation for our life, we must accept the notion that we live in a creative world—things, ideas, and people are constantly changing and producing results that never before existed and could not have been predicted based on the past.

SHIFTING TO A CREATIVE CONTEXT

For a shift of the magnitude we're suggesting to occur, we must adopt a new operating manual to guide our relationships with ourselves, with others, and within our organizations. We invite you to apply each of the natural foundational principles we have presented to create a new underpinning for living a life that will allow you to experience greater joy and fulfillment than you have thought possible.

Nature provided each of us with a wonderful and tenacious internal guidance system for individual transformation. The mechanism is extraordinarily simple. When we are growing and connecting, we feel pleasure and joy. When we are not growing or are disconnecting, we feel pain. These feelings are unerringly accurate signals to guide us. And we all have them.

We do not want to diminish the fact that this is a huge undertaking. Marching to your own drummer and doing what you love to do in the face of a conforming society is not easy. There will be trials and many emotions along the way. However, no pain is greater than living a life without meaning or one filled with regrets. Pain always manifests itself when we refuse to grow. We need to learn to interpret our pain, be it emotional, physical, or spiritual, as a message from our intuitive self to change. Pain arises when something inside us is being denied. Moving beyond the pain, breaking old patterns, letting go of outworn beliefs, and following your heart is how to find true joy.

In the second phase of humanity's development, the logical worldview required that we accept the notion that life is difficult at best. If we hadn't accepted that denial and struggle were essential elements of life, the second phase just wouldn't have functioned. People would have resisted control; the limits it put on personal growth would have been too onerous. So, to reinforce our old beliefs we had to make hardship and misery seem natural: paying for original sin, keeping the divine order, accepting our karma, or the like. Those concepts now belong in a museum of quaint antiquities.

Use joy as your life compass. When you're feeling out of joy—stop. You're probably off track. The signals of pain say you're violating one of the elemental forces. You're existing, not creating; you're stuck in the past, not being pulled by your purpose; you're disconnecting, not openly connecting. Our feelings are nature's compelling way of showing us a path into the uncharted domain of our future destiny.

There will always be numerous, and what may seem like monumental, reasons not to change to a Creative Worldview. Common agreements, society's expectations, doing what others want, conforming and operating under the values and beliefs of culture or religious dogma, the limits of the workplace, and family tradition all can provide a mountain of opposition to one's own journey of personal development. Newspapers, magazines, television, and popular myths remind us that living in this world is a hard, competitive undertaking, filled with traps for the unwary. Anyone who believes that life is easy, that it can be kind, fulfilling, creative, and joyful must be gullible and naive at best.

Moving past these mighty barriers, erected over countless centuries by a fundamental misunderstanding of nature, is not for the faint of heart. To move beyond Breakpoint, every person must release old viewpoints, ways of doing things, and firmly held beliefs. When this happens it often feels, at first, like you are headed downhill. It most often feels like you are losing some part of yourself. Actually, like the crab that sheds its shell and floats helplessly while growing a new and larger one, you are creating yourself anew.

THE SINGULAR OBSTACLE

Why have people and organizations not naturally shifted to a Creative Worldview already? The gigantic catch is that we look at the world, at ourselves, and at change through the lens of our traditional, habitual, and established perceptions of reality. Whether we are consciously aware of it or not, we use ingrained explanations of reality to guide our lives. These assumptions are short and simple and save mental effort. They provide us with set expectations to rely upon.

For over fifty centuries, the traditional and accepted model guiding civilization has been a logical, cause-and-effect worldview. This belief system expects the world to follow orderly, regular patterns that are predictable and rational. Given the same causes, we know what results to expect. Anything that violates this step-by-step progression is "abnormal." This worldview expects the world to be *orderly and routine*.

Yet another worldview has arisen because of the Breakpoint—and seemingly chaotic—changes that have occurred in the past few decades. It attempts to answer the questions that are not addressed by a logical worldview. This mindset maintains that the universe is a random event, strewn with chaos and discord. If the universe has any direction at all, it is toward more disorder. To people who espouse this ethos, evolution or progress of any kind is a temporary exception to the universal rule. Cosmic chaos will catch up with us someday, if it hasn't already. This mindset sees the world as *disorderly and random*, leaving the individual with very little power to create a meaningful life.

What we see around us today is a complicated, interconnected, unpredictable world. A vast majority of people experience obstacles to their lives working well in this constantly changing world because they use either the *orderly* or the *disorderly* explanation of reality to guide, and limit, their decisions.

The *disorderly* view says, "Of course the world is disorderly and it's going to get worse. That's the way things are. We're going to hell in a hand basket; everything is moving downhill." Pessimism and hopelessness prevail. On the other hand, those looking through an *orderly* lens compare the world today with the orderliness of the past and determine that something is wrong. They expend great energy trying to "fix" the problem. They try to force the system Back to Basics, attempting to impose their expected prescription of reality.

Either the orderly or the disorderly worldviews, when used to take snapshots of reality, can appear to be accurate. If you look solely at a first phase situation, you will certainly draw the conclusion that disorder rules. If you focus exclusively on the second phase, you come to the equally valid conclusion that the universe is orderly. In a third phase situation, the system undergoes simultaneous ordering and disordering, constant reordering. The proponents of both order and disorder are confused because they fail to look at the whole dynamic of growth and change.

PARTS VERSUS WHOLES

One cannot draw conclusions about nature by taking snapshots of any singular phase. We are convinced that we must enfold all of the dimensions of change in order to understand our lives and our world. We need to release our current mindset and rely on a worldview that aligns with our intuition, our own internal maps of reality. Our new perceptions can then embrace the context of the natural creative dynamic of change, growth, and evolution.

We face a monumental challenge when current experience does not correspond to our expectations of how things should fit together and work. Very easily, we judge a person or circumstance as good or bad, right or wrong, superior or inferior. As individuals, societies, cultures, and organizations, we are moving toward greater interdependence and connection in civilization's third phase. As yet, we are still prone to constrain the possibilities and potentials of our species within outworn explanations.

So, there are three different belief systems we can choose to adopt about the world: as an inevitable continuation of the past, as headed toward chaos and disorder or as dynamically creative. We suggest that the third is the only realistic view. The belief in a creative universe and the dynamics of three phases of transformational change allow us to approach life with enthusiasm and vitality. In addition, the Creative Worldview and the foundational principles associated with Creativity, Future Pull and Connecting go far beyond the limits imposed by either the logical, cause-and-effect orientation or the random, disorderly mindset. Seeing the world as constantly changing and inevitably creative provides the insight and understanding to transform the future; it endows us with both practicality and promise.

We invite you to see what is happening in the world around you and the world inside of you as vibrantly creative. This allows you to see everything as constantly moving and evolving. No longer will you look at things and only ask, "What is it?" In addition you will ask, "What is it becoming?"

A SOLID BRIDGE TO THE FUTURE

Everything exists in its present state and future potential—being and becoming. With this orientation, each of us can participate as co-creators with nature and with one another in bringing about far deeper, more meaningful relationships as we build an unmatched tomorrow not only in our personal lives but within our organizations.

In our unique era, if we purposefully and knowingly enter in this great natural current of change, every one of us can bring phenomenal possibilities into actuality - in transcending circumstances and recreating our lives, our families, our organizations, and our society. Understanding the creative transformative method of growth and change provides us with a solid foundation—a foundation from which we can soar into the future. As H.G. Wells said:

The past is but the beginning of a beginning and all that is and has been is but the twilight of the dawn.

Together, we can and will create a different world.

About the Authors

Propelled by curiosity as to why the world works as it does, **George Land's** research about nature led him to become a general system's scientist and author with a broad and fascinating background in anthropology, communications, business, and education. His in-depth understanding of creativity and change resulted in his seminal work *Grow or Die: The Unifying Principle of Transformation.* Today his expertise is sought by leaders worldwide. In 1989 he received the Lifetime Creative Achievement Award from the Creative Education Foundation. **Beth Jarman** has been fascinated with the ability of individuals to continuously expand their potential. Her expertise in human development led her to write her first book, *You Can Change Your Life by Changing Your Mind.* Dr. Jarman has been involved throughout her career in widening her experience about human behavior as an educator, businesswoman, and government leader. She has held significant leadership positions as a state legislator and as cabinet secretary to governors in both Utah and Arizona. She is founding partner with George Land of Leadership 2000. Both George Land and Beth Jarman live in Paradise Valley, Arizona.

INFORMATION ABOUT LEADERSHIP 2000

Our Purpose Is to Live the Spirit of the Creative Life and Share Its Possibilities with the World's Communities.

We are confident and optimistic about the capacity of people everywhere to make the Breakpoint shift to live the Creative Worldview. We are commited to make it easier to learn from one another how to fully experience and express the dynamics of a Creative Life.

With our purpose in mind, we enthusiastically respond to opportunities to share our philosophy and concepts.

We offer organizations

- Consulting Services

- Breakpoint Leadership Development

- Organizational Transformation Seminars

- Creativity Development

- Breakpoint Technology—computer-assisted creative processes for group decisionmaking, market research, value analysis, and opportunity discovery

For more information or a catalog of our products and services

contact:

Leadership 2000, Inc.
3333 N. 44th St., Suite Four
Phoenix, Arizona 85018
Telephone: (602)-852–0223 or
FAX: (602)-852–0232

GLOSSARY

Autopoiesis The capability of natural systems to self-organize toward a future goal or purpose.

Back to Basics Bump At the end of the second phase, the natural tendency is to continue doing better those things that have proved so successful in the past. This usually produces a temporary bump where there is an upturn in growth. However, going back to basics ultimately leads to failure.

Bifurcation In the third phase, two simultaneous activities are going on. The growing organism is fulfilling its third phase potential and at the same time a bifurcation or "splitting apart" occurs where a new first phase at a higher level of complexity is occurring.

Breakpoint Change That point in the process of creative growth and change where the rules of successful growth shift abruptly and powerfully, breaking the critical links that connect anyone or anything with the past.

Breakpoint Leadership Being a vital force for creating a new path to the future by living the principles of the Creative Worldview.

Breakpoint Leap   That point where any growing thing, whether it be a person, organization, or an entire society, changes its creative growth potential.

Breakpoint Rules   The specific rules that guide success when a new phase of creative growth and change is encountered.

Breakpoint Thinking   The conscious understanding and application of the rules that create a Breakpoint leap.

Co-creation   The willingness and ability to create with others based on the interdependent sharing of differences which allows something totally new and unexpected to come into being.

Connecting Force   The third cornerstone of the Creative Worldview. Everything defines itself based on its connections or relationships with the world around it.

Convergence   The natural tendency in the creative process to make selections after a wide variety of possible options has been explored.

Creative Drive   The first of three cornerstones of the Creative Worldview. Everything within nature operates in a dynamic, creative way, constantly bringing into being something original and unique.

Creative Learning   Consciously developing an atmosphere where creativity, mutual support, interdependence, and nonjudgment are fostered thereby supporting individuals and groups to discover their potential.

Creative Process   Nature brings about change by going through three phases of growth where three different types of creativity—invention, improvement, and innovation—are encountered.

Creative Worldview   A way of looking at the world based on accepting one's unique, natural creative abilities, knowing that the quality of life is determined based on the quality of relationships and realizing that the pull of the future is more powerful than the push of the past.

Cycle of Growth and Change   A process that encompasses three unique phases of growth and change, where two Breakpoints occur.

Divergence   The natural imaginative process of free and unlimited thinking; a dynamic exploration of an environment where investigation and experimentation is far ranging and comprehensive.

First Phase—Forming   The stage of growth where the type of creativity relies on invention. The growing organism is searching for an initial pattern of successful growth that will connect it with its environment.

Future Pull   The second cornerstone of the Creative Worldview. The most powerful force driving change comes from the future. Nature reveals that complex systems are not controlled or limited by the past, but are being pulled to a future different from the past.

Interdependence A process by which individuals and organizations contribute to a common purpose based on mutually sharing and combining their uniqueness with others.

Logical Worldview With agriculture-based civilization came a relationship between the cause of something and its ultimate effect. This type of thinking embraces the belief that *A* leads to *B* leads to *C* and is past-based, or deterministic. This view of reality has dominated the belief system of the Western World since the time of the Greeks.

Master Pattern of Change All systems found in nature are involved in a similar pattern of evolutionary change and growth where a cycle with three distinct phases of creative growth occurs over time.

Material Particle The concrete, physical aspect of reality.

Nonjudgment The conscious decision to eliminate right or wrong, good or bad, blame or judgment in dealing with a person, situation, or event.

Phase of Growth and Change Describes one of the three intervals within the cycle of change, between Breakpoints.

Purpose Answers the question: How does an organization or individual make the world a better place?

S Curve An "S"-shaped, graphic representation of growth.

Second Phase—Norming Once a first phase pattern has been invented, a Breakpoint is encountered where growth demands that creativity shift to building on the pattern, by repeating, improving, and extending it.

Spirit Guided Worldview A belief system that endowed nature with multiple spirits that guided the actions of large populations—thought to exist in cultures prior to the beginning of agriculture-based civilizations.

Synergy The interaction of elements that when combined produce a total effect that is greater than the sum of the parts.

System A collection of parts that make up a unified whole. The word system can be applied to an individual, a single cell, the history of cell evolution, an organization, or an entire culture.

Third Phase—Fulfilling Following a successful second phase, a system opens up to creative innovation. This requires integrating what was previously excluded and including the new and different within the old pattern.

Transformation Theory An original interpretation detailing nature's dynamic creative growth and change process. First introduced by George Land in *Grow or Die: The Unifying Principle of Transformation*.

Vision The vibrant and compelling picture or image an individual or organization has that portrays the future achievement of the individual's or organization's purpose.

Wave A description of the probable futures of a material particle. All the building blocks that make up our physical world carry in their present material state a wave of future potential. They are both being and becoming at the same time.

Wave Interference Waves of future potential that merge or blend with one another.

Whole Systems Thinking An approach where the world is seen and understood in terms of the universal patterns that pervade everything.

Worldview The beliefs, assumptions, and ways of thinking that determine an individual's view of reality.

NOTES

CHAPTER 1 BREAKPOINT CHANGE

Page

3 "Unprecedented social, political and technological": Lisa Taylor, ed., *The Phenomenon of Change* (New York: Smithsonian Institution, Rizzoli International Publications, Inc. 1984), front cover.

7 "The present situation is unique": Margaret Mead, *Culture and Commitment* (Garden City: Anchor Press/Doubleday, 1970), p. 67.

8 "There is no longer a typical": *1986 Environmental Scan* (Credit Union National Association with CUNA Mutual Insurance Group, Planning and Research Dept., Madison, Wisconsin), p. 12.

11 "Like the stern light of a ship": Samuel Taylor Coleridge, *The Complete Works of Samuel T. Coleridge*, edited by W. G. T. Shedd (New York: Harper & Brothers, 1884), p. 481.

12 "We depended on the creativity": Personal conversations between John Allison and George Land between 1985 and 1989 in North Carolina.

13 "To change the world by": Apple Computer—Mission Statement available at Apple Computer, Cupertino, California.

13 "The world will not evolve": Albert Einstein, *Out of My Later Years* (New York: Philosophical Library, 1934), p. 156.

CHAPTER 2 THE MASTER PATTERN OF CHANGE

Page

14 "Humanity's survival depends on": Buckminster Fuller, *Utopia or Oblivion: The Prospects for Humanity* (New York: Bantam Books, 1969), p. 118.

25 "There is no greater miracle": National Academy of Science, Report to Congress, January 1971.

29 The flying machine: *New York Times* editorial, 1903.

30 "A view in which the accent": Peter Drucker, *Age of Discontinuity* (New York: Harper & Row, 1969), ch. 9.

34 "The greatest riddle of cosmology": John Eccles, *The Self and Its Brain* (Berlin: Springer International, 1972), p. 61.

35 "Everyone is born a genius": R. Buckminster Fuller in Simpson's *Contemporary Quotations*, compiled by James B. Simpson (Boston: Houghton Mifflin, 1988), p. 227.

36 "For the family relationship to grow": James Rumora, "Opportunity in Change," Arthur Andersen's Business Systems Consulting practice (article written for an internal publication, 1991).

CHAPTER 3 DYNAMIC ORGANIZATIONAL CHANGE AND RENEWAL

Page

38 "The whole world is being": Sir Kenneth Durham, Chairman, Unilever Corporation (Presidential Address to the British Association for the Advancement of Science, August 1987).

41 "A Maniac with a Mission": Thomas J. Peters and Robert H. Waterman, Jr., *In Search of Excellence: Lessons from America's Best-Run Companies* (New York: Harper & Row, 1982), p. 225.

41 "They said I was nuts": Daniel Goleman, "The Psyche of the Entrepreneur," *New York Times Magazine*, February 2, 1986, p. 63.

41 "Entrepreneurs never feel they are": Russell Shaw, "Lillian Vernon," *Sky Magazine*, June 1991, p. 57.

44 "Wanted: Impresario to orchestrate": John Sculley with John A. Byrne, *Odyssey* (New York: Harper & Row, 1987), p. 183.

49 "Making money, not cars": Ian Mitroff, *Corporate Tragedies* (New York: Praeger Publishers, 1984), pp. 118–119.

49 "Building the long-term market value": *Southland Corporation Mission Statement*, given to the authors by Southland Corporation.

51 "Fall prey to the equivalent": Samuel Thier, quoted in *The New York Times*, May 5, 1991, p. 16.

55 "In the 1990s corporations": Robert Horton, "Planning for Surprise," *Industry Week*, August 6, 1990, p. 27.

56 "High tech—high touch": John Naisbitt, *Megatrends: The Ten Directions Transforming Our Lives* (New York: Warner Books, 1982), ch. 2.

63 "Companies that fail in diversification": Michael E. Porter, "From Competitive Advantage to Corporate Strategy," *Harvard Business Review*, May 1, 1987, pp. 43–59.

66 "The past is a foreign country": L. P. Hartley, *The Go-Between* (Chester Springs: Dufour Editions, Inc., 1978), prologue.

70 "Many nonprofit organizations": Peter F. Drucker, *Managing the Nonprofit Organization: Principles and Practices* (New York: Harper-Collins, 1990), entire book.

70 "To inspiring girls with the highest": Constitution of the Girl Scouts of the U.S.A.

CHAPTER 4 THE WORLD AT BREAKPOINT

Page

72 "So quickly that few": William Glasser, "The Civilized Identity Society," *Saturday Review*, February 19, 1972, p. 26.

77 "New device quickens and enlarges": Jacob Bronowski, *The Ascent of Man* (Boston: Little, Brown and Company, 1974), p. 74.

79 "His research confirms": J. Bronowski, *The Ascent of Man*, ch. 3.

79 "Lewis Mumford relates": Lewis Mumford, *Technics and Human Development* (New York: Harcourt Brace Jovanovich, 1966), p. 170.

79 "Incalculable changes": Lewis Mumford, *Technics and Human Development*, ch. 9.

80 "Riane Eisler claims": Riane Eisler, *The Chalice and the Blade* (San Francisco: Harper & Row, 1988), p. xvii and ch. 4.

82 "There is a mind in you no magic can touch": Homer, *The Odyssey of Homer*, a modern translation by Richmond Lattimore (New York: Harper & Row, 1965), p. 160.

84 "Simon Kuznets in his Nobel Prize": Simon Kuznets, Nobel Prize Acceptance Speech, December 10, 1971.

86 "We hold these truths": Declaration of Independence, United States of America, quoted from *Magruder's American Government*, revised by William A. McClenaghan (Boston: Allyn and Bacon, 1971), pp. 748–750.

87 "You will quietly and cheerfully": Sam S. Baskett and Theodore B. Strandness, *The American Identity* (Boston: D.C. Heath and Company, 1962), p. 462.

87 "All civilizations we know of": Eric Hoffer, *The Ordeal of Change* (New York: Harper & Row, 1967), p. 33.

88 "The greatest transformation of": Allan Bloom, *The Closing of the American Mind* (New York: Simon and Schuster, 1987), Part 3.

CHAPTER 5 MASTERING THE FUTURE

Page
91 "Nature! We are surrounded": Johann Wolfgang von Goethe, in *Goethes Gespreches*, edited by F. W. von Biedermann (Liepzig: F. W. von Biedermann, 1911), p. 126.

93 "Neils Bohr, one of the": Paul Davies, *Superforce* (New York: Simon and Schuster, 1984), p. 42.

94 "I repeated to myself again": Werner Heisenberg, *Physics and Philosophy* (New York: Harper & Row, 1958), p. 42.

94 "It was entirely new": Max Planck in his Nobel Prize acceptance speech, 1918.

97 "A courageous imagination": Albert Einstein and Leopold Infeld, *The Evolution of Physics* (New York: Simon and Schuster, 1938) pp. 295–96.

100 "It meant a tendency for something": Werner Heisenberg, *Physics and Philosophy*, p. 41.

100 "Whether you believe you can": Nancy Cohen, "Awards Business Leadership," *Restaurant Business*, May 1, 1990, p. 158.

101 "Sören Kierkegaard, the Danish philosopher": Victor M. Parachin, "Motivate to the Max," *Total Health*, December 1990, p. 30.

102 "It's certainly a very exciting prospect": Norman Cousins, "Tapping Human Potential," *Second Opinion*, July 1990, p. 56.

102 "Psyche cannot be totally different": Carl Jung and W. Pauli, *The Interpretation of Nature and the Psyche* (Princeton: Princeton University Press, 1955), p. 61.

NOTES

102 "Stuff of the universe": Sir Arthur Eddington, *Nature of the Physical World* (Ann Arbor: University of Michigan Press, 1978), p. 241.

104 "A system in constant interaction": Harald Fritzsch, *The Creation of Matter*, translated by Jean Steinberg (New York: Basic Books, 1984), p. 262.

104 "A web of relationships between elements": Henry Stapp, "S-Matrix Interpretation of Quantum Theory," *Physical Review*, 1971, p. 1303.

104 "In recent years another": J. S. Bell, *Speakable and Unspeakable in Quantum Mechanics* (New York: Cambridge University Press, 1987), pp. 159–168.

104 "Thus, one is led to a new notion": David Bohm and B. Hiley, *On the Intuitive Validation of Non-Locality as Implied by Quantum Theory* (London: University of London, 1974), p. 103.

107 "Black magic": Alister Hardy, Robert Harvie and Arthur Koestler, *The Challenge of Chance* (New York: Vintage Press, 1975), p. 270.

108 "Driven to opt for some alternative": Alister Hardy et al, *The Challenge of Chance*, p. 272.

109 "One of the fundamental characteristics": Jacques Monod, *Chance and Necessity* (New York: Alfred A. Knopf, 1971), p. 9.

109 "Life is a series of collisions": José Ortega y Gasset, *The Revolt of the Masses, Man and Crisis* (New York: Norton, 1964), p. 21.

CHAPTER 6 PARTING WITH THE PAST

Page

115 "Only through a radical shift": John Sculley with John A. Byrne, *Odyssey*, p. 409.

121 "Ideas by themselves cannot": P. D. Ouspensky and G. I. Gurdjieff as quoted by Susan Hayward in *A Guide for the Advanced Soul* (Crows Nest: In-Tune Books, 1984), p. 171.

121 "The purpose of the school system": Jerry Pournelle, "A User's View", *Infoworld*, November 20, 1989, p. 58.

122 "To help customers achieve": Mission Statement—Branch Bank and Trust, Wilson, North Carolina.

122 "The Body Shop": Bo Burlingham, "This Woman Has Changed Business Forever," *Inc. Magazine*, June 1990, pp. 34–45.

123 "Let them create, let them grow": Tom Melohn, "How to build employee trust and productivity," *Harvard Business Review*, January-February 1983, pp. 4–6.

124 "Dangers and errors": Associated Press story, printed in the *Arizona Republic*, Sunday December 10, 1990, p. G1.

126 "We live in a unique era": Margaret Mead, *Culture and Commitment*, ch. 1.

126 "The ratio of civilians to combatants"; Ruth Sivard, "World Military and Social Expenditures," *World Priorities*, Washington, D.C., 1987–88.

128 "Teaching people how to eat": James Brady, "Jean Nidetch," *Parade Magazine*, May 8, 1988, p. 19.

128 "Victory against disease": Vision of Merck and Company from a letter to Merck employees from Merck Chairman, P. Roy Vagelos, (*Merck Public Affairs Department*, Annual Report, 1990).

128 "Creating a business to change": Alan Hald, Chairman, MicroAge Computer, "When Vision becomes Reality," *The Futurist*, November-December, 1988, p. 27.

129 "Countless books and articles": Rosabeth Moss Kanter, *The Change Masters* (New York: Simon and Schuster, 1983), pp. 303–306; Tom Peters, *Thriving on Chaos* (New York: Alfred A. Knopf, 1987), pp. 398–408; Peter Drucker, *Managing the Nonprofit Organization*, pp. 213–214.

130 "After a long history": "Is the World Bank Financing Impoverishment and Famine," *The Ecologist*, May 6, 1985, pp. 203–301.

131 "We came in the age's most uncertain": Paul Simon, "American Tune" (Warner Brothers Records Inc., New York, 1974).

131 "We want our decisions to be made": Richard M. Smith, et al., "Talking to Gorbachev," *Newsweek*, May 30, 1988, p. 25.

132 "Life is full and overflowing": Eileen Caddy, *Footprints on the Path* (Scotland: Findhorn Press, 1976), p. 31.

CHAPTER 7 CHANGING OUR MINDS

Page

136 "If we believe in the rebirth": Georg Feuerstein, *Encyclopedic Dictionary of Yoga* (New York: Paragon House Publishers, 1990), p. 89.

136 "Dr. Everett Rogers of the University": Everett Rogers, *The Diffusion of Innovations* (New York: Macmillan, 1983), chs. 1 and 2.

136 "The shift overtaking us is not": Marilyn Ferguson, *The Aquarian Conspiracy: Personal and Social Transformation in the 1980s* (Los Angeles: J. P. Tarcher, Inc., 1980), back cover.

136 "Most cultures throughout human history": Denise Shekerjian, *Uncommon Genius: How Great Ideas Are Born* (New York: Viking Press, 1990), p. 52.

138 "A little right of Attila the Hun": Jerry Kammer, "Ted Turner Tells of Attitude Change" *Arizona Republic*, March 10, 1989, F1.

138 "Wayne Townsend, a training manager": From personal interviews between Wayne Townsend and George Land during 1983 to 1990.

138 "John Eisele discovered after": from personal conversations held between 1989 and 1990 in Tucson and Phoenix, Arizona.

140 "Lester Brown founder of Worldwatch": Shekerjian, *Uncommon Genius*, pp. 206–209.

142 "Everything is connected to everything else": Shekerjian, *Uncommon Genius*, p. 86.

CHAPTER 8 THE CREATIVE DRIVE

Page

151 "The creative individual not only": John H. Douglas, "The Genius of Everyman," *Science News*, April 30, 1977, p. 285.

152 "We are living at a time when one age": Rollo May, *The Courage to Create* (New York: Bantam Books, 1976), p. 1.

152 "There is no correlation between": "Excellent Company Report," North American Tool & Die (Draft Report, April 1984).

153 "Dr. Calvin Taylor at the": Calvin W. Taylor, *Creativity: Progress and Potential* (New York: McGraw Hill, 1964), chs. 2–4.

153 "They use the word yes": Robert Fulghum, "A Bag of Possibles and Other Matters of the Mind," *Newsweek*, Special Education Issue, Fall/Winter, 1990, p. 88.

154 "N. C. Wyeth, the great American artist": Richard Meryman, "American Visions, The Wyeth Family," *National Geographic*, July 1991, pp. 79–109.

155 "Abraham Maslow called this place": A. H. Maslow, "Emotional Blocks to Creativity," Lecture before Creative Engineering Seminars—U.S. Army Engineers, Ft. Belvoir, Va., April 24, 1957.

155 "Oliver Wendell Holmes put it well": Marjorie Barrows, *One Thousand Beautiful Things* (New York: Spencer Press, 1955), p. 277.

156 "In order to arrive": T. S. Eliot, *Four Quartets* (New York: Harcourt Brace Jovanovich, 1971), p. 29.

156 "There's no use trying": John Bartlett, *Familiar Quotations* (Boston: Little, Brown and Company, 1968), p. 746.

157 "Carl Jung spent a lifetime": Carl Jung, *Man and his Symbols* (New York: Dell Publishing, 1964), ch. 1; Carl Jung, *Memories, Dreams, Reflections*, edited by A. Jaffe (New York: Vintage Books, 1989) ch. 10.

157 "Alan Huang of Bell Labs": Jason Forsythe, Duncan Maxwell Anderson and Bryan Mattimore, "Breakthrough Ideas: Boost Your Company's Creativity and Blast Your Way to Success," *Success*, October 1990, pp. 31–41.

157 "Courage to Create": Rollo May, *The Courage to Create*, chs. 1–7.

159 "The unexamined life is not": John Bartlett, *Familiar Quotations*, p. 93.

159 "Why he was afraid of certain": Shekerjian, *Uncommon Genius*, p. 208.

159 "Trust me now, baby": Shekerjian, *Uncommon Genius*, p. 221.

160 "Born originals": Edward Young, Eighteenth Century British poet, quoted by President James O. Freedman of Dartmouth on September 17, 1990 at the Convocation opening the College's 1990–1991 academic year.

161 "There are many kinds of risks": Wally "Famous" Amos, "Just Do It," *Journal of Creative Behavior*, Vol. 22, No. 3, Third Quarter 1988, p. 158.

161 "Michael Ray, professor": Michael Ray, "Compassion: Key to Organizational Creativity," *The New Leader*, July/August 1990, p.6.

162 "The traditional management gospel": John Sculley with John A. Byrne, *Odyssey*, p. 184.

162 "Evaluate everyone on his or her love of change": Tom Peters, *Thriving on Chaos*, ch.9.

164 "Chris Argyris, the eminent researcher": Chris Argyris, *Reasoning, Learning and Action* (San Francisco: Jossey-Bass, 1982), parts II and III.

165 "All living is meeting": Martin Buber, *I and Thou*, translation by Walter Kaufman (New York: Charles Scribner's Sons, 1970), p. 66.

166 "Live the questions now": Rainer Maria Rilke, *Letters to a Young Poet*, translated by M.D. Herter Norton (New York: W. W. Norton & Company, 1934), p. 35.

167 "The great artistic inventor": Hans L. C. Jaffe, *Pablo Picasso* (New York: Harry N. Abrams, 1964), p. 12.

168 "Sigmund Freud referred to": Sigmund Freud, *The Future of an Illusion* (New York: W. W. Norton, 1961), p. 27.

168 "The noted psychiatrist, Albert Rothenberg": Albert Rothenberg and Carl R. Hausman, *The Creativity Question* (Durham: Duke University Press, 1976), p. 47.

170 "David Bohm, the well known physicist": Michael Toms, *Interview with David Bohm*, New Dimensions Radio (San Francisco, cassette tapes nos. 2181, 2182).

171 "The liberation from the bondage": Michael Toms, *Interview with David Bohm*, tape no. 2182.

CHAPTER 9 THE POWER OF FUTURE PULL

Page
173 "The purposiveness of all vital": Arthur Koestler, *The Roots of Coincidence* (London: Hutchinson, 1972), p. 112.

174 "Nobel prize winning biologist": Gerald Elderman, lecture entitled "Man and Ideas," Carnegie Music Hall, December 6, 1977.

175 "Jack Nicklaus says that vision": Eugene Raudsepp, *Creative Growth Games* (New York: Pyramid Publications, 1980), p. 142.

175 "I have learned at least": John Bartlett, *Familiar Quotations*, p. 683.

176 "John Mahoney did what others expected": Tom Seligson, "I'm Finally Doing What I Want," *Parade Magazine*, April 9, 1989, p. 8.

177 "Being used for a purpose recognized": John Barlett, *Familiar Quotations*, p. 836.

178 "Jan Carlzon, the president of": Interview with Jan Carlzon, "The Art of Loving", *Inc. Magazine*, May 1989, p. 35.

178 "James Rouse, the great urban planner": Claire Carter, "Yes It Can Be Done," *Parade Magazine*, May 12, 1991, pp. 4–5.

178 "Tom Watson, Jr. of IBM": Tom Watson, Jr, "The Greatest Capitalist in History," *Fortune*, August 31, 1987, p. 34.

178 "Jack Welch of G.E.": Quoted from *Boardroom Reports*, November 1, 1988, p. 2.

179 "A fifty-seven year old chief operating officer": D. Quinn Mills, "Bridging the Corporate Generation Gap," *New York Times*, April 7, 1985, Business Section, p. 5.

179 "The very essence of leadership": Tom Peters, *Thriving on Chaos*, p. 399.

179 "Tormod Bjork, the managing director": Marjorie Parker, *Creating Shared Vision* (Oslo: Norwegian Center for Leadership Development, 1990), entire book.

180 "Debbie Meier is trying to do nothing less": Shekerjian, *Uncommon Genius*, pp. 17–25.

180 "Anita Roddick had a $6,000": Bo Burlingham, *Inc. Magazine*, pp. 34–45.

181 "Joseph Campbell calls the commitment": Joseph Campbell with Bill Moyers, edited by Betty Sue Flowers, *The Power of Myth* (New York: Doubleday, 1988), p. 117.

182 "Alan Hald of MicroAge": Alan Hald, "When Vision becomes Reality," *The Futurist*, November–December 1988, p. 26–27.

183 "The multitalented author and computer guru": Jerry Pournelle, "The Power to Save the Human Species Is Within Our Grasp," *Infoworld*, May 8, 1989, p. 48.

185 "Until one is committed": Goethe, *Faust, A Dramatic Mystery*, translated by John Anster (London: Longman, Rees, Orme, Brown, Green & Longman, 1835), Act 1.

186 "Levi Strauss and Co": Robert Howard, "Values Make the Company: An Interview with Robert Haas", *Harvard Business Review*, September-October 1990, pp. 133–144.

187 "Ivan Blostone, former president of Leaseways": Ivan Blostone interviewed by Beth Jarman, June 1990 in Scottsdale, Arizona.

187 "Robert B. Horton, Chairman of British": Robert Horton, *Industry Week*, p. 27.

187 "What really mattered was getting": Robert Howard, *Harvard Business Review*, p. 135.

CHAPTER 10 THE FORCE OF CONNECTING

Page

190 "The authors of *Creativity in Business*": Michael Ray and Rochelle Myers, *Creativity in Business* (Garden City: Doubleday and Company, 1986), ch. 4.

190 "The Nature Conservancy had no idea": Fact Sheets, Brochures, and Annual Report, 1990 (*The Nature Conservancy*, Arlington, VA).

NOTES

191 "You say it's tainted money?": Sherkijian, *Uncommon Genius*, p. 90.

193 "The ability to connect": Interview with Ruben Cerda, March 1988 at Las Mañanitas, Cuernavaca, Mexico.

194 "Come to the edge, he said": Guillaume Apollinaire, as quoted by Susan Hayward, *A Guide for the Advanced Soul*, p. 170.

197 "We are members of a vast cosmic": J. Allen Boone, *Kinship with All Life* (New York: Harper & Row, 1976), p. 146.

198 "D. Quinn Mill of the Harvard Business": D. Quinn Mill, *New York Times*, p. 5.

201 "Jean Nidetch was at one time": conversations between Jean Nidetch and George Land during the 1970s in New York, NY.

202 "At the first Weight Watchers": James Brady, *Parade Magazine*, p. 19.

202 "It is the assertion of hope": Karl Menninger, M.D., *The Vital Balance* (New York: The Viking Press, 1963), p. 413.

203 "Students at Stanford University enrolled": Michael Ray and Rochelle Myers, *Creativity in Business*, ch. 3.

205 "Not judging is another way of letting": Gerald G. Jampolsky, M.D., *Love is Letting Go of Fear* (New York: Bantam Books, 1985), p. 99.

205 "James M. Kouzes interviewed": James M. Kouzes, "Secret to Success," *Executive Excellence*, December 1989, p. 3.

205 "Jan Carlzon, president of Scandinavian": Interview, *Inc. Magazine*, pp. 35–46.

205 "Joe Kordick, head of Ford's parts": Eric Gelman, "Ford's Idea Machine," *Newsweek*, November 24, 1986, p. 66.

205 "The whole thing comes down to truth and love": "J. Peter Grace," *American Thought Leader* (BB&T Center for Leadership Development, East Carolina University, Greenville, NC), p. 9.

206 "The real essence of leadership": Roger Fritz, "The Real Essence of Leadership," *Boardroom Reports*, March 15, 1989, p. 6.

206 "It boils down to the innate goodness": Tom Melohn, *Harvard Business Review*, p. 23.

206 "In a study conducted by Northwestern": "Employee Burnout: America's Newest Epidemic," *Northwestern National Life* (Northwestern National Life Insurance Company, Research Study, 1991, Section 3).

206 "A recent *Industry Week* survey": "Did You Know That?" *Boardroom Reports* quoting from *Industry Week*, July 1, 1991, p. 15.

207 "I am engaged in trying": Paramahansa Yogananda, *The Autobiography of a Yogi* (Los Angeles: Self Realization Fellowship, 1974), p. 516.

207 "If we wish to give philosophical": Louis de Broglie, *New Perspectives in Physics* (New York: Basic Books, 1962), p. 213.

207 "He found that those who helped": Morton Hunt, "Can Goodness Be Taught?," *Parade Magazine*, May 6, 1990, p. 28.

208 "Allen H. Neuharth, former CEO of Gannett": Alex S. Jones, "Machiavelli Has Nothing on Former Gannett Chief," *The Arizona Republic*, Sept. 17, 1989, p. F 1.

208 "Max DePree, the chairman of": "Try a Little Kindness," *Time*, Sept. 11, 1987, p. 56.

208 "If a company has the attitude": Michael A. Verespej, "Where People Come First," *Industry Week*, July 16, 1990, p. 22.

209 "Everyone has the right and duty": Max DePree, *Time*, p. 56.

209 "Someday, after we have mastered": Teillard de Chardin, *On Love and Happiness* (New York: Harper & Row, 1967), p. 16.

CHAPTER 11 A SOLID BRIDGE TO THE FUTURE

Page

211 "Of all the creatures of earth": William James, *The Will To Believe* (New York: Dover Publications, 1956), p. 27.

212 "The global network of telecommunications": Hugh Henner, "Matter at the End of Its Tether," *BYTE*, February 1990, p. 336.

218 "Men are disturbed not by the things": Epictecus, as quoted in Susan Hayward, *A Guide for the Advanced Soul*, p. 17.

218 "In a conversation with Bill Moyers": Joseph Campbell with Bill Moyers, *The Power of Myth*, p. 161.

219 "To change one's life": William James, as quoted in Susan Hayward, *A Guide for the Advanced Soul*, p. 168.

219 "Betty Friedan, founder of": Betty Friedan, *The Second Stage* (New York: Dell Publishing, 1991), entire book.

220 "A twenty-three-year-old heroin addict": "Against All Odds," *Arizona Republic*, October 23, 1989, p. C3.

220 "We must become the change we seek": Mohandas K. Gandhi, *An Autobiography* (Boston: Beacon Press, 1957), p. 430.

225 "The past is but the beginning": John Bartlett, *Familiar Quotations*, p. 888.

BIBLIOGRAPHY

Andersen, U. S. *The Magic In Your Mind*. North Hollywood, CA: Wilshire, 1961.

Argyris, Chris. *Reasoning, Learning and Action*. San Francisco: Jossey-Bass, 1982.

Asimov, Isaac. *Understanding Physics*. New York: New American Library, 1969.

Barrows, Marjorie, comp. *One Thousand Beautiful Things*. New York: Spencer Press, 1955.

Bartlett, John. *Bartlett's Familiar Quotations*. Boston: Little Brown and Company, 1968.

Baskett, Sam S. and Theodore B. Strandness. *The American Identity*. Boston: D.C. Heath and Co., 1962.

Bell, J. S. *Speakable and Unspeakable in Quantum Mechanics*. New York: Cambridge University Press, 1987.

Bloom, Allan. *The Closing of the American Mind*. New York: Simon and Schuster, 1987.

Boas, George. *The History of Ideas*. New York: Charles Schribner's Sons, 1969.

Bohm, David. *Unfolding Meaning*. London: Ark Paperbacks, 1987.

Bohm, David. *Wholeness and the Implicate Order*. Boston: Routledge & Kegan Paul, 1980.

Bohm, David and B. Hiley. *On the Intuitive Validation of Non-Locality as Implied by Quantum Theory*. London: University of London, 1974.

Bohm, David and F. David Peat. *Science, Order, and Creativity*. New York: Bantam, 1987.

Boone, J. Allen. *Kinship with All Life*. New York: Harper & Row, 1976.

Briggs, John and F. David Peat. *Looking Glass Universe*. New York: Simon and Schuster. 1986.

Bristol, Claude M. *The Magic of Believing*. New York: Pocket Books, 1948.

de Broglie, Louis. *New Perspectives in Physics*. New York: Basic Books, 1962.

Bronowski, Jacob. *The Ascent of Man*. Boston: Little, Brown and Company, 1974.

Buber, Martin. *I and Thou*. Walter Kaufman, trans. New York: Charles Scribner's Sons, 1970.

Caddy, Eileen. *Footprints on the Path*. Scotland: Findhorn Press, 1976.

Campbell, Joseph. *An Open Life*. New York: Larson Publications, 1988.

Campbell, Joseph and Bill Moyers. *The Power of Myth*. Betty Sue Flowers, ed. New York: Doubleday, 1988.

Capra, Fritjof. *The Tao of Physics*. Berkeley: Shambhala, 1975.

Capra, Fritjof. *The Turning Point: Science, Society, and the Rising Culture*. New York: Bantam, 1982.

Carse, James P. *Finite and Infinite Games: A Vision of Life as Play and Possibility*. New York: The Free Press, 1986.

de Chardin, Teillard. *On Love and Happiness*. New York: Harper & Row, 1967.

Clark, Ronald W. *Einstein: The Life and Times*. New York: World Publishing, 1971.

Coleridge, Samuel Taylor. *The Complete Works of Samuel T. Coleridge*. W. G. T. Shedd, ed. New York: Harper & Brothers, 1884.

Dass, Ram. *Journey of Awakening: A Meditator's Guidebook*. New York: Bantam, 1978.

BIBLIOGRAPHY

Dass, Ram. *The Only Dance There Is.* Garden City: Anchor Books, 1970.

Davies, Paul. *Superforce.* New York: Simon and Schuster, 1984.

Davies, Paul. *The Cosmic Blueprint.* New York: Simon and Schuster, 1988.

Davies, Paul, ed. *The New Physics.* Cambridge: Cambridge University Press, 1989.

Davies, P. C. W. and J. R. Brown, ed. *The Ghost in the Atom.* New York: Cambridge University Press, 1986.

Dirac, P. A. M. *The Principles of Quantum Mechanics.* Oxford: Oxford University Press, 1958.

Drucker, Peter. *Age of Discontinuity.* New York: Harper & Row, 1969.

Drucker, Peter. *Managing the Nonprofit Organization: Principles and Practices.* New York: HarperCollins, 1990.

Duncan, Ronald, and Miranda Weston-Smith, ed. *The Encyclopaedia of Ignorance: Everything You Wanted to Know About the Unknown.* New York: Pergamon Press, 1977.

Eccles, John. *The Self and Its Brain.* Berlin: Springer International, 1972.

Eddington, Sir Arthur. *The Nature of the Physical World.* Ann Arbor: University of Michigan Press, 1978.

Eigen, Manfred, and Ruthild Winkler. *Laws of The Game: How the Principles of Nature Govern Chance.* New York: Alfred A. Knopf, 1981.

Einstein, Albert. *Out of My Later Years.* New York: Philosophical Library, 1934.

Einstein, Albert and Leopold Infeld. *The Evolution of Physics.* New York: Simon and Schuster, 1938.

Eisler, Riane. *The Chalice and the Blade: Our History, Our Future.* San Francisco: Harper & Row, 1987.

Eliot, T. S. *Four Quartets.* New York: Harcourt Brace Jovanovich, 1971.

Elvee, Richard Q., ed. *Mind in Nature.* San Francisco: Harper & Row, 1982.

Ferguson, Marilyn. *The Aquarian Conspiracy: Personal and Social Transformation in the 1980s.* Los Angeles: J. P. Tarcher, 1980.

Feuerstein, Georg. *Encyclopedic Dictionary of Yoga.* New York: Paragon House, 1990.

Feynman, Richard P. *QED: The Strange Theory of Light and Matter.* Princeton: Princeton University Press, 1985.

Fine, Arthur. *The Shaky Game: Einstein, Realism and the Quantum Theory.* Chicago: University of Chicago Press, 1986.

Freud, Sigmund. *The Future of an Illusion*. New York: W. W. Norton, 1961.

Friedan, Betty. *The Second Stage*. New York: Dell, 1991.

Fritz, Robert. *The Path of Least Resistance: Principles for Creating What You Want to Create*. Salem: Stillpoint Publishing, 1984.

Fritzsch, Harald. *The Creation of Matter: The Universe from Beginning to End*. New York: Basic Books, 1984.

Fuller, Buckminster. *Operating Manual for Spaceship Earth*. Carbondale: Southern Illinois University Press, 1969.

Fuller, Buckminster. *Synergetics*. New York: Macmillan, 1975.

Fuller, Buckminster. *Utopia or Oblivion: The Prospects for Humanity*. New York: Bantam, 1969.

Gandhi, Mohandas K. *An Autobiography*. Boston: Beacon Press, 1957.

Glansdorff, P., and Ilya Prigogine. *Thermodynamic Theory of Structure, Stability and Fluctuations*. New York: Wiley-Interscience, 1971.

Glasser, William. *The Identity Society*. New York: Harper & Row, 1972.

Gleick, James. *Chaos: Making a New Science*. New York: Viking, 1987.

Goethe, Johann Wolfgang von. *Faustus: A Dramatic Mystery*. John Anster, trans. London: Longman, Rees, Orme, Brown, Green & Longman, 1835.

Goethe, Johann Wolfgang von. *Goethes Gespraches*. F. W. von Biedermann, ed. Leipzig: F. W. von Biedermann, 1911.

Goldsmith, Joel S. *The Infinite Way*. Marina del Rey: DeVorss & Co., 1947.

Goleman, Daniel. *Vital Lies, Simple Truths: The Psychology of Self-Deception*. New York: Simon And Schuster, 1985.

Gorbachev, Mikhail. *Perestroika: New Thinking for Our Country and for the World*. New York: Harper & Row, 1987.

Gregory, Bruce. *Inventing Reality*. New York: John Wiley & Sons, 1990.

Gribbin, John. *In Search of Schrödinger's Cat: Quantum Physics and Reality*. New York: Bantam Books, 1984.

Guillemin, Victor. *The Story of Quantum Mechanics*. New York: Charles Scribner's Sons, 1968.

Hardy, Alister, Robert Harvie, and Arthur Koestler. *The Challenge of Chance: A Mass Experiment in Telepathy and its Unexpected Outcome*. New York: Vintage Books, 1973.

Harrison, Edward. *Masks of the Universe*. New York: Macmillan, 1985.

Hartley, L. P. *The Go-Between*. Chester Springs: Dufour Editions, Inc., 1978.

BIBLIOGRAPHY

Hayward, Susan. *A Guide for the Advanced Soul: A Book of Insight.* Crows Nest: In Tune Books, 1984.

Heisenberg, Werner. *Across the Frontiers.* New York: Harper & Row, 1974.

Heisenberg, Werner. *Physics and Beyond.* New York: Harper & Row, 1971.

Heisenberg, Werner. *Physics and Philosophy.* New York: Harper & Row, 1958.

Herbert, Nick. *Quantum Reality.* Garden City: Anchor Press, 1987.

Hey, Tony and Patrick Walters. *The Quantum Universe.* Cambridge: Cambridge University Press, 1987.

Hoffer, Eric. *The Ordeal of Change.* New York: Perennial Library, 1952.

Hofstadter, Douglas R. *Godel, Escher, Bach: An Eternal Golden Braid.* New York: Vintage Books, 1979.

Homer, *The Odyssey of Homer.* Richmond Lattimore, trans. New York: Harper & Row, 1965.

Jaffe, Hans L. C. *Pablo Picasso.* New York: Harry N. Abrams, Inc., 1983.

James, William. *The Will to Believe.* New York: Dover Publications, 1956.

Jammer, Max. *The Conceptual Development of Quantum Mechanics.* New York: McGraw-Hill, 1966.

Jampolsky, Gerald G. *Love is Letting Go of Fear.* New York: Bantam Books, 1985.

Jantsch, Erich. *Design for Evolution: Self-Organization and Planning in the Life of Human Systems.* New York: George Braziller, 1975.

Jeans, Sir James. *The Universe Around Us.* New York: Macmillan, 1929.

John, Robert and Brenda Dunne. *Margins of Reality.* San Diego: Harcourt Brace Jovanovich, 1987.

Joy, W. Brugh. *Joy's Way: A Map For the Transformational Journey.* Los Angeles: J. P. Tarcher, 1979.

Jung, Carl G. *Man and His Symbols.* New York: Bantam, 1968.

Jung, Carl G. *Memories, Dreams, Reflections.* A. Jaffe, ed. New York: Vintage Books, 1989.

Jung, Carl and W. Pauli. *The Interpretation of Nature and the Psyche.* Princeton: Princeton University Press, 1955.

Kanter, Rosabeth Moss. *The Change Masters.* New York: Simon and Schuster, 1983.

Kitchener, Richard F., ed. *The World of Contemporary Physics: Does it*

Need a New Metaphysics? Albany: State University of New York Press, 1988.

Koestler, Arthur. *Janus: A Summing Up.* New York: Vintage Books, 1978.

Koestler, Arthur. *The Roots of Coincidence.* London: Hutchinson, 1972.

Koestler, Arthur. *The Sleepwalkers.* New York: Grosset & Dunlap, 1963.

Kuhn, Thomas S. *The Structure of Scientific Revolutions.* Chicago: The University of Chicago Press, 1962.

Kunkel, Fritz. *Selected Writings.* John A. Sanford, ed. New York: Paulist Press, 1940.

Land, George A. *Grow or Die: The Unifying Principle of Transformation.* New York: John Wiley & Sons, 1973. Buffalo: Creative Education Foundation, 1992.

Laszlo, Ervin. *Evolution: The Grand Synthesis.* Boston: New Science Library, 1987.

Marshack, Alexander. *The Roots of Civilization.* New York: McGraw-Hill, 1972.

Massey, Sir Harry. *The New Age in Physics.* New York: Basic Books, 1960.

May, Rollo. *The Courage to Create.* New York: Bantam Books, 1976.

McClenaghan, William A. *Magruder's American Government (rev.).* Boston: Allyn and Bacon, 1971.

Mead, Margaret. *Culture and Commitment: The Relationships Between the Generations in the 1970s.* Garden City: Anchor Books, 1970.

Menninger, Karl, M. D. *The Vital Balance: The Life Process in Mental Health and Illness.* New York: The Viking Press, 1963.

Mitroff, Ian. *Corporate Tragedies.* New York: Praeger Publishers, 1984.

Monod, Jacques. *Chance and Necessity.* New York: Alfred A. Knopf, 1971.

Morris, Richard. *The Nature of Reality.* New York: The Noonday Press, 1987.

Mumford, Lewis. *The Myth of the Machine: Technics and Human Development.* New York: Harcourt Brace Jovanovich, 1966.

Naisbitt, John. *Megatrends: Ten New Directions Transforming Our Lives.* New York: Warner Books, 1982.

Ortega y Gasset, José. *The Revolt of the Masses: Man and Crisis.* New York: W. W. Norton & Co., 1964.

Pagels, Heinz R. *The Cosmic Code.* New York: Bantam, 1983.

Parker, Marjorie. *Creating Shared Vision.* Oslo: Norwegian Center for Leadership Development, 1990.

BIBLIOGRAPHY

Patent, Arnold M. *You Can Have It All*. Piermont: Money Mastery Publishing, 1984.

Pauling, Linus and E. Bright Wilson. *Introduction to Quantum Mechanics*. New York: McGraw-Hill, 1935.

Peat, F. David. *Einstein's Moon: Bell's Theorem and the Curious Quest for Quantum Reality*. Chicago: Contemporary Books, 1990.

Peck, M. Scott. *The Different Drum: Community Making and Peace*. New York: Simon and Schuster, 1987.

Peck, M. Scott. *The Road Less Traveled*. New York: Touchstone Books, 1978.

Peters, Tom. *Thriving on Chaos: Handbook for a Management Revolution*. New York: Alfred A. Knopf, 1987.

Peters, Thomas J. and Robert H. Waterman, Jr. *In Search of Excellence: Lessons from America's Best-Run Companies*. New York: Harper & Row, 1982.

Pfeiffer, John E. *The Creative Explosion*. New York: Harper & Row, 1982.

Prigogine, Ilya. *From Being To Becoming: Time and Complexity in the Physical Sciences*. San Francisco: W. H. Freeman and Company, 1980.

Prigogine, Ilya. *Thermodynamics of Irreversible Processes*. New York: Interscience Publishers, 1955.

Prigogine, Ilya, and Isabelle Stengers. *Order Out of Chaos: Man's New Dialogue With Nature*. New York: Bantam, 1984.

Raudsepp, Eugene. *Creative Growth Games*. New York: Putnam, 1980.

Ray, Michael and Rochelle Myers. *Creativity In Business*. Garden City: Doubleday, 1986.

The Reader's Digest Association. *The Last Two Million Years*. New York: The Reader's Digest Association, 1973.

Reeves, Hubert. *Atoms of Silence*. Cambridge: The MIT Press, 1984.

Rilke, Rainer Maria. *Letters to a Young Poet*. M. D. Herter Norton, trans. New York: W.W. Norton & Company, 1934.

Rogers, Everett. *The Diffusion of Innovations*. New York: Macmillan, 1983.

Rothenberg, Albert and Carol R. Hausman, eds. *The Creativity Question*. Durham: Duke University Press, 1976.

Schumacher, E. F. *A Guide for the Perplexed*. New York: Harper Colophon Books, 1977.

Sculley, John with John A. Byrne. *Odyssey*. New York: Harper & Row, 1987.

Shekerjian, Denise. *Uncommon Genius: How Great Ideas Are Born.* New York: Viking Press, 1990.

Sheldrake, Rupert. *A New Science of Life: The Hypothesis of Formative Causation.* Los Angeles: J. P. Tarcher, 1981.

Siegel, Bernie. *Love, Medicine and Miracles.* New York: Harper & Row, 1986.

Simpson, James B. *Simpson's Contemporary Quotations.* Boston: Houghton Mifflin, 1988.

Siu, R. G. H. *The Tao of Science.* Cambridge: The MIT Press, 1957.

Spigelman, Joseph H. *Toward a New Foundation for Physics.* New York: Kips Bay Press, 1987.

Strömberg, Gustaf. *The Soul of the Universe.* Philadelphia: David McKay, 1940.

Talbot, Michael. *Beyond the Quantum.* New York: Macmillan, 1986.

Talbot, Michael. *Mysticism and The New Physics.* New York: Bantam, 1981.

Taylor, Calvin W., ed. *Creativity: Progress and Potential.* New York: McGraw Hill, 1964.

Taylor, Lisa, ed. *The Phenomenon of Change.* New York: Rizzoli International Publications, 1984.

Thom, Rene. *Structural Stability and Morphogenesis.* D. H. Fowler, trans. Reading: W. A. Benjamin, 1975.

Toffler, Alvin. *Future Shock.* New York: Bantam, 1976.

Toffler, Alvin. *The Third Wave.* New York: Bantam, 1980.

Whitehouse, Ruth and John Wilkins. *The Making of Civilization.* New York: Alfred A. Knopf, 1986.

Wilber, Ken, ed. *The Holographic Paradigm and Other Paradoxes.* Boulder: Shambhala, 1982.

Wilber, Ken, ed. *Quantum Questions: Mystical Questions of the World's Great Physicists.* Boston: New Science Library, 1984.

Wilson, Edward O. *On Human Nature.* Cambridge: Harvard University Press, 1978.

Wilson, Larry. *Changing the Game: The New Way to Sell.* New York: Simon and Schuster, 1987.

Wolf, Fred Alan. *Taking the Quantum Leap.* San Francisco: Harper & Row, 1981.

Yankelovich, Daniel. *New Rules.* New York: Random House, 1981.

BIBLIOGRAPHY

Yogananda, Paramanansa. *Autobiography of a Yogi*. Los Angeles: Self-Realization Fellowship, 1946.

Zeeman E. C. *Catastrophe Theory*. Reading: Addison-Wesley, 1977.

Zeleny, Milan, ed. *Autopoiesis: A Theory of Living Organization*. New York: Elsevier North Holland, 1981.

Zukav, Gary. *The Dancing Wu Li Masters: An Overview of the New Physics*. New York: William Morrow and Company, 1979.

INDEX